Meaning and Mind

Meaning and Mind

An Examination of a Gricean Account of Language

Anita Avramides

A Bradford Book
The MIT Press
Cambridge, Massachusetts
London, England

This book was set in Palatino by Achorn Graphic Services and printed and bound by Halliday Lithograph in the United States of America.

Library of Congress Cataloging-in-Publication Data

Avramides, Anita.
 Meaning and mind : an examination of a Gricean account of language
/ Anita Avramides.

    p. cm.
    "A Bradford book."
    Bibliography: p.
    Includes index.
    ISBN 0-262-01108-5
    1. Semantics (Philosophy)—History—20th century. 2. Meaning
(Psychology)—History—20th century. 3. Languages—Philosophy—
History—20th century. 4. Grice, H. P. (H. Paul) I. Title.
B840.A94 1989
121'.68'0924—dc19   88-28602
                                                                    CIP

To the memory of my father

Contents

Chapter 4
Meaning and Mind   127

Preface

This book examines Gricean accounts of meaning. My interest in this topic goes back to 1979, when I was bringing together thoughts for a D.Phil. thesis. I was struck by two things. The first was the essential richness of Grice's original ideas on meaning. The second was what appeared to be a rejection of those ideas by many whose work I admired. Counterexamples to Grice's analysis of meaning excited most attention in the literature that followed the publication of Grice's 1957 paper. My own interest never lay in counterexamples, but the more I learned about the development of the analysis of meaning in response to the counterexamples, the more perplexed I became by the rejection of the analysis. I wanted to understand what was wrong with an analysis that seemed to work so well. This is the reason for chapter 2, which outlines the development of the analysis in some detail. It is no exaggeration to say that this is one of the most successfully developed analyses in the philosophical literature.

One needs to draw a firm distinction between two different interpretations of the analysis of meaning, the one reductive and the other reciprocal, as I labeled it. I became convinced that it was only the reductive interpretation that many were rejecting, and that because no distinction was made between interpretations, it appeared that the analysis itself was being rejected. This tendency was encouraged by the writings of the early followers of Grice's work, Stephen Schiffer and Brian Loar, who took Grice's original analysis in a reductive direction. Schiffer wrote his book *Meaning* in 1972, but not until the early 1980s did he become explicit about his program, which he called "intention-based semantics." The aim of the program is to reduce the semantic to the psychological, and to make this reduction part of the even larger program of reducing the semantic and the psychological to the physical. (See chapter 1, section 5.) While Schiffer and Loar developed this program in their newer work, I concentrated on what was *wrong* with the reductive interpretation of Grice's early work.

Ideas in this area developed rapidly. Not only were Schiffer and

Loar exploring intention-based semantics in enormous detail; Grice himself after a long silence contributed a couple of articles to the discussion of the analysis. Yet Grice has never embraced intention-based semantics. In 1986 Richard Grandy and Richard Warner brought out a collection of papers devoted to Grice's work, some of which contributed to the issue of meaning. Schiffer himself has now written *The Remnants of Meaning*, repudiating his work in intention-based semantics. I have tried to incorporate much of this new literature into my work, but Schiffer's most recent ideas appeared too late for me to comment on them here.

The style and structure of the first two chapters are rather different from the later ones. Chapter 1 explores the place of Grice's work on meaning in the larger context of other approaches to the problem, introduces the distinction between reductive and reciprocal interpretations of the analysis, and explains the program of intention-based semantics. Chapter 2 deals with the analysis itself. In chapters 3 and 4 I explain my interpretation of what is involved in the claim to reduce the semantic to the psychological, and I present my reasons for thinking that such an approach to the understanding of meaning and mind is misguided.

The heart of the book is chapter 3. There I argue that the Gricean does not aim to support his reductive claim with the observation that we can come to know another's beliefs and intentions in advance of understanding his language. This is significant since at least some of those who reject Grice's work appear to do so on the grounds that such an epistemological asymmetry is false. But if this asymmetry does not support the reduction, what does? I argue that we must find an asymmetry advocated by the reductive Gricean but rejected by his antireductionist opponent. I consider the suggestion that the dispute centers on the ontological issue of whether there can be thought without language: the Gricean accepts such an asymmetry, and the antireductionist rejects it. I argue that the antireductionist need not reject ontological asymmetry. The dispute, I suggest, is not over the issue of ontological symmetry versus asymmetry, but over the *conception* of mind. I argue that to reduce the semantic to the psychological is to commit oneself to the idea that the mind is an essentially objective phenomenon that can be comprehended from an external, detached, and impersonal perspective. To understand meaning, we must first be clear about the conception of mind with which we are working. It is easy to argue that specific reductive Griceans are committed to a conception of mind as an objective phenomenon; the more difficult task is to argue that a Gricean is committed by his reduction of the semantic to the psychological to such an objective conception of mind. Yet I believe this to be true, and I argue my case in chapter 4. I also suggest an alternative, subjective conception of mind, which, I argue, is incompatible with a Gricean reduction.

Over the years I have worked on this topic I have benefited from discussion with several people. In shaping the material for an Oxford D.Phil., I was supervised first by Michael Woods and then by John McDowell. John McDowell greatly aided the development of my ideas, especially in chapters 3 and 4. John Biro, Hartry Field, Adrian Moore, Stephen Schiffer, and Galen Strawson read some very early drafts. Stephen Schiffer also provided helpful comments on the completed manuscript. Both of my thesis examiners, Paul Snowden and P. F. Strawson, made helpful and encouraging comments. Katherine Morris commented usefully on chapter 4. I am grateful to several anonymous referees of the manuscript and most especially to Richard Warner, whose detailed reading of the completed manuscript proved invaluable. I would like to thank the Queen's College, Oxford for a sabbatical leave. I am indebted to Colin McGinn for years of discussion and support. Finally, I would like to thank Karen Zaffos and Steven Zaffos for their invaluable help in preparing the index.

Meaning and Mind

Chapter 1
Approaches to Meaning

1 Historical Perspective

The problem is to give an adequate and illuminating account of the concept of meaning. In the past there have been many varied attempts to do this. There is no easy nonmisleading way to summarize or classify these attempts, but some rude organization of the material may help to provide a place for the account of meaning that H. P. Grice introduced into the philosophical world in 1957 and that is the subject of this book.[1]

It is unclear whether or not it is useful to view Grice's work as furthering some preexisting approach to the problem of meaning. What is true is that Grice, in his first paper on the topic, considers and rejects the causal approach to meaning found in the writings of C. L. Stevenson.[2] This approach has its roots in the stimulus-response theories of J. B. Watson.[3] The causal approach to meaning is thus directly associated with the school of radical behaviorism that became prominent in the first part of the twentieth century. Causal theorists recognize that to account for meaning one must pay attention to the role of speakers and hearers. Their behaviorist roots require that whatever it is about speakers and hearers that is relevant to meaning should be accessible to observation. The initial idea, drawn from Pavlov's work on conditioned responses in dogs, is to identify the meaning of a word with the response a certain sound (or mark) induces in the hearer. This idea is in need of substantial modification, however, if for no other reason than that in this crude form the constancy of meaning is lost in the welter of possible responses.

Stevenson identifies the dilemma confronting the theorist of meaning in the following way: on the one hand, if a word is divorced from the "psychological habits" of those who use it, it "becomes devoid of any referent [and] no more interesting than any other complex noise"; on the other hand, the meaning of a word is (relatively) constant, while the psychological states of speakers are in constant flux.[4] Stevenson suggests that the way out of this dilemma is to identify

meaning with a dispositional property of a word; the crucial psychological processes come in as responses to the word. Meaning, then, is
said to be a disposition of a sign to affect certain responses in a hearer.
Stevenson is careful to add: "A sign's disposition to affect a hearer is
to be called a 'meaning' . . . only if it has been caused by, and would
not have developed without, an elaborate process of conditioning
which has attended the sign's use in communication."[5] In other
words, not just anything that has a tendency to produce a certain
response in another is a case of meaning. To see this consider Grice's
example:[6] Putting on a tail coat may lead some observer to conclude
that the wearer of the coat is about to go to a dance. But we would not
want to say that putting on a tail coat *meant* anything (in the sense
these philosophers are interested in).[7] Grice is aware that his
counterexample would be ruled out by Stevenson's insistence that
the conditioning which leads to the response be the result of "the
sign's use in communication." However, as Grice points out, this
excludes the unwanted case only at the cost of introducing a circularity into the proposed account of meaning. We want an account of
precisely what makes something a *communicative* use of a sign.

Having offered a few perfunctory criticisms of causal theories,
Grice then proceeds to offer a "different and . . . more promising
line."[8] The most notable feature of this "new line" is its unselfcon-
scious employment of such concepts as intention and belief. For reasons having nothing to do with the antimentalistic scruples of Grice's
predecessors and contemporaries, some of the most difficult problems with Grice's account of meaning still center around the understanding of these concepts, as I shall soon explain.

It is interesting to consider what relation Grice's account of meaning has to the "ideational theories" of the sixteenth to eighteenth
centuries.[9] Such a theory is to be found, for example, in the writings
of John Locke. In his *Essay Concerning Human Understanding* Locke
speaks as if language is essentially an instrument for the communication of some preformed and otherwise invisible thought. Words are
"marks for the ideas within [the speaker's] own mind," and where
those "internal conceptions" are absent, the sounds we associate
with language are as insignificant as the articulations of a parrot.[10]
According to Locke the speaker uses words as signs (or marks) of his
ideas; communication is achieved when the words excite the same
ideas in the hearer as they are made to stand for in the speaker. In this
way the content of the utterance (what it is about) is said to derive
from the content of the thoughts with which it is associated. Locke
thus writes:

The comfort and advantage of society not being to be had without communication of thought, it was necessary that man should find some external signs, whereof those invisible ideas, which his thoughts are made up of, might be known to others. . . . The use, then, of words is to be sensible marks of ideas; and the ideas they stand for are their proper and immediate signification.[11]

This account of meaning is part of Locke's general empiricist account of concepts: words are associated with ideas, and all ideas derive ultimately from experience. According to Locke and the empiricists, then, one accounts for the meaning (signification) attached to utterances by reference to the ideas for which they stand.[12] But this raises the question of how we are to understand the signification that *ideas* have. To say that all ideas are derived from experience is to gesture in the direction we should look, but it alone provides few answers. Furthermore, since ideas depend on the subject, it is hard to see how reference to them can be used to explain the commonality of language. This account of meaning also raises the question of how that signification that ideas are said to have is conveyed from the idea to the utterance. To say that words are "external signs" of ideas, to suggest that words serve to encode ideas,[13] is merely to describe the phenomenon; it provides no explanation of how it occurs.[14]

It was questions like these that led to much criticism of ideational theories in the late nineteenth and early twentieth centuries. According to Michael Dummett, this conception of language was "first clearly repudiated by Frege."[15] Frege's criticism was closely followed by Wittgenstein's.[16] Grice's work on meaning was published after these criticisms were well established, yet it is not entirely clear how to place Grice's work with respect to them. The issue is pressing owing to the central role allotted to speakers' psychological states in Grice's account of meaning. Consideration of ideational theories and criticism of them raise several specific questions about Grice's work. First of all, what account are we to give of the intentions and beliefs that are mentioned on the right-hand side of the analytic biconditional?[17] As we consider this question, another, more fundamental question arises: if we say that the way meaning attaches to utterances can be analyzed in terms of speakers' intentions to produce certain beliefs in an audience, what are we to say about what is meant? It looks as if the theorist of meaning can be seen as having two tasks: one is to say how utterances have meaning; the other is to say something about that meaning. If this is right, we can ask which task Grice saw himself as discharging. I would argue that Grice's concern is not with the issue of content per se but with understanding how utterances have their content. His suggestion is that to understand how utterances have their content we must understand how intentions and beliefs have their content, for the former is definable in terms of the latter. Understood in this way, Grice's work still leaves open a very important issue: how is it that intentions and beliefs have their content?

Understanding how Grice's work relates to ideational theories is far from a straightforward matter. It requires first that we understand how to interpret Grice's work. In sections 3 and 4 of this chapter I discuss different possible interpretations of Grice's analysis. In chapter 3 I proceed to investigate one prominent interpretation in some depth. It is not until I have done this that I return in chapter 4 to the question of the relation Grice's work has to ideational theories of meaning.

Frege's work in the philosophy of language is sometimes thought to mark a shift from ideational or code conceptions of language to a more formal approach. In the first half of the twentieth century the logical apparatus developed largely by Frege and Russell was brought to bear on language. The formal semanticists were interested not in natural language as such but in a purely formal structure, which may or may not be abstracted from natural language. Their concern was mainly with the sentences of this abstract and formal language and with the entailment relations that hold between them. From Frege onward these formal philosophers insisted that the job of any adequate theory of meaning was to give an account of the following features of language: (1) that the sentence is the primary bearer of meaning; (2) that the sense of a sentence is determined by the sense of its constituent elements; and (3) that the sense of a sentence constituent is determined by its contribution to the sense of any sentence in which it occurs.[18] The second of these features is what accounts for the property often thought to be most distinctive of language, namely, that from a finite stock of semantic primitives a language user can understand and construct a potentially infinite variety of sentences.[19]

Around the 1950s purely formal theories came under attack. The attack is to be found in the work of the later Wittgenstein and J. L. Austin. Whereas the formal theorists had concentrated on the structure and interrelations among sentences in the indicative mood, abstracting from the ambiguity and imprecision of natural languages, these use theorists, as they came to be called, argued that imprecision and ambiguity are of the essence of the expressive power of language, that the use of language to describe the world is only one among many of its uses, and that language cannot properly be studied in abstraction from its daily use. Despite their differences, formal theorists and use theorists concurred in at least one thing: both agreed that the sentence is the primary bearer of meaning. However, in the shift of emphasis from words to sentences, use theorists took the opportunity also to emphasize the role of speakers. John Searle writes that the influence of the later Wittgenstein and Austin "recasts the discussion of many of the problems in the philosophy of language into the larger context of the discussion of human action and behaviour generally. . . . Instead of seeing the relations between words and the world as something existing *in vacuo*, one now sees them as involving intentional actions by speakers."[20] It is natural to locate Grice in this tradition.

Clearly Grice's account of meaning does bring the philosophy of language within the scope of the philosophy of mind and the theory of action. His account may be said to have its roots in the simple observation that noises and marks have meaning only insofar as they are the expression of some individual's intention to communicate.[21] Donald Davidson also draws on this observation when he writes:

> Someone who utters the sentence "The candle is out" as a sentence of English must intend to utter words that are true if and only if an indicated candle is out at the time of utterance, and he must believe that by making the sounds he does he is uttering words that are true only under those circumstances. These intentions and beliefs are not apt to be dwelt on by the fluent speaker. But though they may not normally command attention, their absence would be enough to show that he was not speaking English, and the absence of any analogous thoughts would show that he was not speaking at all.[22]

Observations such as these suggest that it must be right to bring the philosophy of language within the scope of the philosophy of mind. However, in recognizing this important feature of language one must not lose sight of another, equally important feature: the fact that the meaning of a sentence is built up from the meanings of words, in accordance with the rules of combination governing the language. Formal theorists may have erred in their apparent omission of any mention of the beliefs and intentions of speakers in their account of meaning, but in correcting this omission use theorists must not lose sight of the fact that any adequate account of language must give an account of its structural and recursive features.

Now if one looks at Grice's 1957 paper on meaning, one finds no mention of structure. One thing that might be said to explain the omission is the following: Grice is concerned primarily with meaning, a phenomenon which occurs both in language and outside it.[23] But the kind of structure emphasized and so well understood by the formal semanticists is only found in language.[24] As one Gricean writes: "The notion defined is intended to be fully general, and to cover all communication, from a caveman's tentative grunts to the orations of Cicero."[25] An account wide enough to cover meaning quite generally may be one that can relegate the question of structure to secondary status. It is arguable that this is Grice's strategy. Grice never denies the importance of structure to language, and it is clear that Grice intends his account of meaning to serve as an account of linguistic meaning.[26] Nevertheless, his primary purpose is to give an account of the more general feature of meaning.

Once Grice's strategy is understood, it is less clear whether he is solely a use theorist.[27] Indeed, it is unclear whether anyone was or is solely a use or solely a formal theorist of meaning. Neither the structural features of a language nor the obvious connections with speakers' psychological states can ultimately be ignored when giving an account of meaning. In fact several philosophers have thought that formal semanticists and use theorists are not really in direct competition. David Wiggins writes: "Nothing that has happened since J. L. Austin's 1950 lectures 'Words and Deeds' or their publication [1962] seems to me to have undermined or made obsolete the kind of semantic theory typified by Frege or Russell or, in our times, by Carnap."[28] And Searle echoes this: "Although historically there have been sharp disagreements between practitioners of these two approaches [one which concentrates on the use of expressions in speech situations and one which concentrates on the meaning of sentences], it is important to realize that the two approaches . . . are complementary and not competing."[29]

It is easy to see that some reconciliation is necessary; it is much harder to explain how that reconciliation is to proceed. If we think of the program of accounting for meaning as the wider enterprise of which giving a Gricean account of use is only one part, while some more formal theory accounting for structure is another part, then we must ask how these parts fit together. There is no quick answer to this question. I believe that this question compels us to reflect upon our general conception of the semantic and the psychological, both individually and as part of a larger whole. This conceptual issue determines which interpretation we choose to give of the Gricean analysis, and the interpretation we give will determine our view of the reconciliation. The question of interpretation, then, is prior to that of reconciliation.

However, when the concept we seek to understand is meaning, we can address the question of interpretation only after we agree that the method of analysis is appropriately applied. Some philosophers have argued that our concept of meaning is one that the method of analysis does not suit. Obviously, such an argument would, if correct, completely undermine Grice's work on meaning. In the next section I shall consider some of these arguments. In section 3 I consider the question of interpretation, and in section 4 I discuss reconciliation. It is not until chapter 3 that I fully explain my claim that interpretation is affected by one's general conception of the semantic and the psychological.

2 Two Approaches to the Problem of Meaning

The problem of meaning is not the problem of giving an account of the meaning of the words and sentences in this or that particular language. The problem is a more general one. The question is: how are we to understand the obvious fact that certain noises and marks have significance for individuals, that they can be used to convey information, command another to act, and much more? This phenomenon, so familiar to us, remains elusive to our understanding.

It has been the view of some more recent philosophers of language that the problem should be approached indirectly. Rather than attempting to say what meaning is, these philosophers choose to ask: what form should a *theory* of meaning take? This method has been adopted by philosophers of language as different as Davidson and Dummett.[30] The latter writes, "Once we can enunciate the general principle in accordance with which such a construction [of a theory of meaning] could be carried out, we shall have arrived at a solution to the problems concerning meaning by which philosophers are perplexed."[31] Once such a theory has been constructed we can say the following: meaning is what a theory of meaning is a theory of.

This indirect approach to the problem of meaning chosen by the theory builders stands in stark contrast to the more direct method chosen by Grice. In the latter's work there is no mention of general principles or of theories. Rather, Grice sets out in a quite straightforward way to elucidate our concept of meaning in terms of various beliefs and intentions of speakers and hearers.[32] Such elucidation is common in philosophy: one takes the concept one is interested in and analyzes it in terms of other concepts whose joint application is both necessary and sufficient for its application.[33]

The theory builders are doing more than considering a different approach to the problem. Many of them argue that the method of analysis is unsuited to the concept of meaning. I want to take a brief look at their method, and to consider some of their reasons for rejecting analysis when the concept in question is meaning. I hope to show that the pessimism of the theory builders is either premature or unfounded.

Davidson has said that when the problem is to understand the phenomenon of meaning, our strategy should be to accumulate requirements which any theory purporting to be a theory of meaning for a language should meet. These requirements are thought to give us the shape of our concept. Davidson suggests that any adequate theory of meaning for a language should meet the following requirements: (1) the theorems of the theory must be such that they are recognizable by any speaker of the language as expressing what he knows in virtue of being a speaker of that language; (2) the account must make clear how we can generate an unlimited number of sentences from a finite stock of semantic primitives; and a related point, (3) the account must be one that explains the systematic contribution words make to the sentences in which they figure. Davidson then points out that there already exists a method for constructing theories which meet these requirements, viz. Tarski's approach to truth.[34] "To know the semantic concept of truth for a language is to know what it is for a sentence—any sentence—to be true, and this amounts, in one good sense we can give of the phrase, to understanding the language."[35]

Dummett follows Davidson's method, but it leads him to somewhat different conclusions. Dummett too believes that the best way of approaching the philosophical problems that surround the concept of meaning is to enunciate general principles (compare Davidson's requirements) that must govern the construction of a theory of meaning, a theory that is "a detailed specification of the meanings of all words and sentence-forming operations of the language, yielding a specification of the meaning of every expression and sentence of the language."[36] The principles Dummett enunciates, however, lead him to reject a theory of meaning based on truth conditions in favor of one based on verification conditions. Dummett begins with the observation that "philosophical questions about meaning are best interpreted as questions about understanding."[37] In another place he writes, "What a theory of meaning has to give an account of is what it is that someone knows when he knows the language."[38] Dummett observes that someone who knows a language has a straightforward practical ability, the ability to use the language to communicate with others. So whatever it is the speaker who knows a language knows, that something must be manifested in, and recoverable from, his use of expressions of that language, or else communication cannot take place. It is this practical ability that the theory seeks to represent. These, then, are the general principles in accordance with which Dummett sees the theory of meaning being formed, and he cannot see that a theory based on a realistically interpreted notion of truth (compare Davidson's theory) can meet them.

Now my concern is not to adjudicate between alternative general conceptions of what theories of meaning should be. Rather, it is to contrast the method of theory building and the method of analysis for the concept of meaning. On this issue of analysis versus theory building Dummett compares our concept of meaning with that of knowledge. He observes that although the indirect method of theory building is well tried in the philosophy of language, no one has so much as suggested a parallel way of proceeding in epistemology. When the question is, How are we to understand our concept of knowledge? philosophers do not begin by constructing a theory of knowledge which would serve as a detailed specification of what every individual knows who has knowledge. Analysis seems more suited to *this* concept. This is Dummett's explanation of the difference in our approach to these two concepts:

> Our grasp on the concept of knowledge is rather more secure than our grasp on the concept of meaning. . . . At least we are quite certain [with respect to our concept of knowledge] *which* are the sentences whose logical form and whose truth conditions we are seeking to analyse. By contrast, while most of us . . . would agree that the concept of meaning is a fundamental and indispensable one, we are unclear even about the surface structure of statements involving that concept. What kind of sentence, of natural language, should be taken as the characteristic form for an attribution of a particular meaning to a given word or expression? Not only do we not know the answer to this: we do not even know whether it is the right question to ask. . . . It is precisely because, in this area of philosophy, we know even less what it is that we are talking about than we do in other areas that the proposal to approach our problem by considering how we might attempt to specify the meanings of the expressions of an entire language does not appear the waste of time that an analogous proposal would seem to be within epistemology.[39]

John Wisdom has said, "The first precept for philosophic analysing is this: Know clearly what it is you propose to analyse."[40] What Dummett seems to be suggesting in the passage quoted above is that fulfilling this precept is possible when the concept is knowledge but difficult when the concept is meaning. Hence, we require an alternative method to analysis when the concept is meaning.

But is Dummett right to think that it is not possible to meet Wisdom's precept when the concept in question is meaning? To be fair, Dummett does preface his discussion of this matter with the claim that although he believes theory building to be the most fruitful approach to the problem of meaning, he "should not feel capable of giving a demonstration that this was so to someone who denied it."[41] The contrast between the concepts of meaning and knowledge is meant as an attempt to give some reason for his preference for theory building. This attempt to give support to his preference raises interesting and important issues, and the comparison with the concept of knowledge is illuminating. Nevertheless, I shall argue that Dummett's reasons, insofar as I understand them, are unpersuasive, and his preference for theory building remains a mere preference.

It is certainly true that the word "means" is used in many connections other than linguistic ones (e.g., "She means to leave him," "I mean what I say," etc.).[42] And even within language we find such phenomena as speaker meaning, word meaning, sentence meaning, meaning on a particular occasion, and meaning over time. But perhaps there is some recognizable order in all this apparent chaos. After all, "know" also is an expression with varied uses (e.g., "knows how," "knows that," "knows Tom"). It does seem that the linguistic promiscuity of the latter expression is tamer than that of the former, but we may ask whether this observation is sufficient to warrent such substantially different approaches to the philosophical problems that each concept raises. Perhaps what is needed is some sentence form with which one can begin one's analysis of meaning, a sentence form that will serve the function for the concept of meaning that "x knows that p" has traditionally served for the concept of knowledge.

Grice's suggestion is that we begin with speaker meaning on an occasion, that we provide an analysis of this concept in terms of the psychological states of the speaker and the hearer, and that we reconstruct such notions as meaning over time and the meaning of words and sentences on the basis of this basic notion. By drawing attention to such distinctions as that between sentence meaning and speaker meaning, and that between timeless meaning and occasion meaning, Grice is able to clear the ground sufficiently to find the starting point that is needed for analysis. The suggestion, then, is that the sentence form that captures some central use of our concept of meaning, to which all other uses are related, and that can serve as the focus of an analysis is this: Speaker S means on an occasion that p.[43] If the linguistic promiscuity of "means" is the problem Dummett is concerned with, I cannot see that Grice (and others) have not clarified matters sufficiently to allow for the possibility of an analysis of our concept of meaning. And I might add that work relating the various uses of the expression "knows" is far less developed.

It is, of course, possible that Dummett's animadversions on the analysis of our concept of meaning extend beyond anything with which this logical ordering of priorities can help. For in the same place he writes:

> Perhaps it is impossible, in general, to *state* the meaning of an expression: perhaps we ought, rather, to inquire by what linguistic means, or possibly even non-linguistic means, it is possible to *convey* the meaning of an expression other than by explicitly stating it. Or perhaps even this is wrong: perhaps the question should be, not how we express that a particular expression has a certain meaning, but how we should analyse sentences which involve the concept of meaning in some different way.[44]

But I cannot see that these problems are confined to the concept of meaning. Perhaps, it will ultimately prove fruitless to aim to determine conditions necessary and sufficient for knowledge; perhaps we will find that to explain how a creature comes to have knowledge and subsequently to manifest it is all philosophers can hope to do. If there is something wrong with the analytic approach to meaning, I do not think that Dummett has said enough to locate the difficulty.

Can anything explain the fact that some philosophers reject analysis in favor of theory building when the concept is meaning? And can anything explain the divergence of method by these same philosophers when the concept is, for example, knowledge? I believe we do better to ask not why the method of analysis has no application to the concept of meaning but rather why the method of theory building has application to the concept of meaning and not, for example, to a concept like knowledge. Putting the question this way around leaves it open whether analysis is applicable to the concept of meaning, as well as whether theory building is. Once we have fulfilled Wisdom's first precept of analysis (*pace* Dummett), analysis may be viewed as a harmless enterprise potentially applicable to all concepts. Theory building, on the other hand, may be thought to have a place with only some concepts. As Dummett quite rightly points out, no one would proceed in epistemology by constructing a theory that would serve as a specification of what every individual knows who has knowledge. What Dummett does not do is to say *why* no one would proceed in this way with the concept of knowledge. It seems to me that the reason is that such a theory would in no way further our understanding of that concept. When we want to further our understanding of linguistic meaning, the sort of thing a theory could exhibit would be helpful. One of the most important things the theory would do is to show how it is that the meanings of sentences depend on the meanings of the words that compose them. Relatedly, the theory would make it clear how it is that from a finite stock of semantic primitives speakers of a language are able to generate an infinite variety of new sentences. These are very important features of language, and it is hard to see how analysis alone can explain them.[45] As far as I can see there are no analogous features of knowledge to be explained.[46]

Dummett is not the only theorist of meaning who has explicitly opposed the analysis of the concept. John McDowell indicates opposition to the analysis of meaning in several of his papers. In a relatively recent paper McDowell writes, "We lack an argument that meaning constitutes the sort of philosophical problem which requires analysis for its solution."[47] This is just as well, for McDowell foresees a problem for the analytic approach to the concept of meaning.

The problem in its most general form is this: after we provide an analysis of meaning in terms of something else, we cannot rest content until this something else is, in its turn, accounted for. McDowell is especially concerned with philosophers who accept Davidson's suggestion that we look to a theory of truth for a language when we seek to find a theory of meaning for it and then argue that such a theory is crucially incomplete until we can provide an account of what a theory of truth is for a language, for *any* language.[48] McDowell argues that there is an appearance of incompleteness here only if we understand the appeal to truth along the lines of an analysis; theorists who make this appeal, however, are not engaged in an analysis of the concept of meaning (see the discussion of direct versus indirect approaches above).

McDowell suggests that we abandon the direct approach of analysis altogether and rest content with a more indirect approach to the problem of meaning. Rather than ask, What is meaning? McDowell suggests that we change tack and consider what is involved in *understanding* a language.[49] As he sees it, what one wants from a theory of understanding is this: the theory must take a possessor of it from an uninterpreted description of marks and sounds to a description of them as speech acts with a certain content, and it must do this in such a way as to reveal how the meanings of the parts, the words, contribute to the meaning of the whole, the sentence. To fulfill the latter requirement, we employ a suitable theory of truth, and to fulfill the first requirement we must construct this theory so as to make the overall behavior of speakers of the language intelligible.[50] Nowhere in this do we need to appeal to analysis, according to McDowell. What we have in place of an analysis is "a perspicuous mapping of interrelations between concepts which, as far as the exercise goes, can be taken to be already perfectly well understood."[51] And McDowell notes: "It is a striking fact that in the mapping offered by my theorist the concept of meaning as such does not even appear. So far from analysing the notion of meaning, he suggests the radical thought that in describing the understanding of a language we can get along without it."[52]

McDowell has suggested one way of bringing the philosophy of language within the scope of the philosophy of mind, but I cannot see that he has given any reason yet to reject the alternative of a Gricean analysis of meaning. McDowell seems to be suggesting that the method of analysis is incompatible with something which provides "a perspicuous mapping of interrelations between concepts which . . . can be taken to be already perfectly well understood," but this need not be the case. It depends upon the interpretation we choose to give of the analysis. In this chapter, section 3, I suggest that there is a strong, reductive interpretation of the analytic biconditional and a weak, nonreductive interpretation of it. As far as I can see, everything McDowell says about analysis is true only of the strong, reductive interpretation of it. Under its weak reading, an analysis is the statement of conditions necessary and sufficient for the analysandum concept to apply; there is no requirement that the concepts in the analysandum reduce to those in the analysans.[53]

What is needed is an account of meaning that does the following two things: (1) relates utterances to speakers of them; and (2) carries out (1) so as to reveal a relevant structure in the process. One way to fulfill the first of these requirements is to spell out precisely which psychological states are the ones that relate speakers to their utterances. According to the weak, nonreductive interpretation of the analysis, specifying this relation is just what we may take Grice's analysis to be doing. In his work McDowell offers an alternative, nonanalytic approach to (1); I cannot see, however, that McDowell has yet given us a good reason to choose his approach over Grice's.

Pending a workable argument against analysis, it may be wise to leave ourselves open to its merits. The analytic method may prove useful in providing some understanding of our concept of meaning.[54]

In another place, and in conjunction with Gareth Evans, McDowell does put forward another argument, which if correct, would count against even a weak, nonreductive interpretation of Grice's analysis.[55] Accepting the need to bring the philosophy of language within the scope of the philosophy of mind, McDowell and Evans consider Grice's work as providing "a richer set of constraints, imposed, not necessarily in a reductive spirit, by bringing general psychological principles to bear upon determinations of meaning in order to make the constructed theory fit the data on the basis of which it was constructed."[56] They reject this suggestion for the following reason: Grice's analysis, even under this weak interpretation, does not properly reflect the "phenomenology of language." The phenomenology of language is habitual and unreflective, while the analysis is rather complex and suggests a highly reflective form of behavior. That is to say, Grice's account of the relations meaningful utterances bear to the psychological states of the speakers of a language is inaccurate in its spelling out of necessary and sufficient conditions: it can never be brought to square with how things seemed to the speaker at the time of speaking.

Grice and Griceans have had much to say about this matter. As far as I know, all Griceans accept the observation that the phenomenology of language is as McDowell and Evans describe. They would agree with their critics that the complexity reflected in their analysis is not matched by any conscious processes in speakers. However, Griceans have made various suggestions that accommodate this observation.

Against this charge of imposing too complex a psychological life upon the ordinary linguistic behavior of individuals, Stephen Schiffer has argued that the case under consideration is very similar to the explanation of nonlinguistic behavior more generally by citing certain and in some cases highly complex beliefs, desires, and intentions.[57] Schiffer gives the following example. Janet sees a dog threatening to menace her garden and smacks the book she happens to be reading in order to scare off the intruder. This behavior (like ordinary linguistic behavior) is done quite unreflectively. Nevertheless, we might choose to give the following account of Janet's behavior: Janet's primary intention in smacking the book was to get rid of the dog; she also intended to produce a sharp noise that would startle the dog and intended the dog's being startled to cause it to run off. Now consider the case of Janet's telling John that there is a vicious dog in the garden by uttering the words, "There is a vicious dog in the garden." According to the Gricean, for Janet to tell John that there is a vicious dog in the garden is for Janet to utter "There is a vicious dog in the garden" with the primary intention of informing John that there is a vicious dog in the garden.[58] Furthermore, Janet intends the satisfaction of her primary intention to be achieved, at least in part, because John believes (1) that "There is a vicious dog in the garden" is related in a certain way to there being a vicious dog in the garden, (2) that Janet uttered what she did with the intention of informing John that there is a vicious dog in the garden, and at least partly on the basis of this, (3) that Janet believes that there is a vicious dog in the garden, and partly on the basis of this, (4) that there is a vicious dog in the garden. The Gricean account of linguistic behavior requires, then, the plausibility of attributing to the speaker certain *tacit expectations* about her audience. In this case what is at issue is the plausibility of attributing to Janet the tacit expectation that (1) John believes that the words "There is a vicious dog in the garden" bears a conventional relation to their being a vicious dog in the garden, (2) at least in part because of this convention John will believe that Janet uttered the sentence intending to inform him that there is a vicius dog in the garden, (3) John will believe at least partly on the basis of his recognition of her intention that Janet believes that there is a vicious dog in the garden, and (4) John will believe partly as a result of (3) that there is a vicious dog in the garden.

Complex though such attributions are, it is hard to see how any account of communication can omit them. The reasons are as follows: First of all, without expectations concerning John's knowledge of the conventions of English, Janet would not have chosen those particular sounds to convey the information that there is a vicious dog in the garden. Furthermore, without expectations about John's beliefs concerning her intentions in producing the utterance, Janet might not have chosen this way of conveying this information to John (if, for example, she expected that John would take her to be joking or teasing). Also, without expectations about John's belief that she believed that there is a vicious dog in the garden (i.e., without the expectation that John would not take her to be lying), Janet might not have spoken. And finally, without expectations that at least in part on the basis of (1) through (3) John would come to believe that there is a vicious dog in the garden, Janet might not have spoken at all.

Those that find the attribution of such tacit expectation to speakers implausible sometimes add another objection, this time about the Gricean picture of audiences. On the Gricean view, an audience's understanding of an utterance is a process of inference from a string of uttered noises to the intentions of the utterer, and from there to a piece of information or knowledge about the world. The objection to this view of understanding as a process of inference appears to be the other side of the objection that Griceans attribute too much psychological complexity to speakers. In reply the Gricean could simply adapt what was already said in defence of tacit expectations to serve as a defence of the Gricean picture of understanding. P. F. Strawson may be thought to have summed up the Gricean position on this matter when he wrote:

> Only a very naive, a far from mature, audience would be quite unaware of the possibility of honest mistake, or of intention to mislead or of sheer casualness or carelessness, on the part of the communicator; and only a very naive communicator would be unaware of the audience's awareness of these possibilities. And if this is so, it seems hardly too much to say that it is a part, though normally a subdued or submerged part, of the genuine communication intentions, that the audience's response to his performance should be governed by certain (normally subdued or submerged) assumptions regarding his (the communicator's) sincerity and reliability.[59]

Once again, the claim is that we need not think of such inferences as there may be as conscious or explicit.

Talk of tacit expectations and implicit inference is in effect a defence of the psychological reality of certain states in speakers and their audiences. Some Griceans, however, go so far as to suggest that we needn't think in terms of psychological reality at all in order to support the proposed analysis. In one short passage David Armstrong suggests that it may be a matter of "rational reconstruction rather than psychological reality."[60] Talk of rational reconstruction has recently been attributed to Grice himself.[61] Basing their remarks on Grice's John Locke lectures, Grandy and Warner suggest that a speaker or an audience may be held to reason from a particular premise to a particular conclusion without ever having entertained an argument linking that premise and that conclusion either explicitly or implicitly. Rather, if the speaker or audience is to be correctly described as having reasoned from premise to conclusion, then he must at least intend that there be some sequence of propositions that constitute an argument from the premise to the conclusion.

Evans and McDowell continue to balk. They refuse to accept that communication involves any ratiocination, explicit, implicit, or reconstructed.[62] They insist that the phenomenological facts exclude anything along Gricean lines. But what they offer is not so much an argument as an alternative. They write, "Our understanding of meanings should normally be perception of meaning, and hence precisely *not* a matter of inference."[63] Evans and McDowell offer here an extremely interesting alternative to a Gricean account of communication. Adjudicating between different accounts of communication, however, is not my purpose. My interest here is to find a workable argument against the Gricean approach. Without such an argument the Gricean account remains an option.

One Gricean chooses to modify the analysis of meaning in order to accommodate the problems I have been discussing. Jonathan Bennett formulates the problem in the following way.[64] On Grice's picture of things, communication relies on the speaker's expectation that his audience can discover, through the speaker's use of a particular utterance, what the speaker's communicative intentions are. That is, communication involves the speaker's intentions and the hearer's recognition of the speaker's intentions. Bennett proposes for our consideration a community of speakers which uses a communication system that does not seem to rely on Grice's mechanism of beliefs and intentions. He labels this system "Plain Talk." It is a characteristic of users of plain talk that speakers rely on their audiences' belief in the following generalization: whenever a particular utterance, U, is uttered, a particular proposition, p, is true. In this way the route of communication does not need to pass through the speaker's intentions. Bennett then proposes the following challenge to the Gricean: "If the facts will accommodate that simpler diagnosis of how A came to believe p, then we should prefer it to the more complex one which says that he followed the sophisticated Gricean route."[65]

Bennett believes the Gricean can meet this challenge. He points out that the facts about communication may not seem to point in the direction of Grice's analysis because we are overlooking what he calls "the crucial background fact."[66] That fact is that any communication system must be at least indirectly dependent on the intentions of speakers. Of course, once a language is established, the audience may simply rely on the generalization that whenever U is uttered, p is true, but this is possible because of the intentions of past U utterers.[67] We see this once we realize that "if the speaker had not intended to communicate p when he uttered U, it would have been inappropriate to bring his utterance of U under the generalization that whenever U is uttered p is true."[68]

Consideration of plain talk thus does not lead Bennett to reject Grice's analysis of meaning. It does, however, lead him to modify it. His modification is designed to emphasize this "background fact" in communication without excessive reliance on the speaker's intentions in any given case of communication. Bennett's modification involves omitting the mention of complex propositional attitudes in the analysis, and substituting instead something along these lines: a speaker intends to communicate the proposition that p to an audience by offering the audience intention-dependent evidence that p.[69] But it is not clear that any modification is necessary. One could simply say that Grice's original analysis of meaning captures this "crucial background fact." The analysis is not meant to capture the way things seem; it is just a statement of the way things must be. In keeping with the defence discussed earlier, Brian Loar responds to Bennett's modification thus: "But not only is that economy not necessary for a realistic theory; to eliminate the alleged intentions eliminates something that seems fundamental to communication once one notices it. That the intentions, expectations, and beliefs of ordinary communication and personal relations are simple appears so improbable that it puzzles me why it should be thought to be the more realistic view."[70]

Whatever the outcome of this debate, we should note that objections to what I have called the weak, nonreductive interpretation of Grice's analysis are not objections to the method of analysis as such. What is being objected to is a *particular* proposed analysis. Even if the objections should succeed and communication not be what the Gricean says it is, there may still be room for *some* analysis of the concept of meaning.[71] It is important to notice this, as it is often the analytic approach to meaning in general that is assumed to be the casualty of such considerations.

My purpose in this section has been to show that those who reject analysis in favor of theory building for the concept of meaning may have a preference, but they do not have an argument.[72] Dummett contrasts philosophers' approach to the concept of meaning with their approach to the concept of knowledge. Our more secure grasp on the latter leads Dummett to conclude that analysis may suit it, but an insecurity in our grasp of the former concept makes theory building a more suitable approach here. I can see no reason in what Dummett says for different approaches to these concepts. McDowell too suggests that we should turn away from analysis when our concern is with the concept of meaning. He suggests that we seek in the place of analysis an account that will provide "a perspicuous mapping of the interrelations between concepts which . . . can be taken to be already perfectly well understood." I pointed out that a nonreductive interpretation of the method of analysis can give McDowell what he is looking for. Finally, I turned to an argument designed to show that a *Gricean* analysis of meaning, even on a weak interpretation, yields a mistaken account of that concept. Here the defender of analysis need only reply that squaring with how things seem to the speaker at the time of speaking is not his primary concern. His concern is with how things are, and if they turn out to differ from the way things seem, there is no cause in this to turn away from the analysis. And an appeal to tacit expectations or reconstructed reasoning can help to make the results of a Gricean analysis more palatable.

This last point is clearly not meant to be decisive. The issue is not one I shall pursue here (though, as we shall see in section 4 of this chapter, the issue is relevant to the reconciliation of Gricean and more formal approaches to meaning). As I said, my primary purpose in this section has been to show that there are no good reasons for rejecting the method of analysis as unsuited to the concept of meaning. If one is impressed by McDowell's appeal for "a perspicuous mapping of interrelations between concepts . . . ," one need only reject an interpretation of Grice's analysis. And even one who goes so far as to reject the weak, nonreductive interpretation of Grice's analysis need not reject the method of analysis per se. Analysis may not provide the whole story about meaning, but it may turn out to provide a valuable piece in a very difficult puzzle.[73]

3 Two Kinds of Analysis

I have on several occasions now referred to the possibility of two quite different interpretations of the method of analysis. In discussing McDowell's proposal for understanding meaning, I had cause to distinguish a strong, reductive interpretation of analysis from something much weaker. In section 1, I suggested that how one reconciles a Gricean account of use with a more formal theory revealing structure depends upon which interpretation of Grice's work one is prepared to defend. Related to this, I also suggested that each interpretation of Grice's work is bound up with a radically different conception of the psychological and of the semantic, and of the relationship between the two. In this section I want to explain what is involved in each of these interpretations of the analytic method.

The most straightforward and least controversial thing that can be said about an analysis is that it is represented by a biconditional, the right-hand side of which gives conditions necessary and sufficient for the application of the concept in which we are interested on the left-hand side. I shall take it that analysis is a method philosophers engage in to further our understanding of some given concept. It can equally be said that analysis helps us to get clearer about a certain concept.

Compare this with what G. E. Moore says in his paper "The Justification of Analysis." In that paper Moore considers two uses of analysis: the first is to relieve puzzlement about some concept; the second is to make our thoughts clearer. Moore cites Broad as a champion of the first of these two uses of analysis. According to Broad, we are puzzled by the obscurity which surrounds certain concepts, and this puzzlement leads us into various difficulties. Providing an analysis reduces obscurity and helps us to avoid these difficulties.[74] Moore, on the other hand, believes that analysis has very little to do with the relief of puzzlement and has much more to do with the business of making our thoughts clearer. Moore does not think that the clarification which analysis can bring can help us live our ordinary lives, nor does he think it can help us to avoid difficulties. Rather, Moore believes that "the chief use of analysis in the way of clearness, is only the clearness which it produces when you're doing philosophy itself."[75] In saying this, Moore is keen to emphasize that he believes that it is a mistake to think of analysis as useful for the sake of something else.

There exists a much more radical opposition to Moore's view of analysis than Broad's. John Wisdom, for example, has argued that the aim of analysis is to reach another level of concepts, concepts that are more basic, more fundamental, than the ones under analysis. This kind of analysis is sometimes called "new-level analysis," and Wisdom contrasted it with Moore's sort, which he labeled "same-level analysis."[76] For instance, Wisdom and others have claimed that an analysis of nations reveals that individuals are more basic than nations, and that an analysis of individuals reveals that sense data and mental states are more basic than individuals.

Moore's view of analysis is certainly to be contrasted with Wisdom's, and yet one cannot deny that moving to a new level of concepts in the way Wisdom envisages would be *one* way of achieving the clarity about a concept that Moore is after. What Moore needs to do is explain how a same-level analysis produces clarity. I want to suggest that one way of achieving clarity without moving to another level of concept would be to discover interdependencies among concepts. It can be clarifying to see the place a concept holds in our system of (same level) concepts. To put the same thought in a slightly different way, it can help us to understand what is involved in our grasp of one concept to be told that it is inextricably bound up with our grasp of some other concept or concepts. This interrelationship in its precise detail is what analysis reveals.

Drawing on the ideas of both Moore and Wisdom, we can now say that the method of analysis in general is concerned with the clarification and understanding of concepts. One way analysis can clarify our concepts (and here I follow Wisdom) is by revealing that certain concepts are, in a sense to be explained, less basic or less fundamental in our scheme of concepts than some other concepts. Such an analysis would show that our grasp of certain concepts could be broken down into elements (other concepts) that could replace the originals in our general scheme of concepts without loss (other than that of simplicity perhaps). But there is another way in which analysis can clarify our concepts (and here I follow and develop Moore): by revealing precisely how those concepts are related to others in our overall scheme of concepts. The concepts mentioned on either side of the analytic biconditional have to be thought of as on a par (in a sense I shall discuss in chapter 3 below). Neither set of concepts would be more basic or fundamental than the other.

One could think of these two ways of achieving clarity as two kinds of analysis, each kind distinguished by the sort of understanding it reveals of a particular concept. In terms of understanding, then, we may say that one kind of analysis reveals that understanding some particular concept is to be achieved by understanding some other concepts. The other sort of analysis tells us that understanding a certain concept is to be gained only by discerning its place in a system of interrelated concepts. I shall call the first sort of analysis "reductive" and the second "reciprocal."

When I say that there are two kinds of analysis, I do not mean to imply that one constructs the biconditional in two different ways. The difference lies only in the interpretation we give of the analytic biconditional that *any* analysis produces: are we to see the concepts mentioned on either side of the biconditional as, in Wisdom's words, on the same level or on different levels? We can ask the same question in a slightly different way: is there a symmetry between the concepts mentioned on either side of the analytic biconditional, or are there some grounds for claiming an asymmetry between these concepts?

Thus, when presented with an analysis, Grice's analysis of meaning, for example, we must ask what kind of analysis it is; how is that analysis to be interpreted? Because of the connection between understanding and analysis, we find that how we should interpret the analysis depends upon the kind of understanding possible of the concept in question. This means that the concept itself determines the kind of understanding we may have of it, and hence, the kind of analysis we may give of it. Presented with an analysis, we need to ask whether the concepts mentioned on either side of the biconditional are on the same or different levels. Or as I prefer to put it: we need to ask whether there is a symmetry between the concepts mentioned in the analysans and those in the analysandum, or whether there is some ground for claiming an asymmetry. Of course, talk of symmetry is hardly less obscure than talk of levels. What we need to understand is what lies behind any claim of symmetry or asymmetry. It is the central work of this book to explore what such a claim amounts to in the case of the semantic and the psychological. In chapter 3 I discuss various kinds of asymmetry which might be claimed by those who propose a reductive interpretation of Grice's analysis of meaning. Once the relevant asymmetry is established, we must return to conceptual investigation and ask whether the proposed asymmetry is really true of the concepts of semantics and psychology. I do this in chapters 3 and 4. If that investigation does reveal the relevant asymmetry, the analysis in question may be considered reductive; if it does not, then the analysis must be considered to be of the weaker, reciprocal sort, if it is to be maintained at all.

Let us now consider how the analytic biconditional may register the distinction I have just drawn. So far I have said that any analysis will provide conditions necessary and sufficient for some given concept to apply. Now if this is all that we can find to say about analysis, then biconditionals of the following sort will have to be accepted as analyses: p if and only if p. What this sort of biconditional reveals is that we need to say something more about an analysis than that it provide conditions necessary and sufficient for some given concept to hold. We need some principled way of ruling out a biconditional which merely repeats the concept in question on its right-hand side. If we return to Moore's discussion of analysis, we find that he stipulated that an analysis must meet the following three conditions: (1) philosophical analyses must be analyses of concepts or propositions;[77] (2) the concepts susceptible of analysis must be of an entirely *general* nature;[78] and (3) the phrases or expressions employed on the right-hand side of the analytic biconditional must be more complex than those on the left-hand side, more complex in the sense of possessing a greater number of symbols each of which has a separate meaning.[79] The last of these conditions provides a rather mechanical way of ruling out, *inter alia*, the trivial biconditional under discussion. Since we analyze a concept to further our understanding of it, we can also give an explanation of *why* such a rule should exist: such an analysis would not further our understanding of the concept mentioned on the left-hand side of the analytic biconditional.[80]

Say, then, that we have before us an analysis of concept C_1 in terms of concepts $C_2, \ldots, C_n$. In the case of Grice's analysis of meaning, C_1 is some semantic concept (e.g., speaker meaning on an occasion), and C_2 through C_n are various psychological concepts (e.g., intention, belief, etc.). The unavailability of the kind of asymmetry that would support a reductive analysis of the semantic is reflected in the analytic biconditional in one of two ways. (1) We may find that it is not possible to put together a set of *other* concepts which will add up to conditions necessary and sufficient for C_1, and that the only thing which will complete the analysis is an outright injection of C_1 into its own analysans. Or (2), we find that further attention to C_2 through C_n reveals that C_1 must play a part in the understanding of some (or all) of these concepts. The first way should be obvious from a cursory glance at a completed analysis; the second is much more difficult to detect. Until such time as philosophers turn their attention to the further understanding of the concepts mentioned on the right-hand side of the analytic biconditional, there will be nothing to suggest that C_1 will or will not reappear in this way.

When the analysis is reductive rather than reciprocal, one tends to envisage a chain of analyses proceeding, as it were, in one unchanging direction: the analysandum of some previous analysis does not show up in some succeeding analysans. The chain must come to an end at some point, however, and it is important to consider the limiting case, the case where the end of the analytic "chain" is reached with the very first analysis. In other words, although an analysis of C_1 may be forthcoming, it may turn out that none of C_2 through C_n are susceptible of analysis. Nothing I have said thus far requires that analysis be our method of understanding C_2 through C_n. Whatever our method of understanding these concepts, in order to assess the status of our original analysis of C_1 we must ask the following: is it possible to understand C_2 through C_n without reference to C_1? If we can, we may accept the original analysis as a reduction; if we cannot, we know that the original analysis must be considered reciprocal.[81] A rather more dramatic conclusion may strike us once we realize that we cannot *further* analyze the analysans concepts: we may reconsider the appropriateness of the *original* analysis. It may be that we do better to think of the relationship between these concepts in some way other than as the analytic spelling out of necessary and sufficient conditions.[82]

I have been arguing that there are two kinds of analysis, or two very different interpretations that can be given of the analytic biconditional. However, many philosophers write as though analysis can only be of one kind, namely reductive.[83] The idea of analysis may connote a move toward, or resolution into, the simpler elements of which something is composed. To speak as I have, then, of a reductive analysis may appear to be pleonastic. On the other hand, to speak of a reciprocal analysis may strike some as a contradiction in terms: reciprocity connotes a relationship of mutual give and take, where talk of hierarchy would appear to have no place. This may explain why analysis is often equated with reduction, and why analysis is held to be an inapplicable method of understanding when a more reciprocal relation is discerned among the concepts involved. I can see no good reason, however, to limit the method of philosophical analysis in this way, nor do I think that talk of "reciprocal analysis" is a contradiction in terms. This is clear if in those cases where a reduction is not suited to the concept, we think of the analysis as applying not to the analysandum concept alone but to the *relationship* that the concept has with the analysans concept. So, for example, a reciprocal analysis of the concept of meaning may be thought to apply not strictly to the concept of meaning alone but to the relationship meaning has to the psychological states of speakers.[84] If we see the analysis to be of this relationship, we should be less prone to reject the reciprocal interpretation of it.

In his book *Meaning*, which is a development of Grice's work, Schiffer briefly considers further analysis of the analysans concept in Grice's original analysis of meaning. He writes:

> I do not believe that psychological states such as believing and desiring are best analysed as being attitudes towards sentences. Indeed, I think this view false. However, since I cannot prove that this view is false, I will leave a discussion of this important issue for some other occasion. But assume that propositional attitudes are attitudes towards sentences. It would not follow from this that Grice's account of S[peaker] meaning . . . is false, nor would it show that an account of utterance-meaning in terms of such an account is false. The most that would follow, if it does follow, is that the concept of S[peaker] meaning is not logically prior to the concept of utterance-meaning, and that an analysis of meaning along Gricean lines is in a peculiar way like "a closed curve in space."[85]

What Schiffer is responding to here is the possibility that the analysis of the propositional concepts used in Grice's analysis of meaning requires a return to some semantic concept (beliefs turn out to be "attitudes towards sentences").[86] Schiffer writes here as if there is only one kind of analysis, and he considers just how problematic a discovery of the need for such a return would be for this analysis. Schiffer is in effect worried that Grice's analysis of meaning should prove to be circular. His response to this possibility is to point out that in such an event Grice's analysis of meaning must no longer be taken to show that the concept of speaker meaning (which is analyzed in terms of the psychological states of speakers) is logically prior to that of utterance meaning. So it must also no longer be taken to show that psychological concepts are logically prior to semantic ones. We must conclude that an analysis of meaning along Gricean lines is "in a peculiar way like 'a closed curve in space.' " Circularity, then, is a problem for the analysis of meaning only if our aim was to exhibit logical priority among concepts. Discovery of a circularity need not force us to abandon the project of analysis; we need only modify our claims.

What Schiffer is saying here can perhaps be understood more clearly in terms of the distinction I drew between kinds of analysis. The problem of circularity plagues only *reductive* analyses.[87] One cannot have succeeded in breaking up a concept into simpler or more basic components if those components require the original concept for their explication. If beliefs *are* attitudes towards sentences, the goal of achieving a new level of concepts must be abandoned, but this need not compel us to abandon analysis altogether. Rather, we must accept that our analysis is of another kind, namely, reciprocal. What the analysis shows is how in precise detail our psychological and semantic concepts fit together. Here the analysis is like "a closed curve in space."

In section 2 I defended Grice's proposed analysis of meaning against attacks aimed at showing that analysis is a method unsuited to the concept of meaning. In this section I suggested that two interpretations of any analysis are possible: reductive or reciprocal. There are those, however, who reject conceptual analysis as a legitimate exercise, not just under its reductive interpretation and not merely in application to the concept of meaning. Quine's doubts about the possibility of an analytic/synthetic distinction cast a shadow over any attempt to explicate, or analyse, concepts. Such doubts may even have affected Schiffer, who at one point appears to want to abandon the spirit, if not the letter, of Grice's original work. Schiffer writes: "Certain intention-theoretic writings have, unwittingly, tended to foster the misleading impression that the program was an exercise in conceptual analysis, the aim and the end of which was the definition of various ordinary language semantic idioms in terms of certain complexes of propositional attitudes. . . . In fact, the program need have no truck with conceptual analysis."[88]

The tone of this quotation strikes me as somewhat disingenuous. I do not think that earlier writers (Schiffer included) unwittingly fostered the impression that the exercise was one of conceptual analysis. It seems to me that Grice was clearly in the business of giving a conceptual analysis, and insofar as his followers thought about the matter at all, their work was also in this tradition. Conceptual investigation was, and continues to be, what much philosophical work is about.[89]

Of course, nothing Quine has said requires that philosophers abandon the method of analysis. Analysis and explication are still a philosopher's business; it is only how this should be understood that Quine sought to alter.[90] It is over the *understanding* of the method of analysis that consideration of the viability of an analytic/synthetic distinction are relevant. Of course, Grice and Quine take very different views of the viability of that distinction and hence understand analysis differently.[91] Schiffer and also Loar[92] clearly choose to follow Quine and not Grice on the interpretation of analysis.

It is not clear, however, that the attitude Schiffer expresses towards his earlier work in the above quotation is a reflection of Quine's qualms. It seems more likely that Schiffer is reinterpreting his earlier work in the light of his later interests. In his 1981 and 1982 papers Schiffer acknowledges that he sees Grice's work as one step on the road of providing a physicalist explication of both mind and meaning.[93] From the standpoint of this larger enterprise it is perhaps unsurprising that Schiffer would prefer to reinterpret Grice's work and his own along Quinean lines. But this is not necessary. One could equally well arrive at a physicalism like Schiffer's as a result of conceptual investigation. It might be argued that such investigation reveals that our semantic concepts are nothing but a special case of our psychological ones, and that our psychological concepts are nothing but a special case of our physical ones.[94] Grice's work is, I believe, best understood in the way he conceived it: as an exercise in conceptual analysis. The real question is whether it is to be interpreted as a reductive or a reciprocal analysis of meaning.

4 The Place of Grice's Work in an Overall Account of Meaning

In this section I want to return to the question: how does Grice's analysis of meaning bring the philosophy of language within the scope of the philosophy of mind and the theory of action? I want to suggest a reply to this question which, at the same time, settles the question of how a Gricean account of meaning is to be reconciled with a more formal approach which uncovers the structural and recursive features of language.

David Wiggins has suggested that we adopt a layered or composite view of what in its entirety may be called a "theory of meaning."[95] Such a theory at its first level would isolate what is strictly and literally said and attempt to account for this in terms of, for example, truth conditions. At the next level we proceed to account for the utterance's force and at subsequent levels to account for such things as perlocutionary effect, conversational implicature, and tone. Wiggins writes, "If we persist in bringing all these things together in an undifferentiated notion of meaning it seems hopeless to look for a systematic theory to account for such meaning."[96] Using this model of a layered theory of meaning, Wiggins then suggests that we reconcile formal and use theories by allocating each to a different level within our overall theory of meaning. Formal theories account for things at the first level, the level of sense; use theories account for things at the next level, the level of force. If we take semantics to be the theory of what is strictly and literally said, and pragmatics as the theory of force, we can, on this model, locate Grice's analysis within pragmatics.[97]

In what can be seen as a development of Wiggins's suggestion, John McDowell sets out two different ways in which we might think of the interaction between the different layers of such a composite theory of meaning; he discusses in particular the way the theory of sense interacts with the theory of force.[98] One way is this: we begin by setting up a theory of sense—for McDowell this will be a theory which uses truth as its central notion—and then we develop a theory of force that supplements this original core theory. The other way is to start with a picture of the whole, which includes both sense *and* force, and then to work one's way back to the core theory of sense. Such a theory works to explain the structural and recursive features of language. Now the first picture seems to imply that the work of each theory is carried out in isolation from the work of the other, and that a complete account of meaning is the result of somehow bringing these theories together in the end. This raises the question of whether it is really plausible to think of a theory at the first level as being developed in such isolation. Is it really plausible to postpone any mention of the relation that utterances have to speakers until the *next* level is reached?

It was once argued that theories of truth conditions fail to serve as theories of *meaning*, since as far as purely extensional truth theories are concerned, the following are perfectly good theorems for the theory to turn out:

(1) "Snow is white" is true if and only if grass is green.

(2) "Hesperus is bright" if and only if Phosphorus is bright.

(3) "Snow is white" is true if and only if snow is white and $2 + 2 = 4$.

These may serve as adequate theorems of a truth theory, but they clearly will not serve as the results of a theory of *meaning*.[99] The problem in (1) is more easily solved than that in either (2) or (3). It is usually accepted that attention to the axioms of the theory, together with the fact that the theory aims systematically to match truths with truths, will help solve the problem in (1).[100] Any residual problem here will make (1) like (2) or (3). To solve the problem *these* raise it is necessary to recall the three requirements that Davidson explicitly places on any theory that aims to be an adequate theory of meaning (see section 2, above). The first of these requirements is that the results of the theory be such as to be recognizable by any speaker of the language as expressing what he knows in virtue of being a speaker of that language. Clearly, a theory which resulted in theorems (1) to (3) would not meet this requirement for the average English speaker. But to say that a theory does not meet certain requirements is not yet to say how those requirements are to be met. In this case the requirement itself provides the hint: to discover *which* truth theory will serve as our theory of meaning, we must pay attention to the *speakers* of the language.

Exploiting this hint, McDowell suggests that we see the problem arising in the first place because we are thinking of the relationship between the theory of sense and the theory of force in the first of the two ways of theory building outlined above. However, if we turn away from this picture and see the relationship between sense and force in the second of the two ways mentioned above, the problem disappears. We must begin by seeing our project to be that of making the best overall sense of the people in question. Part of this process will be to see the noises these people make as speech *acts* of a certain kind, and then to proceed to offer an account of the truth conditions of these utterances. In this way the truth theory we finally end up with will be one guaranteed to be a proper theory of meaning for these people. This is because of the constraints on the theory of having to fit in with an appropriate theory of force.[101]

Consider the following:

> *Objection:* It makes no sense to say that a mere string of sounds or of marks can bear a meaning or a truth-value. The proper bearers of meaning and truth-value are particular speech acts.

> *Reply:* I do not say that a mere string of types of sounds or of marks, by itself, can bear a meaning or truth-value. I say it bears a meaning or truth-value relative to a language, or relative to a population.[102]

The objection here is similar to the one I considered in the preceding paragraph. The passage is from David Lewis. Lewis's reply to his objector is in the same spirit as McDowell's reply to his objector. Lewis, however, is working with a slightly different model from that of McDowell. Rather than speaking of a layered theory of meaning, Lewis speaks of giving a general account of the meaning of various possible languages and then proceeding to explain what makes one such language the actual language of a given population. Only when discussing this relation to the actual language do the psychological states of speakers come into play. On Lewis's model there is also the temptation to ask how one can speak of possible languages in isolation from speakers. Lewis's reply to this objection is to point out that in a sense speakers and their psychological states are never far from view when the topic is meaning. One might say that to speak of doing one thing and *then* another is merely a heuristic device which orders the activities of philosophers; it does not reflect any actual or possible separation of language from its speakers.

One philosopher working within the Gricean tradition who has tended to favor Lewis's model over the one adopted by Wiggins and McDowell is Loar.[103] Loar explicitly rejects the model that both separates semantics and pragmatics and places Grice's work squarely within the realm of pragmatics. He insists that it is not possible to carry on work in semantics without an immediate injection of psychological concepts. As far as Loar is concerned, Grice's account operates at the *first* level in the theory of meaning. He writes: "There *is* a distinction between semantics and pragmatics, and where the line gets drawn is a hard question. Pragmatics is to be defined negatively, relative to the definition of semantics; the pragmatics of the language of a population is all the facts of a certain kind about language use in that population which are not semantic facts."[104] Semantic facts are, according to Loar, facts about what a sentence means in a language for a population, and Grice's account is an account of such facts.

I should note that Loar's distinction between semantics and pragmatics is not the standard one. The standard use of these terms is taken from Charles Morris in his book *Foundations of the Theory of Signs*. There Morris distinguishes three areas of study grouped together under the heading of semiotics, or the general study of signs: syntax (the study of the relations of signs to one another), semantics (the study of the relation between signs and what they are signs of), and pragmatics (the study of the relation between signs and their interpreters). Any study, then, that includes speakers would, for Morris, fall squarely within pragmatics. This clearly includes Grice's work. In drawing the distinction in the way he does, Loar is breaking with this standard way of drawing the distinction between semantics and pragmatics. On the other hand, the model of the relationship between the theory of sense and the theory of force that Wiggins and McDowell adopt is in keeping with Morris's picture of the relation between semantics and pragmatics. Perhaps in part for this reason Loar finds it necessary to reject their model. He appears to prefer the model of Lewis. But it is unclear to me that anything is gained by such a move. Loar seems to hold the distinction between possible and actual languages as a distinction *within semantics,* and pragmatics is something over and above semantics. But another way of seeing Lewis's model is as follows: the distinction between actual and possible languages is directly parallel to the semantic/pragmatic distinction as Morris drew it. The former is simply a fresh way of thinking about the latter, old distinction.

It seems to me that Loar's rejection of the old distinction between semantics and pragmatics—and with it his rejection of the Wiggins and McDowell model of the relation between the theory of sense and the theory of force and his refusal to see Lewis's distinction as in keeping with this model—can be traced to a misinterpretation. Loar seems to be under the impression that if we accept a layered conception of meaning, we must also hold that the work done at each level is carried out in complete isolation from the work at the other levels. Hence Loar's fear that on this model of things, Grice's work will come to be seen as contributing *merely* to pragmatics, isolated (at least temporarily) from semantics.[105] On McDowell's favored interpretation of the distinction, however, this is not so. On that interpretation, as we have seen, philosophers of language are taken to be working with an overall picture that includes *both* semantics and pragmatics, within which we can develop a core theory (call it "semantics") that will reveal the structural and recursive features of the language. This interpretation does not leave a place for Loar's fears to get a grip. On this picture of things, pragmatics, far from being banished, is at the very heart of the matter. Also, once we adopt this interpretation of the old semantics/pragmatics distinction, there seems little reason to see Lewis's distinction between possible and actual languages as anything other than a new way of thinking about that old distinction.

Once we accept a layered or composite view of the theory of meaning we would seem to have an easy solution to the problem of how to reconcile a Gricean account of use with a more formal theory of meaning. It will be remembered from section 1 that some sort of reconciliation seemed desirable after we noticed that the defect of one kind of account of meaning was the virtue of the other: on the one hand, formal theorists concentrate on giving an account of the structural and recursive features of a language, but in such a way that leaves speakers of the language aside; on the other hand, use theorists (including Gricean use theorists) stress the importance of speakers, while relegating the task of giving an account of structure to a position of secondary importance. The envisaged solution would take the form of assigning each theorist his proper place in a composite theory of meaning.

As we saw from section 1, the idea that formal and use theories be accepted as complementary and not competing is not a new one. And the idea has been resuscitated in recent years by philosophers who wish to bridge the gap between Davidson's work on meaning and Grice's.[106] The idea is a good one, but we must be careful about the proposal. We must clarify certain details and background facts. And we must be sure that the reconciliation is acceptable to both sides.

First of all, there is the issue I have just been discussing between Loar's view of the place of Grice's work and the view of Davidsonians like Wiggins and McDowell. The question of whether Grice's work should be taken as a contribution to semantics or to pragmatics may seem to some to be a merely terminological matter, but, as we have just seen, this is not at all how at least one Gricean sees it. I have suggested that Loar's worries about placing Grice's work in pragmatics may be alleviated if one understands the interrelation between semantics and pragmatics in the way suggested by McDowell. However, Loar will likely still jib. As he says in the passage I quote in footnote 105: "The nature of the semantics/pragmatics distinction is no mere terminological matter, but involves the fundamental nature of semantic concepts."

Echoing the aim of many a use theorist of meaning, Loar writes, "What I want to show is that the theory of meaning is part of the theory of mind, and not the other way around."[107] For Loar, then, we can understand the fundamental nature of our semantic concepts by reference to psychological concepts. In other words, Loar is adopting a reductive interpretation of the biconditional in Grice's analysis. Under a reductive interpretation we find that all questions about public-language meaning concern some complex of speakers' psychological states.[108] It would seem that Loar sees the battle over where to place Grice's work in a layered "theory of meaning" as crucial to the interpretation of that work. For Loar, Grice's work belongs within semantics, and its purpose is to reduce semantics to psychology.

If we seek to reconcile this reductive kind of Gricean analysis with a formal theory of meaning, what we find is the following: the structure of sentences so rightly emphasized by the formal semanticists becomes the structure of certain propositional attitudes; and the insight that the meaning of a sentence can be specified by giving its truth conditions has to be reinterpreted: rather than map sentences directly onto truth conditions, there has to be an intermediate mapping of sentences onto beliefs and intentions. The reductionist attitude towards reconciliation is perhaps summed up by this passage from a more recent work of Loar's:

> Without doubt, there are interesting systematic correlations between utterances and the obtaining of states of affairs we count as their truth conditions. But such correlations would *also* be explained by communication intention regularities; while to leave the latter out of the picture simply fails to account for our seemingly fundamental conception of public language meaning as involving the goal directed use of language in communication.
> The foregoing considerations imply that conventional regularities involving communication intentions are central in public language semantics—indeed, that they *constitute* sentential meaning.[109]

Loar's concern to make the philosophy of language part of the philosophy of mind pushes him in the direction of a reductive interpretation of Grice's work. Loar appears to assume that unless we take psychological notions as basic in our account of meaning, those notions will end up being ignored or omitted from that account. This, however, is a non sequitur. Adopting a reciprocal interpretation of the biconditional in Grice's analysis affords us another way of bringing the philosophy of language within the scope of the philosophy of mind. This nonreductive interpretation of the analysis would allow a part of the account of meaning autonomy from the philosophy of mind, though loosely it would fit under the umbrella concept of intentional action. Not all questions having to do with public language meaning turn out to be, strictly speaking, questions in the philosophy of mind. Reconciliation of a formal theory with Grice's analysis understood in this way is a much more straightforward affair. The point of the analysis would be to specify the propositional attitudes in the light of which these truth conditions must be specified.

Those working toward a reconciliation starting from something like, for example, a Davidsonian formal theory would favor a reconciliation based on a reciprocal interpretation of Grice's analysis. But there are those who would resist even this. As we saw in section 2, some theory builders reject analysis applied to the concept of meaning. For some, this is just the rejection of a reductive interpretation of the analysis, but for others the rejection extends even to the reciprocal interpretation of Grice's analysis. To accept a reconciliation of more formal work with Grice's would allow the possibility that analysis may have *some* part to contribute to the overall understanding of our concept of meaning. The question of whether a reconciliation based on a weak, nonreductive interpretation of the analysis is acceptable or not may be seen to be the question of whether a Gricean account of communication is acceptable. As we have seen, analysis isn't required if all we want to do is to give an account of the relationship meaningful utterances have to their utterers.[110] For this reason further discussion is needed to explain why it is thought that employing the analytic method is the best way of filling out the formal theory in question.

We thus see that although reconciliation between Gricean use theories and more formal theories of meaning is desirable in principle, achieving such reconciliation is a delicate matter. Certainly, those who speak of reconciliation from either side of the debate can be seen to have different ideas about how to interpret such an enterprise. And although Griceans appear to be content to accommodate formal theories,[111] it is not always clear that all formal theorists would be content to accommodate Gricean analyses.

5 A Reductive Analysis of Meaning

In section 3 I began considering Grice's work by introducing a distinction between two different kinds of analysis, reductive and reciprocal. As we have seen, each kind of analysis raises somewhat different issues. One of my reasons for drawing this distinction between kinds of analyses, or interpretations of Grice's analysis, is so that I can place one kind, the reciprocal, to one side and concentrate my attention on the other, the reductive.

It is not altogether clear which interpretation Grice himself intended of his work.[112] However, some of those who have worked most closely with Grice in developing the analysis have been more forthright about the way they see matters.[113] They take Grice's analysis to effect a reduction of the semantical to the psychological. So we find Schiffer, for example, writing, "The definability of meaning in terms of thought, without the reducibility of meaning to thought, is barely of passing interest, a curious fact in need of no explanation, certainly no account of what meaning is."[114]

That Schiffer is so insistent upon a reductive interpretation of Grice's work may seem odd if we recall the remark I quoted in section 3 from his first book, *Meaning*, to the effect that the discovery that psychological concepts are not logically prior to semantic ones need only commit us to viewing the analysis of meaning along Gricean lines as "in a peculiar way like 'a closed curve in space.' " Schiffer's later view, however, is not that such a discovery would invalidate Grice's work; he just thinks that such a discovery would make that work less interesting. The reason for this is to be found in the role that Schiffer has allocated to Grice's work on meaning in the larger program of providing a physicalist account of both mind and meaning. Schiffer is interested in reducing the psychological to the physical as well as in reducing the semantic to the psychological. And he admits that these interests are not unrelated: "I believe that *the only viable reduction of the semantical and the psychological to the physical is via the reduction of the semantical to the psychological*" (Schiffer's italics).[115] The program is clear: first we find that our concept of the semantic is replaceable by certain psychological concepts, and then we find that our physical theory of the world can explain even our concept of the psychological. Once we have the former, Gricean reduction, the task that the physical theory is called on to do is somewhat easier. A Gricean analysis reduces two troublesome concepts to one, and in the end some physical theory will sweep away the problem posed by that remaining troublesome concept.[116]

Compare Schiffer's interpretation of Grice's analysis with Loar's when the latter writes: "The point is not that the pragmatic concept of meaning for a person or population cannot be explicated within a physicalist framework; on the contrary. Rather it is that the only promising explication requires an *independent* explication of propositional attitudes."[117] So Loar too sees the overall program as one of giving a *physicalist* explication of our concept of meaning. When he says that the only promising physicalist explication of the semantic requires an independent explication of the propositional attitudes, what he means is this: Loar believes that the only way of reducing the semantic to the physical is by first reducing the semantic to the psychological. He also recognizes that the latter reduction cannot succeed unless it proves possible to provide an explication of the propositional attitudes that makes no mention of the concept of meaning. In other words, for the analysis of meaning to count as a reduction, it must not prove viciously circular. A physicalist explication of the propositional attitudes would, of course, avoid circularity in the original, Gricean analysis of meaning; it would provide the needed *independent* explication of the propositional attitudes. With a workable analysis of the concept of meaning in terms of propositional attitudes already present, a physicalist explication of the propositional attitudes would not only allow for a reductive interpretation of the analysis, it would *eo ipso* be a physical explication of the semantic as well.

We should note that not all philosophers interested in a physicalist explication of the semantic choose to exploit the route offered by Grice. There are other suggestions for reducing the semantic to the physical, ones that do not require an *intermediate* reduction of the semantic to the psychological.[118] It is fair to say that Schiffer and Loar adopt the line they do because of their independent commitment to intention-based semantics.[119] Moreover, their further commitment to physicalism forces both Schiffer and Loar to adopt a *reductive* interpretation of Grice's analysis of meaning.

Early work stimulated by Grice's account of meaning tended to be concerned with specifying conditions necessary and sufficient for speaker meaning and accommodating counterexamples. Griceans like Schiffer and Loar who wanted to vindicate a reductive interpretation of Grice's original analysis began to concentrate less on the analysis of meaning and more on the explication of the propositional attitudes mentioned on the right-hand side of the analytic biconditional. Each in his own way believed that he would advance the program of intention-based semantics by developing a functionalist account of propositional attitudes. As Loar quite candidly admits, "This all implies that much of the 'theory of meaning' has not been about *meaning* but about the *content* of the propositional attitudes."[120]

The requirement that a reductive interpretation of Grice's analysis rely on an explication of the propositional attitudes that has no recourse to semantic concepts needs careful formulation. "Semantics" in the widest sense covers a range of concepts including meaning, truth, and reference; that is, the term may be used to cover any relation between words and the world. In its more narrow use it is roughly equivalent to "meaning." Concepts like truth and reference will likely play a part in any account we give of the propositional attitudes, so it is semantics in the *narrow* sense of the term that concerns us when the issue is the reduction of the semantic to the psychological. And here another distinction must be drawn, this time between public-language semantics and the semantics of the language of thought. If propositional attitudes are taken to be attitudes toward sentences with meaning in a *public* language, reduction is threatened.

In one place Loar distinguishes between what he calls "strong Griceanism" and "modest Griceanism."[121] The strong Gricean holds that Grice's analysis suffices to explain all the semantic properties of natural language, whether used in communication or not. The weak

Gricean restrains his claim; Grice's analysis suffices to explain all the concepts of the semantics of language in communication: sentence meaning, illocutionary force, what makes a language the language of a population, and the like. The modest Gricean presupposes an independent account of the language of thought. Strong Griceanism is not only reductive; it is complete. Loar claims to be a modest Gricean; Schiffer is as well. Of course, the modest Gricean is far from modest in the claims he wants to make about the relationship of the semantic to the psychological, for he advocates a reductive interpretation of Grice's analysis of meaning. In summary, then, the reductive Gricean is committed to giving a nonsemantic account of the propositional attitudes, but he is not committed to an account of them that makes no mention of truth, reference, or meaning in the language of thought. He is restricted by his commitment to reduction to an account of the propositional attitudes that makes no mention of public-language semantic concepts.

Before the issue of interpretation arises, philosophers may be content simply to hone the analysis in response to counterexamples. Once reductive ambitions come into play, attention focuses on the explication of the propositional attitudes mentioned on the right-hand side of the original biconditional. Attempts to reduce the semantic to the psychological raise another issue: Is it really plausible to hold that there is an *asymmetry* between semantic concepts and psychological ones? Is it true that psychological concepts are, in Wisdom's words, "more fundamental" or "more basic" than semantic concepts in our overall scheme of concepts? This is not just the question of whether we can provide an explication of propositional attitudes that makes no mention of public-language semantic concepts. It concerns our conception of mind and of meaning.

Turning to this larger issue is, I suggest, the next stage in the development of the analysis first put forward by Grice in 1957. The first stage concentrates on the biconditional alone, the next raises the issue of the interpretation of the analysis, and the third stage investigates how appropriate a given interpretation of the analysis is to the concept in question. Central to the work at this third stage is an explanation of what this talk of symmetry versus asymmetry amounts to in the case of the concepts of semantics and psychology. Equally important is a conceptual investigation that would reveal whether such a claim of symmetry or asymmetry is in fact plausible.

I believe that after this work is done, it will be apparent that reduction is not suited to our concept of the semantic. A reductive analysis not only misrepresents the relationship that exists between the semantic and the psychological; it also forces us to have the wrong view of the *psychological*. Indeed, I would say that because philosophers like Schiffer and Loar have a mistaken picture of the psychological, they entertain the possibility of reducing the semantic to it. A proper conception of the psychological would rule out a reductive account of the semantic. This is what I hope to show in chapters 3 and 4. Like Schiffer and Loar, I shall thus be concerned with the reductive interpretation of Grice's analysis of meaning rather than the reciprocal one. But unlike Schiffer and Loar, I want to explain why I think the analysis under this interpretation is mistaken.

Loar explains the pressures that he sees forcing him into the position of looking for a physicalist explication of both mind and meaning in the following way. As theorists we are faced with a dilemma whose components are as follows: a theoretical framework A (e.g., a physical theory); an imperialist inclination to accept A as adequate for expressing all truths about a certain subject S; a set of propositions, B, within S but not in A that we have a strong inclination to accept (e.g., propositions about beliefs and desires, or meaning, etc.).[122]

There are several responses one may have to this dilemma: (1) one could say that the propositions of B are really equivalent in meaning to some of those in A; (2) one could give up the imperialist pretentions of A to express all truths about S and set to work constructing a new framework better suited to B; or (3) one could simply cease to accept the propositions of B. Like Schiffer, Loar rejects response (1), which he identifies with classical (he calls it "Moorean") analysis. Like Quine, Loar prefers response (3), but Loar proposes a variation on this Quinean theme: allow that the propositions of A have been replaced by those of B but insist that nothing has changed thereby in people's views about things. In particular, allow that the propositions of some physical theory have replaced propositions about beliefs, desires, and meaning but don't let this change the way we think about one another. Loar calls this "conservative explication," and he says about it: "The theorist for whom explication is conservative may have achieved the happier resolution of the dilemma—not exactly because he hasn't changed any beliefs. . . . But his cognitive situation is *as though* he hasn't changed any beliefs. How can that be? I can suggest no more detailed account of the phenomenon of conservative explication; but it *occurs* and can serve as a cognitive resolution to what is perceived as a serious theoretical problem."[123] Whether or not one is able to make sense of conservative explication with the dilemma at hand, one thing about it is clear: "For the replacement to be correct, the truths of B must give way to the truths of A."[124]

As I propose to show why I think the reductive interpretation of Grice's work is misguided, I must reject response (3) to Loar's proposed dilemma; I cannot accept that the truths of B *must* give way to the truths of A. As I hope to be able to show in chapters 3 and 4, the reasons we have for clinging to the propositions of B (meaning or belief) are reasons which should force us to give up the imperialist pretentions of A (physicalism). This is along the lines of Loar's response (2). Furthermore, whether one adopts response (2) or Loar's preferred response (3), I see no reason entirely to reject response (1). As I said in section 3 above, *whatever* one's interpretation of Grice's explication of meaning, it is possible to accept it as an instance of classical philosophical analysis.

Now the position I intend to defend is blatantly antireductionist. Loar says about any such position, "To make a concept sacrosanct, not illuminable by reconstruction, may simply make it *uninteresting* in the light of ongoing theory; and, in any case, the drive towards explication may be irrepressible."[125] What is irrepressible may not always be correct, and I see nothing *uninteresting* about the possibility of providing a reciprocal analysis of meaning (that is, an account that shows how the semantic depends upon, without reducing to, the psychological). Some "ongoing theory" (like A) may be interesting and exciting, but the question of whether it is suited to account for a set of propositions like B is a question that can only be answered after careful investigation into the concepts employed in both A and B.

Reductionists like Schiffer and Loar insist that objections to their program must not come from any general prejudice one may have against reductions, nor from a reliance on the proven failure of *other* reductions (e.g., behaviorism and phenomenalism). They fail to see any specific objection that can be brought to bear on their reductive program. My objection will be entirely specific; it will proceed from a careful consideration of our pretheoretic grasp of our concepts of the semantic and the psychological. I believe that it is only this kind of consideration that can determine whether the concept of meaning can be understood by understanding some other concepts, as the reductive interpretation of Grice's analysis suggests, or whether that concept is better understood by discerning its place in a system of interrelated concepts, as a reciprocal interpretation of Grice's analysis would suggest. Even if in the end the reductive Gricean remains unconvinced by my arguments, I hope to make clear the picture of mind and meaning to which his reduction commits him.

Chapter 2
The Analysis of Meaning

Grice's original work on meaning is, I believe, of a hearty nature and can endure alteration and modification without becoming obsolete. For this reason it is important to understand how the analysis works. Unfortunately, early discussions of the analysis tend to be complex and baroque, while more recent discussions either assume acquaintance with the program or offer only the briefest sketch of it. Many discuss Grice's work or criticize it without clarifying how they interpret the work. As I explained in chapter 1, philosophers more often than not reject the reductive interpretation of Grice's work. Yet Grice's work can survive the rejection of the reductive interpretation. There have been more fundamental objections to Grice's work, but such objections are, I believe, less common than has often been supposed.[1] By saying this I do not deny that there are many difficulties that need to be addressed by anyone wishing to accept even the weakest interpretation of Grice's work.[2] But there is a difference between objections indicating modification in a work and objections that seek to supplant it. Setting aside reduction, we need to see just what the analysis offers us as a supplementation to or part of an overall "theory of meaning." Understanding how the analysis works should, I believe, make philosophers more open to what it can tell us about meaning. Many criticize the analysis for its complexity, but we must be careful not to close our eyes to the problems that the complexity is designed to meet. It is easy to sweep aside a complex analysis, harder to come up with an alternative way of meeting the problems. In any case, understanding the work that Grice and others have put into constructing the analysis is an excellent way of coming to see just what the problems are.[3]

In this chapter I aim to provide an overview of the basic analysis that gives as much detail as is necessary to highlight the basic strategy of the analysis.[4]

1 The Basic Analysis

After we agree that analysis of one sort or another can provide us with some understanding of our concept of meaning, we must decide which sentence involving that concept we want to analyze.[5] Denis Stampe writes, "Skepticism concerning the integrity of the concept of meaning may be inspired by the polysemy of the verb 'means', or again by the grammatical promiscuity of [that] verb."[6] The sceptic will be struck by the variety of sentences which employ the verb "mean." For example:

(1) She means to leave him.

(2) He means a lot to her.

(3) He means what he said.

(4) The occurrence of thunder means that there will be a storm.

(5) By uttering "Your face is red," she meant that your face is red.

Stampe has suggested that we rely on the diverse syntactic contexts where "means" occurs to provide a guide to the word's semantic diversity. His aim is to clear a path for Grice's analysis of the concept of meaning, an analysis that may reveal "such univocity as the concept possesses."[7]

Exploiting grammatical hints, Stampe proposes the following understanding of sentences (1) through (3): in (1), where the verb is followed by an adverbial occurrence of an infinitive, we can replace "means" with "intends"; in (2), where the verb is followed by an adverbial of quantity (Stampe's term), we can replace "means" with "matters"; in (3) where the verb is followed by a pronomial expression referring to something the agent in the subject place said (wrote, etc.), we can replace "means" with "is serious and sincere in saying" ("writing," etc.). The uses of "means" in (4) and (5), however, look not to be replaceable by anything other than what are clearly trivial variants (e.g., "signify"). Perhaps, then, the analysis should cover these *two* uses of the word. Yet surely, we may protest, the use of "means" in (4) is less concerned with either communication or language than its use in (5), and it is its use in communication or language with which the analysis should be concerned. Is there any more that we can say about the difference between these two ineliminable uses of the word "means" that can help us further to isolate the usage that will serve as the starting point of the analysis?

In the opening pages of his 1957 paper Grice assumes that intuition can help us to decide whether in a sentence ineliminably containing the word "means," it is like the use in (4) or the use in (5). He labels these uses "natural" and "nonnatural" respectively, and makes the following observations concerning the two uses:

Natural (n): "x means that p" entails that p.

Nonnatural (nn): "x means that p" does not entail that p.

Natural: We cannot argue from "That thunder means that there will be a storm" to any conclusion about what was meant by that thunder.

Nonnatural: We can argue from a sentence like "Your face is red" to a conclusion about what was meant by those words.

Natural: We cannot argue from "That thunder means that there will be a storm" to any conclusion about what someone meant by that thunder.

Nonnatural: We can argue from a sentence like "Your face is red" to a conclusion about what someone meant by those words.[8]

Without saying any more, Grice assumes that we will have caught onto this distinction between natural and nonnatural meaning.[9] He then sets himself the following task for the rest of the paper: to see what more he can say about those cases in which we claim that "means" is being used in its nonnatural sense as opposed to its natural sense. The sentence schema that Grice takes to involve the concept he wants to analyze is:

(1) x means$_{nn}$ something   (where x is an utterance).

However, sentence schema (1) is not the only one that contains the concept of nonnatural meaning with which Grice is concerned. That concept is also contained in the following schema:

(2) S means$_{nn}$ something   (where S is a speaker).

Once we notice this, it seems less clear that Grice *has* found a starting point for his analysis. And the difficulty is compounded once we notice that each of these schemata, (1) and (2), is similarly ambiguous. That ambiguity may resolve itself in either of the following two ways. In Grice's terms,

(1a) x means$_{nn}$ something (on a particular occasion),

(1b) x means$_{nn}$ (timeless) something,

(2a) S means$_{nn}$ something by x (on a particular occasion),

(2b) S means$_{nn}$ (timeless) by x something.

And further, when the grammatical subject is an utterance, i.e., in cases (1a) and (1b), we must always allow for the possibility of structure.[10] Hence, we get the following:

(1a') x (a whole utterance) means$_{nn}$ something (on a particular occasion),

(1a'') a (an utterance part) means$_{nn}$ something (on a particular occasion),

(1b') x (a whole utterance) means$_{nn}$ (timeless) something,

(1b'') a (an utterance part) means$_{nn}$ (timeless) something.

Thus, even when limited to cases of nonnatural meaning we are faced with a multitude of possible sentence schemata with which to begin the analysis. One may be excused for sharing the pessimism of some of the theory builders regarding the possibility of providing an analysis of our concept of meaning. Grice, however, remains undaunted. He suggests an ordering of all these uses of the concept of nonnatural meaning that provides the starting point for an analysis of it.

First of all Grice suggests that we solve the problem of whole-utterance meaning before approaching that of part-utterance meaning. So Grice will be concerned with (1a') and (1b') before (1a'') and (1b''). Notice that this decision is in keeping with Grice's proposal to employ the term "utterance" in an artificially wide sense. That is, it reflects the observation that not all utterances are semantically structured, that not all meaning occurs in language. Under Grice's broad reading of "utterance" can be included such things as flag waving, air raid whistles, nods of the head, hand waving, etc., as well as sentences of a language.[11]

Grice next suggests that we account for the meaning of a whole utterance on a particular occasion before attempting to say what it is for a whole utterance timelessly to mean something. In other words, Grice proposes to analyze the meaning of an utterance on an occasion before concerning himself with the *standard* meaning an utterance may have. Notice that this priority too is in keeping with Grice's concern with the wider phenomenon of nonnatural meaning. Standard or timeless meaning is of particular concern when our interest is language, but as Grice wants to emphasize, not all meaning occurs in language. Outside language, meaning is a property of an utterance on an occasion.[12] As this is so, we should be concerned with (1a) and (2a) before (1b) and (2b).

Finally, Grice suggests the following: "x means something (on a particular occasion)" is roughly equivalent to "S means something (on a particular occasion) by x."[13] Notice that this equivalence is plausible only if one allows Grice that occasion meaning has priority over timeless meaning, and that such a priority is plausible only if one agrees that the phenomenon of meaning is not essentially language bound.[14] It is in this *wider* phenomenon, represented by the sentence schema "S means something (on a particular occasion) by x," that Grice finds the starting point he needs for the analysis of nonnatural meaning.

The way is then clear for an analysis of our concept of nonnatural meaning. Grice's first proposal is:

> (1) "S means$_{nn}$ something by uttering x" would be true if and only if S uttered x intending to induce a response in some audience (and to say what the response was would be to say what S meant).[15]

Immediately we are faced with a very long series of counterexamples to the analysis. The counterexample to formulation (1) is as follows: A may leave B's handkerchief by the scene of a crime in order to induce in the detective on the case the response of believing that B was the criminal involved.[16] The conditions of formulation (1) are here satisfied, and yet we would not want to say that the handkerchief meant anything, or that A meant anything by leaving the handkerchief in the way that he did. The reason why not is important. What the described case leaves out is any *communication* between A and the detective. This becomes clear if we compare a case where A intentionally leaves B's handkerchief in the appropriate place with a case where B unintentionally drops his handkerchief while fleeing the scene of the crime. In both cases the detective will have the same response (i.e., the belief that B was the criminal), and he will come to have his response in the same way (i.e., by relying on the evidence). But if this is correct, we cannot be said to have captured the difference between natural and nonnatural meaning, which was Grice's aim in producing the analysis.

Perhaps the above-mentioned counterexample can be avoided if we rewrite the analysis in the following way:

> (2) S meant something by uttering x if and only if S uttered x intending
> (a) that S's utterance of x produce a certain response, r, in a certain audience, A, and
> (b) that A recognize S's intention.

Adding to the analysans a condition specifying that the audience recognize the speaker's intention does seem to avoid the particular counterexample considered above, but formulation (2) still fails fully to capture the communicative aspect of nonnatural meaning. This is brought out by the following counterexample:[17] King Herod presents Salome with the head of Saint John the Baptist on a charger, intending Salome to have the response of believing that Saint John is dead and intending also that Salome recognize that he intends her to believe that Saint John is dead. Both conditions of the analysis as stated in formulation (2) above are thus satisfied, and yet, intuitively, this does not look to be a case of meaning$_{nn}$. What again seems to be missing is a communicative link between Herod and Salome. This is clear once we realize that Herod's intention may be incidental to Salome's response. It is most likely that Salome comes to have the belief that Saint John is dead simply because she has seen his head on a charger and she knows that a man does not survive once his head has been severed from his body. What is missing is some link between the audience's recognition of the speaker's intention and the response the audience is intended to have. We need in the analysis a condition ensuring that communication is essentially dependent upon the audience's recognition of the speaker's intention. Without such a firm anchoring in the psychological, there will be no difference between "letting someone know" (or "getting someone to think") and "telling." It is the latter that is crucial to understanding nonnatural meaning. To capture this aspect of meaning, another condition must be added to the analysis:

(3) S meant something by uttering x if and only if S uttered x intending:

(a) that S's utterance of x produce a certain response, r, in a certain audience, A,

(b) that A recognize S's intention (a), and

(c) that A's recognition of S's intention (a) shall function as at least part of A's reason for r.[18]

Stated in this way, the analysis does establish a link between the audience's recognition of the speaker's intention and the response that the audience is intended to have. With the addition of this third condition the analysis will have moved one step closer toward capturing the communicative aspect of nonnatural meaning.

With these three conditions, however, we have by no means reached the completed analysis; counterexamples continue to multiply, as I shall show in sections 2 and 3 below. Nevertheless, there is enough before us at this point for the *strategy* of the analysis to be apparent. Grice's analysis of nonnatural meaning begins with the following rather obvious observation: the difference between a mere sound and an act of communication is that when there is communication, human beings with appropriate audience-directed beliefs and intentions produce the sounds. To capture this difference Grice makes it a condition of the analysans that the audience's response be occasioned by its recognition of the speaker's intentions. As Grice explains, it must make a difference to the effect the utterance has on A (i.e., a difference to A's response) that A takes the utterance to have been produced with a certain intention to convey information.[19] Although it seems correct that such a condition should be added to the analysis, its addition appears to lead to a difficulty. Grice himself illustrates the difficulty with the following example. If I spontaneously frown in the ordinary course of events, someone seeing me may very well have the response of coming to believe that I am displeased. Similarly, if I frown with the intention of conveying my displeasure to some particular person, and he recognizes the intention, this person will have the response of coming to believe that I am displeased. Exactly the same information is conveyed, then, whether or not the speaker has an intention to communicate that the hearer recognizes. Looking only at the response produced (or the information conveyed), we seem to have no ground for drawing a distinction between natural and nonnatural meaning. Must we conclude, then, that the deliberate frown does not nonnaturally mean anything?

Grice's reaction to the problem is to point out that we are looking in the wrong place for a difference in the audiences' responses in the two cases. There is no difference in *what* the audience ends up believing in each case, but we can still say that the belief-producing capacity of the frown in each case is different. That is, "if we take away the recognition of the intention, leaving the other circumstances (including the recognition of the frown as deliberate), the belief-producing tendency of the frown must be regarded as being impaired or destroyed."[20] The difference between the two cases thus has to do with what the one who frowns can *expect* the observer to believe in each case.[21] It is in this sense that it makes a difference to the audience's response that the audience recognize the speaker's intention and that the intention functions at least in part as the audience's reason for this response; without the recognition of S's intention, A might not have had that response.

One can come to have a firmer grip on the distinction Grice is drawing here if one imagines two sorts of individuals: the one can have only self-regarding intentions, the other can have both self-regarding and other-regarding intentions. Say that you come across a creature of the former sort intentionally making the sound "danger" (for whatever reason). Now even if you are an English speaker, if you *know* that this creature can have no other-regarding intentions, you will have no inclination to believe that there is danger. The matter will be very different if you recognize that the individual producing this sound is of the latter sort, of the kind that can have, and in this case does have, communication intentions. In the first case the belief-producing tendency that sound has (because of its association for you with the English word) is destroyed by the absence of an intention to communicate. For nonnatural meaning it is never sufficient that an utterance have a tendency to produce a response of a certain sort in a hearer of it. The utterance must be produced with the appropriate intentions to communicate and those intentions must be recognized by the audience for there to be a genuine case of nonnatural meaning.[22]

2 Is the Analysis Sufficient?

Although the basic idea behind the analysis is captured by the third formulation of it in the previous section, the three conditions there listed cannot be said to be either necessary or sufficient for speaker (nonnatural) meaning. The counterexamples I shall consider in this section all aim to show that these three conditions alone do not suffice for speaker meaning.

Here is the first case designed to show that satisfying conditions (*a*) through (*c*) alone is not sufficient for speaker meaning. A prisoner of war possessing vital information has been captured by the enemy. The prisoner knows that his captors want the information that he possesses. The captors, in order to induce him to give it up, subject the prisoner to torture by thumbscrews. In this example the three conditions of the third formulation of the analysis are satisfied: the captors apply the thumbscrews to the prisoner with the intention of producing the response of his offering up the information that he possesses (condition (*a*)); they intend that the prisoner recognize that they intend their torture to have this effect (condition (*b*)); and they intend that should the prisoner give in under torture and reveal the information, it should be due at least in part to his recognition of his captors' intentions (condition (*c*)).[23] And yet it does not seem correct to say that by applying the thumbscrews the captors *meant* that the prisoner should tell them the information, or indeed that they meant anything at all. The reason we hesitate to say that the captors meant anything here is that the thumbscrews do not reveal the captor's intentions. The prisoner already knows his captors' intentions; the thumbscrews are merely an inducement.

What we need to avoid such a counterexample is a condition in the analysis stipulating that the audience recognize the speaker's intentions at least in part from the utterance. This condition can be built into the analysis in the following way:

(4) S meant something by uttering x if and only if S uttered x intending:
   (a) that x have a certain feature f,
   (b) that A recognize that x has f,
   (c) that A infer at least in part from the fact that x is f that S uttered x intending:
   (d) that S's utterance of x produce response r in A and
   (e) that A's recognition of S's intention (d) should function as at least part of A's reason for r.[24]

By ensuring that the audience's recognition of the speaker's intention is based on the audience's recognition of some feature of the utterance, the analysis is made to square more firmly with our intentions about what is to count as a genuine case of meaning$_{nn}$.

Two things should be noted in connection with the introduction into the analysis of some feature of the utterance. First, an utterance may have several features, such as the feature of being uttered softly. The feature of the utterance relevant to our concerns is what has been called its *meaning-bearing* feature. Here are two examples of different kinds of meaning-bearing features that an utterance may have: (1) S utters "grr" intending A to recognize that this sound has the feature of resembling the sound made by an angry dog, and intending A to infer from this that S intends A to believe that S is angry. (2) S utters "The cat is in the garden" intending A to recognize that this string of sounds has the feature of being a sentence of English which means that the cat is in the garden, and intending A to infer from this that S intends A to believe that the cat is in the garden. Second, notice that it is a condition of the analysis that S intends A to recognize the utterance's meaning-bearing feature, and that S can do this only if he believes that A speaks his language or understands certain natural signs. Thus, the analysis as it stands in formulation (4) captures the surely undeniable fact that a basis for communication between individuals is a certain common understanding.[25]

Counterexamples to the sufficiency of the analysis of speaker meaning may be thought to fall into two broad categories. There are those like the prisoner example just discussed that are fairly easily accommodated with the introduction of utterance features. The other kind of counterexamples indicate a more fundamental flaw in the analysis as it stands in formulation (4), and how they are to be accommodated is a somewhat more controversial matter. The issue is whether counterexamples of this second kind can be blocked by the analysis without appeal to implausible conditions and without introducing undue complexity into the analysis.

The problem was first discovered by Strawson, and the counterexample which illustrates it is to be found in his 1964 paper. Strawson's counterexample is as follows: S intends by an action of his to induce in A the belief that p (condition (d)). S arranges convincing-looking evidence that p in a place where A is bound to see it (condition (a)). In fact S arranges this evidence knowing that A is watching him work and knowing also that A does not know that S knows that A is watching him. S realizes that A will not take the arranged "evidence" as natural evidence that p, and intends that A take S's arranging of the "evidence" as grounds for believing that S intends to induce in A the belief that p (conditions (b) and (c)). And finally, S knows that A is convinced of S's reliability, and that A believes that S would not want A to believe that p unless it were the case that p; hence, A's recognition of S's intention to induce in him the belief that p is his reason for believing that p (condition (e)). Strawson concludes that although all the conditions of formulation (4) are satisfied, we do not in this case have an instance of attempted communication. Strawson identifies as the impediment to communication in this case the fact that A is not intended to know that S knows that A is watching him arrange the evidence. Strawson then suggests, "It seems a minimum further condition of his trying to do this [communicate with A] that he [S] should not only intend A to recognize his intention to get A to think that p, but that he should also *intend A to recognize his intention to get A to recognize his intention* to get A to think that p" (p. 29). This condition is then built into the analysis in the following manner:

> (5) S meant something in uttering x if and only if S uttered x intending:
> (a) that x have a certain feature f,
> (b) that A recognize that x has f,
> (c) that A infer at least in part from the fact that x is f that S uttered x intending:
> (d) that S's utterance of x produce response r in A,
> (e) that A's recognition of S's intention (d) should function as at least part of A's reason for r,
> (f) that A should recognize S's intention (c).

Strawson ends his discussion of Grice's analysis by suggesting that even with this sixth condition the analysis may not suffice for meaning$_{nn}$. Unfortunately, Strawson was right; the counterexamples do not stop with his. Schiffer has constructed another counterexample to the analysis as it stands in formulation (5).[26] S, who sings very badly, intends to get A, who has an extremely sensitive ear, to leave the room that he is presently occupying along with S. S intends to do this by singing "Moon Over Miami." Furthermore, S intends that A should recognize that S is singing "Moon Over Miami," and that A should infer from this that S is singing with the intention of getting A to leave the room (conditions (a) through (c)). Also, S intends that A recognize S's intention to get A to leave the room, for S wishes to show his distain for A. (Thus, Strawson's condition (f) is satisfied.) And finally, although S intends that A believe that S plans to get A to leave the room by means of his repulsive singing, at the same time S intends that A's *reason* for leaving the room will be A's recognition of S's intention (d) to get him to leave the room (condition (e)). In other words, S expects that A will think as follows: S wants me to leave because of his repulsive signing, but in fact I shall leave only because I am unwanted in this room. I do not care to be where I am unwanted. Thus, A will be conforming to S's plan without being aware that he is doing so.

The question is whether in this example S can be said to have meant something (that A was to leave the room) by singing "Moon Over Miami." The example fulfills the conditions of the proposed analysis of speaker meaning. So if formulation (5) is an adequate account of speaker meaning, S must indeed have meant something by his singing. But Schiffer argues that this is not an instance of communication and, hence, that the Gricean analysis as it stands in formulation (5) is inadequate. This is not a case of meaning$_{nn}$, since there is an intended discrepancy between the reason A was intended to have for leaving the room and the reason A was intended to think he was intended to have. In the above example the discrepancy is this: on the one hand, A is intended to *think* that S intends him to leave the room because of his repulsive singing, yet on the other hand, A is intended to *have as his reason* for leaving the room the recognition that S wants him to leave. To rule out this discrepancy, Schiffer suggests that we add yet another condition to the analysis as it stands in formulation (5), thus:

(6) S meant something in uttering x if and only if S uttered x intending:

(a) that x have a certain feature f,

(b) that A recognize that x has f,
(c) that A infer at least in part from the fact that x is f that S uttered x intending:
(d) that S's utterance of x produce response r in A,
(e) that A's recognition of S's intention (d) should function as at least part of A's reason for r,
(f) that A should recognize S's intention (c),
(g) that A should recognize S's intention (e).

Difficult though it is to grasp the intricacies of the counterexamples, one might worry, as Strawson did for formulation (5), that it may be possible to construct further counterexamples to the analysis even as it stands in formulation (6). And again, it would be right to worry. Schiffer has proposed yet another counterexample to the analysis as it stands in formulation (6).[27] It is less important to understand the intricacies of the counterexamples than to understand the reason they arise. Considering Strawson's and Schiffer's counterexamples alone, one can see that there is a diagnosable pattern in these challenges to the sufficiency of the analysis. In each case genuine communication is frustrated because of an element of deceit. It is true that more and more ingenuity is required at each stage to manage the deceit but it is also true that the analysis, as it stands, lends itself to such exploitation and thus is not an adequate analysis of our concept of nonnatural meaning.

Just as there is a pattern in the counterexamples, so too there is a pattern in the moves to counteract them. Schiffer found it sufficient to tag onto the analysis a condition, (g), that mimicked Strawson's suggested condition (f). Similarly, it seems that we can accommodate succeeding counterexamples by further mimicking Strawson's original suggestion. We may thus formulate the following rule: with the appearance of further counterexamples to the analysis as it stands in formulation (6), simply add to the existing set of intentions, n, the further intention, $n + 1$, that A recognize S's $(n - 1)$th intention. Adding such a condition will restore each time the missing ingredient that transforms a case of someone's merely getting something across to another into a genuine case of communication by eliminating a particular deceit.

There are several problems with this solution. One problem is that it threatens a regress. Grice suggests a way around the potential regress by allowing that after a certain point speakers cannot have such complex intentions, because audiences cannot be expected to recognize them.[28] As Grice recognized, the problem with this is that determining a simple cut-off point may always lead to counterexamples, while allowing the cut-off point to vary from speaker to speaker is theoretically unacceptable.[29] I suggest a problem deeper than either of these with this proposed solution. The postulation of backward-looking intentions is an essentially *defensive* measure. The problem it is designed to solve is this: at any point in such an analysis a wedge of deceit can be driven between the analysis and our intuitive notion of communication. The possibility of such deceit seems woven into the very fabric, so to speak, of the analysis. What is needed is a way of blocking the feature of the analysis that allows for deceit.

Both Grice and Schiffer suggest a way around the problem that seeks to root out the source of the counterexamples. Both recognize that the possibility of deceit is causing the problem, and both recognize that the possibility of such deceit arises for the following reason. As the analysis stands in formulations (4) and (5), there exist two avenues of communication: information can be passed on either as a result of A's recognition of S's intention that A recognize the meaning-bearing feature of S's utterance, or it can be passed on as a result of A's recognition of some wider intention that S possesses. In each of the counterexamples the speaker takes advantage of the possibility of such a split in his intentions in order to deceive his audience. Thus, the audience is directed toward the utterance's meaning-bearing feature and away from the speaker's true intentions. What Schiffer and Grice propose, each in his own way, is that a condition be built into the analysis that would force the speaker's communication intentions into line with the utterance's meaning-bearing feature. Such a condition would ensure that there is only one line of communication available. Grice does this by building into the analysis a condition prohibiting the speaker from having a certain sort of intention; Schiffer does this by introducing the condition of mutual knowledge. Both suggestions are essentially *offensive*: they rule out the possibility of deceit before it can get a grip.

Let us look at Grice's suggestion first. Using the analysis as it stands in formulation (4) as a base, Grice suggests that we add a further condition to the analysis so that it reads thus:

(7) S meant something in uttering x if and only if
  (1) S uttered x intending:
    (*a*) that x have a certain feature f,
    (*b*) that A recognize that x has f,
    (*c*) that A infer at least in part from the fact that x has f that S uttered x intending:
    (*d*) that S's utterance of x produce response r in A and
    (*e*) that A's recognition of S's intention (*d*) should function as at least part of A's reason for r, and

(2) there is no inference-element E such that S uttered x intending both

(a) that A's determination of r should rely on E and

(b) that A should think S to intend that (a) be false.[30]

The purpose of condition (2) is to guarantee that the speaker does *not* have certain deceitful intentions.

Grice defends this way with this counterexample in his more recent writings. In "Meaning Revisited" Grice explains just why condition (2) is a plausible (and indeed, essential) condition of speaker meaning.[31] His explanation relies on the acceptance of a certain notion in semantics: the notion of value. Value, Grice suggests, enters semantics with the idea of an optimal state, and appeal to an optimal state is just what Grice believes we find in the analysis of speaker meaning. Let us return for a moment to the analysis in formulation (6). First we notice the counterexample, and then we notice that the counterexample can be met by introducing "backward-looking intentions." Further counterexamples are then met by further backward-looking intentions. Then we notice that the counterexamples may continue and that we are now committed to the introduction of a potentially infinite number of backward-looking intentions. But if the number of intentions is infinite, it cannot be realized. Communication comes to be seen to rely on an optimal state that is impossible (and in this case logically impossible) to realize. This, claims Grice, should be taken as a mark in *favor* of the analysis rather than against it. The analysis reveals communication to be an ideal that any particular act of communication never strictly attains. This, Grice argues, is the way with ideal limits.

Grice gives two examples. Perhaps for some reason there cannot be anything that is strictly circular in what Grice calls the "sublunary world." Nevertheless, we may continue to call things circular when they approximate that ideal. Think of philosophers who hold that strictly speaking, one can only be said to know something one cannot be wrong about. They may still allow application of the word "knows" to cases where that ideal is not reached. All that is necessary is that the case at hand in some way approaches or approximates to the ideal.[32] The analysis of speaker meaning reveals communication to be such an ideal. In the counterexamples under discussion the speaker has deceitful, or what Grice calls "sneaky," intentions, and the existence of these intentions disqualifies the act as one of communication. Sneaky intentions mar the optimal. For this reason we need to build some condition into the analysis that would bar sneaky intentions and ensure that a particular act may qualify as a sublunary performance of communication. This is the function of condition (2).

Schiffer believes that Grice's condition (2) fails to block the original counterexample.[33] Schiffer proposes another way of blocking the problem. He suggests that we supplement the analysis as it stands in formulation (4) with what he calls a "mutual-knowledge condition." Roughly, speaker S and audience A mutually know that p if and only if S knows that p, and A knows that p, and S knows that A knows that p, and A knows that S knows that p, and S knows that A knows that S knows that p, and A knows that S knows that A knows that p, and so on. Schiffer offers the following very common example to illustrate the phenomenon. Two people, A and B, are seated at a table and between them is a candle. Assuming that A and B have normal sense faculties, normal intelligence, and normal perceptions and that they both have their eyes open, we can say: both A and B know that there is a candle before them. Given these same assumptions, we can also say: both A and B know that the other knows that there is a candle before him, and so on.

On the basis of this example we can see, Schiffer claims, that we can iterate knowledge operators indefinitely, and more important that the regress involved here is perfectly harmless. It is harmless because it involves an amount of knowledge that two (or more) people may uncontroversially be said to have about one another given certain situations and certain general features of those situations. In the candle case the relevant general feature of the situation is that both A and B are visually normal, i.e., each has his eyes open, has a perfectly intact optical system, has his head facing the candle and his partner, and can recognize all this about the other. Schiffer is, of course, not claiming that any individual explicitly articulates such complicated thoughts, only that it would be true to say of the individual that he has them.[34]

Having presented this case, Schiffer urges us to notice that the phenomenon illustrated in the case of two people seated before a candle is an entirely general one; it does not depend upon any features peculiar to viewing a candle. Indeed, the phenomenon can also be found in instances of communication. It is the *absence* of such mutual knowledge, Schiffer claims, that gives rise to the counterexamples from Strawson onward to the sufficiency of the Gricean analysis.

Drawing on the candle example, and in particular on the fact that A and B are visually normal, Schiffer observes the following. First, in general, if one knows, one knows *how* one knows. This knowing how, Schiffer claims, can be construed as knowing that having a certain property is sufficient for anyone to know that p. Let's label this property H. Now if one knows that p and one knows that having property H is sufficient for knowing that p, then one will know that one knows that p. Also, if one knows that property H is sufficient for anyone to know that p, one also knows that whoever is H knows that p. Putting all this together, Schiffer formalizes the conditions for mutual knowledge thus:

> S and A mutually know that p if and only if there are properties F and G such that
> (a) S is F,
> (b) A is G,
> (c) being F and being G are each sufficient for knowing that p, that S is F, and that A is G, and
> (d) for any proposition q, if being F and being G are each sufficient for knowing that q, then being F and being G are each sufficient for knowing that being F and being G are each sufficient for knowing that q.[35]

Property F may be, for example, the property of being a visually normal, open-eyed, conscious person who is identical with S and who is directly facing, at close distance, a candle and A—where A is a person who is visually normal, open-eyed . . . and who is directly facing a candle and S at close distance. Property G is similar to property F, only with the substitution of "S" for "A" and "A" for "S."

Condition (c) says that possessing properties F and G is sufficient for knowing that p (e.g., for knowing that there is a candle on the table), and that possessing these properties is sufficient for knowing that S is F and that A is G as well. Condition (d) relies on properties F and G being instances of property H, together with the following principle (which draws on the properties of property H). If two properties (in this case F and G) entail the same purely general properties and if both properties are such that: for any proposition p, it is true of each property that if it is sufficient for knowing that p, it is sufficient for knowing that it is sufficient for knowing that p; then for any proposition q, if either property is sufficient for knowing that q, then that property is sufficient for knowing that the *other* is sufficient for knowing that q. Thus, since S and A share all of the purely general properties entailed by either property F or property G, the two properties do not differ in any relevant respect. Condition (d) captures this fact.

Incorporating the condition of mutual knowledge into the analysis of speaker meaning must be done so as to ensure that all communicative intentions are out in the open. Schiffer proposes the following formulation:

> (8) S meant something by uttering x if and only if S uttered x intending thereby to realize a certain state of affairs E that S intends to be such that if E obtains, S and a certain audience mutually know that E obtains and that E is conclusive (or at least good) evidence that S uttered x intending:
> (a) to produce a certain response, r, in A,
> (b) that A's recognition of S's intention (a) function as at least part of A's reason for A's response r, and
> (c) to realize E.[36]

I said earlier that Schiffer's proposal, which would avoid the need to supplement the analysis with a series of backward-looking intentions, involves the introduction of a condition of mutual knowledge into the analysis as it stands in formulation (4). Yet if one compares formulations (4) and (8), one finds a substantial alteration in the form of the analysis. Upon closer inspection, however, one will see that (8) does contain the same conditions as (4) along with the addition of a mutual-knowledge condition. Condition (d) in (4) has become condition (a) in (8); condition (e) in (4) has become condition (b) in (8); and conditions (a) to (c) of formulation (4) have become the prelude and condition (c) of formulation (8). Feature f, which was introduced into the analysis in formulation (4) to avoid an earlier counterexample, has been incorporated into the state of affairs E in formulation (8). That this is so is clear from the explanation that Schiffer offers of E: "Typically, E will essentially involve the fact that S, a person having such and such properties, uttered a token of type x having a certain feature(s) f in the presense of A, a person having such and such properties, in certain circumstances, C."[37]

At this point another relatively minor revision must be made to the analysis. As it stands in formulation (8), the analysis has the undesirable consequence that whenever anyone means that p he will mean a lot more as well. According to (8) S means by uttering x that p *and S means* that he uttered x intending to produce in A a certain response. Clearly, S means too much. Schiffer proposes a minor alteration to the analysis to avoid this. He suggests that we distinguish between those intentions *with which* the person uttered x and the intentions the person had *in* uttering x and that we stipulate the following asymmetry: if i is an intention with which one uttered x, i will be an intention one had in uttering x, but not conversely. The intention with which one uttered x is the *primary* intention. Building this distinction into the analysis we get:

(9) S meant something by uttering x if and only if S uttered x intending thereby to realize a certain state of affairs E that S intends to be such that if E obtains, S and a certain audience mutually know that E obtains and that E is conclusive (or at least good) evidence that S uttered x with

(a) the primary intention to produce a certain response, r, in A,

(b) the intention that A's recognition of S's intention (a) function as at least part of A's reason for A's response r, and

(c) the intention to realize E.

In this way excess meaning is eliminated.

Returning to the problem of deception, which threatens the sufficiency of the analysis of speaker meaning, we find that there are two potential solutions: either build a condition into the analysans that requires that intentions of a certain sort be absent (Grice's way) or build in a condition of mutual knowledge (Schiffer's way).[38] Whichever way we choose, questions will have to be answered. Schiffer's way has gained a certain orthodoxy and has also acquired a proportional amount of substantial opposition. Here questions concerning the psychological plausibility of mutual knowledge loom large. Some may choose to defend the idea by appeal to tacit knowledge, but the complexity of this knowledge (its essentially regressive character) make such a defense implausible. Loar has suggested that we need only appeal to grounds that would suffice for further knowledge: "Often one has sufficient grounds for thinking things one does not think, which may even be too complex to think."[39] Perhaps another solution to the problems raised by the condition of mutual knowledge would be to adapt Grice's appeal to an optimal state.[40]

It has been argued, however, that even with the introduction of a condition of mutual knowledge, the analysis is not sufficient for speaker meaning. Harman, in his review of Schiffer's *Meaning*, points out that as the analysis stands in formulation (8), it may still be possible for some kind of deceit to gain a foothold.[41] He does not construct a counterexample, but merely points out that under one interpretation of formulation (8), although S intends to realize E and intends that if E, S and A mutually know that E obtains etc., the analysis says nothing about S intending A to *recognize* that S intends to realize E and intends that if E, S and A mutually know that E obtains etc. To avoid this Harman proposes the following emendation of formulation (8):

(10) S meant something by uttering x if and only if for some possible state of affairs E whose "obtainment" is sufficient for S and a certain audience A to mutually know (or believe) that E obtains and that E is conclusive (or at least good) evidence that S uttered x intending

    (a) to produce a certain response r in A,

    (b) that A's recognition of S's intention (a) function as at least part of A's reason for A's response r,

    (c) to realize E,

S uttered x intending thereby to realize E.

At this point Harman asks whether there are any possible states of affairs of the sort the analysis requires for communication, and he gives this answer: "If something like self-referential states of affairs are possible, E might be the conjunctive state of affairs, *S's uttering x intending (a)–(c) and S and A mutually knowing that E obtains.*"[42] Harman then throws the following dilemma at the Gricean. Either self-referential states of affairs are possible or they are not: if they are, why not return to the beginning and use self-referential *intentions* in the analysis; if they are not, it is not clear that the proposed analysis is sufficient for speaker meaning.

Harman proposes that we sweep away the complexities of the analysis as it is formulated in (8) and that we accept the following:

(11) S intends that an audience A will respond in a certain way r at least partly by virtue of A's recognition of S's intention.

According to Harman, both Grice and Schiffer avoid formulation (11) as a statement of the analysis because they want to avoid self-referential intentions.[43] It is this desire, according to Harman, that leads them into the complexities of the analysis as formulated in (7) and (8). If self-referential intentions are not allowed, then we might begin the analysis of speaker meaning by ascribing to S the intention:

    (a) to produce in audience A a certain response, r.

But of course, this is not sufficient for speaker meaning, so we add that S intends

    (b) that S's intention (a) be realized at least in part because of A's recognition of S's intention (a).

But this leaves open the possibility that A not recognize S's intention (b), and so we add that S intends

    (c) that S's intention (b) be realized at least in part because of A's recognition of S's intention (b).

And of course, the problem that arose after intention (*b*) had been added can arise again after intention (*c*) has been added. So we are forced to postulate a regressive series of backward-looking intentions. In order to avoid this problem, we are led, for example, to employ Schiffer's condition of mutual knowledge. All this is the result of avoiding the introduction of self-referential intentions into the analysis. Under the circumstances a reassessment of self-referential intentions is in order. Such a reassaessment is even more imperative if we agree with Harman that the analysis as it stands in formulation (8) is not yet sufficient for speaker meaning.[44]

Self-referential intentions (intentions that have themselves within their scope) will be enormously appealing to anyone who wishes to avoid the complexity of Schiffer's analysis.[45] To some, the simplicity of such intentions make their psychological reality relatively unproblematic.[46] Others, however, find the psychological reality of self-referential intentions not one jot less problematic than an explicit regress of intention.[47]

Our options appear to be as follows: accept Schiffer's way, introduce a condition of mutual knowledge into the analysis of speaker meaning, and find a way of meeting Harman's alleged problem; or embrace self-referential intentions and defend the position that such intentions are unproblematically grasped by speakers. But these are not the only options. We may return to Grice's way and avoid the possibility of deception with a condition in the analysans that prohibits a certain intention.[48]

I believe that the specificity of the problem that plagues the sufficiency of the analysis, in conjunction with the various ways that have been developed to meet the difficulty, should convince us that the prospects look good for eventually establishing conditions that will suffice for speaker meaning.

3 Is the Analysis Necessary?

In this section I shall briefly consider whether the Gricean analysis as it stands in formulation (9) provides conditions necessary for speaker meaning. Throughout sections 1 and 2 I formulated the analysandum thus: *S* meant something by uttering *x*. Schiffer has argued that *S* meant something by uttering *x* if and only if either in uttering *x*, *S* meant that such and such was the case, or for some *A*, in uttering *x*, *S* meant that *A* was to do such and such.[49] If these equivalences are correct, we can now formulate two distinct analysanda thus: First, in uttering *x*, *S* meant that *p*. Second, for some *A*, in uttering *x*, *S* meant that A was to do ψ. (Substituends for "p" are sentences, and substituends for "ψ" are descriptions of actions.) Such specificity in the analysandum requires analogous specificity in the analysans. Rather than continue to speak in a general way of "a certain response r," we can now specify the particular response. In sections 1 and 2 above, the nature of some of the examples considered made it natural for me to speak of the intended response as a belief. Had the utterances in the examples been not in the indicative mood but in the imperative, the intended response would be an action. We can thus formulate two different analyses, each in accordance with the same general principles.

For the indicative we have:

(8a) S meant that p by uttering x if and only if S uttered x intending thereby to realize a certain state of affairs E that S intends to be such that if E obtains, S and a certain audience mutually know that E obtains and that E is conclusive (or at least good) evidence that S uttered x intending:

(a) to produce the belief that p in A,

(b) that A's recognition of S's intention (a) function as at least part of A's reason for believing that p, and

(c) to realize E.

And for the imperative we have:

(8b) S meant that p by uttering x if and only if S uttered x intending thereby to realize a certain state of affairs E that S intends to be such that if E obtains, S and a certain audience mutually know that E obtains and that E is conclusive (or at least good) evidence that S uttered x intending:

(a) that A should ψ,

(b) that A's recognition of S's intention (a) function as at least part of A's reason for ψing, and

(c) to realize E.

In considering counterexamples to the claim that the analysis is necessary for speaker meaning, I shall consider those aimed at the analysis as it is formulated in (8a). To be brief, I shall ignore the formulation of the analysis in (8b).[50]

The general form of each counterexample in this section is this: there are cases that one would at least prima facie classify as cases of meaning$_{nn}$ but that do not satisfy the conditions of (8a). Here are some examples (in each case the B speaker produces a meaningful utterance but does not satisfy the conditions of the analysis as stated in formulation (8*a*)):

(1) The Examination
   A (teacher): "Who won the American Civil War?"
   B (student): "The North won the war."

(2) The Confession
   A (man): "It's no good trying to deny it; you spent the night with him."
   B (woman): "Yes . . . I did."

(3) Reminding
   A: "Let's see, what *was* the name of that restaurant?"
   B: "The Four Seasons"

(4) Reviewing Facts
   A and *B* are together studying for, say, a history exam.
   A: "The American Revolution took place in 1776."
   B: "Yes, and the French Revolution took place in 1789."
   A: "Right, and the Russian Revolution took place in 1917."

(5) The Inference
   A: "You believe that *p*, and you believe that *q* . . ."
   B: "Ah, yes, I can see now that *r* follows from the conjunction of *p* and *q*.

(6) Countersuggestion
   In some areas of belief *A* regards *B* as being almost invariably mistaken. *B* knows that *A* thinks this. *B* then says, "My mother thinks very highly of you," with the intention that *A* (on the strength of what *B* says) should think that *B*'s mother has a low opinion of *A*. Here there is an inclination to say that although *B*'s intention is that *A* should think that *B*'s mother has a low opinion of *A*, what *B* *meant* was that his mother thinks very highly of *A*.

(7) Indifference about Whether the Audience Believes
   A (stranger): "Where is Madam Tussaud's?"
   B (passerby): "Just around the corner."

(8) The Inadvertent Slip
   A (mother): "And where have you been?"
   B (daughter): "To the cinema with Tom." (To herself: "Damn, I didn't want her to know that. Why can't I keep quiet?")

(9) Accusation

A: (child): "I've just had a very busy day at school."

B: (parent): "That's a lie; your teacher called here today to ask where you were."

Grice considers cases of types (1) through (6) and offers two different suggestions for modifying the analysis in order to avoid them.[51] Working with the analysis as it stands in formulation (7), Grice first suggests that we accommodate the counterexamples by rewriting condition (c) thus:

(*c'*) that *S*'s utterance of *x* produce in *A* the activated belief that *p*.

Because of certain difficulties with this suggestion, Grice moves on to a second, preferred emendation of the analysis. Instead of (*c'*) Grice suggests that we rewrite condition (c) of formulation (7) as follows:

(*c''*) that *S*'s utterance of *x* produce in *A* the belief that the speaker believes that *p*.[52]

Schiffer adopts and develops the first of these suggestions, (c), adapting it to his preferred analysis, formulation (8). Schiffer argues that condition (*c''*) is false in certain cases, and suggests some adjustments to the analysis that will allow us to use (*c'*) while avoiding the difficulties envisaged by Grice. Furthermore, Schiffer's way of handling these counterexamples removes an implausibility from the analysis. As the analysis stands in either formulation (8*a*) or Grice's preferred formulation (7), communication involves the production of a certain response in an audience via the audience's recognition of the speaker's intention. The implausibility here is that often speakers (or writers) do not intend to produce beliefs in their audience in this way. A speaker does not always intend his audience to believe something because the speaker intends the audience to. In the case of assertions of a conceptual or theoretical nature, for example, the speaker intends his audience to see what is true by understanding how certain beliefs follow from certain other beliefs or, one might add, by understanding how things are in the world. Such assertions are not covered by the analysis as it stands in formulation (7). Schiffer aims to remove this implausibility from the analysis and to avoid the counterexamples listed above by rewriting the analysis in the following way:[53]

(12) *S* meant that *p* by uttering *x* only if *S* uttered *x* intending thereby to realize a certain state of affairs *E* that *S* intends to be such that if *E* obtains, *S* and a certain audience mutually know (or believe) that *E* obtains and that *E* is conclusive (or at least good) evidence that *S* uttered *x* intending

(a) to cause in A the activated belief that p and
(b) to realize E.

The analysis as it stands in formulation (12) reveals the basis for handling counterexamples (1) through (9), but the analysis is no longer sufficient. With formulation (13) Schiffer once again constructs a complete analysis that he believes will provide conditions both necessary and sufficient for speaker meaning. We need first of all to build back into the analysis the observation that in cases of genuine communication the audience has a reason for its belief that p and is not merely caused to believe that p. Furthermore, the reason the audience has for its belief that p should be its belief that the speaker's utterance x is related in a certain way R to the belief that p, i.e., either naturally or conventionally. Finally, we need to distinguish primary from secondary intentions. We thus get:

(13) S meant that p by uttering x if and only if S uttered x intending thereby to realize a certain state of affairs E that S intends to be such that if E obtains, S and a certain audience mutually know (or believe) that E obtains and that E is conclusive (or at least good) evidence that S uttered x with
   (a) the primary intention that there be some p such that S's utterance of x causes in A the activated belief that p/ρ (t),[54]
   (b) the intention that satisfaction of (a) is achieved at least in part by A's belief that x is related in a certain way R to the belief that p, and
   (c) the intention to realize E.

The analysis as it stands in formulation (13) is not quite the final version. One further qualification is needed to avoid one further kind of counterexample. Nevertheless, formulation (13) fends off all counterexamples so far considered. In particular, formulation (13) avoids cases (3) through (5) in the above list of counterexamples to the necessity of the analysis. In cases of reminding, reviewing the facts, and inference it is clear that the audience already has the beliefs in question and that the speaker's remarks are intended merely to bring that belief to mind. Rather than further adjust the anaysis to accommodate cases (1), (2), and (6) through (9), Schiffer chooses to look more closely at these cases to see whether they are genuine counterexamples.

Schiffer concludes the following. Case (7), indifference, and (8), the inadvertent slip, only *appear* to be counterexamples because the intention the second speaker has to inform his or her audience that p is fleeting or momentary. Once we see that the intention, however fleeting, *is* present, we can no longer see the example to run counter to the analysis of meaning as it stands in formulation (13). Cases (1), examination, (6), countersuggestion, and (9), accusation, are not really counterexamples to the analysis, because, argues Schiffer, they are not genuine cases of meaning. In these cases the second speaker means something only in an extended sense, in a sense "derivative from and dependent upon the primary sense captured in the definition."[55] The case of confession, (2), is not clear: sometimes meaning in such cases is derivative; at other times, however, the speaker confesses with the intention of activating or strengthening A's belief that p. These latter cases are straightforwardly accommodated by the analysis as it stands in formulation (13). But those cases of confession that do not fit this paradigm are not straightforward cases of telling; rather, they—along with cases of examination, accusation, and countersuggestion—are cases in which the speaker pretends to tell his audience that p or acts as if he were telling his audience that p.[56]

It would appear that Schiffer's analysis, in which the speaker intends the audience's response to be the activated belief that p, meets the challenge of counterexamples (1) through (9). Harman, however, has proposed a counterexample designed to force us back to Grice's second suggested response to this kind of counterexample, (c''). Here is Harman's counterexample:

(10) Personal Dignity
Suppose that D knows that his interrogators, A, B, and C, are firmly convinced that p is false. Say that p is the utterance "The earth revolves around the sun." Suppose also that A, B, and C want D to deny that p, and threaten to torture him if he does not. D nonetheless continues to uphold and to say that p.[57]

In this counterexample, D does not produce his utterance to activate the belief in his audience that the earth revolves around the sun. After all, D knows that A, B, and C firmly believe that this proposition is false. Indeed, we can assume that D is not even *trying* to convince his audience that the earth revolves around the sun. Yet D's utterance is clearly meaningful. Harman claims that if D were to continue to say that the earth revolves around the sun under these circumstances, his intention must be to uphold his own personal dignity. Harman also points out that this description of the case is in keeping with Grice's suggestion, mentioned just after the counterexamples, that the intended response is that the audience should believe that the speaker actively believes that p.

There is, however, another way of accommodating Harman's counterexample. I think that in Harman's case the speaker is not really speaking to an audience at all. I thus think that this counterexample should be grouped with another list of outstanding counterexamples to the necessity of the Gricean analysis of meaning. I turn now to these further counterexamples and the different suggestions made by Grice and Schiffer to accommodate them. I will then return to Harman's counterexample and explain why I think that it should be considered along with this second list of counterexamples.

This second list of counterexamples all have one thing in common: they are all cases of speaker meaning in which the speaker does not intend to produce a response in a particular audience. This list includes the following:[58]

(a) Entries in diaries,
(b) Rehearsing a part in a projected conversation or speech,
(c) Silent thinking,
(d) Writing notes to clarify a problem,
(e) Soliloquies,
(f) Leaving a note for a friend on the off chance that he will stop by,
(g) Muttering, "This is an incredible view," on a lone hike on a Grand Canyon trail,
(h) A sign that says, Private Property, Keep Out,
(i) A purist typing out "Snow is white" as an exercise in saying only true things,
(j) A science teacher, realizing that he has a naive, over-zealous, eager-to-please student in his class, takes delight while alone in saying aloud, "The earth is the farthest planet from the sun, and the sun revolves around it."

These counterexamples seem to fall into two categories: those in which the speaker S produces his utterance with the intention that some person *may* encounter it either at the time of the utterance or in the future; and those in which the speaker produces his utterance with *no* audience-directed intention whatever.

In his 1969 paper Grice explicitly considers six of these ten counterexamples. To accommodate the first sort of counterexamples, Grice suggests that we modify the analysis so as to allow for the possibility that the intended audience may not be present or may not be specified. If we incorporate this suggestion into Schiffer's analysis, (13), we get the following:

(14) S meant that p by uttering x if and only if S uttered x intending thereby to realize a certain state of affairs E that S intends to be such that if E, then:

(1) if anyone who has a certain property F (e.g., reads the diary or the note or the sign) knows that E obtains, that person will know that S knows that E obtains;

(2) if anyone who is F knows that E obtains, that person will know that (1); and so on;

(3) if anyone who is F knows that E obtains, that person will know (or believe), and know that S knows (or believes), that E is conclusive (or at least good) evidence that S uttered x with:

    (*a*) the primary intention that there be some p such that S's utterance of x causes in anyone who is F the activated belief that $p/\rho(t)$;

    (*b*) the intention that the satisfaction of (*a*) be achieved at least in part by the belief that x is related in a certain way R to the belief that p; and

    (*c*) the intention to realize E; and finally

(4) if anyone who is F knows that E obtains, that person will know that S knows that (3); and so on.

Formulation (14) covers counterexamples (*a*), (*b*), (*f*), (*g*), and (*h*). To accommodate cases (*c*), (*d*), and (*e*), cases where there is *no* intended audience, Grice suggests that we say that the speaker produced his utterance with the intention of uttering something that *would* produce an activated belief in a certain audience if uttered in appropriate circumstances.

Schiffer follows Grice's suggestion for the cases in which the audience is unspecified or not present but rejects it for the cases in which there is no intended audience. His reason for rejecting Grice here is this: Suppose we were to accept that in cases in which there is no intended audience, the speaker intends, nevertheless, to provide something that *would* produce an activated belief in an audience under certain circumstances. We would then be committed to accepting that the purist in counterexample (*i*) meant that snow is white when typing out his sentence, and that the teacher in counterexample (*j*) meant that the sun is the farthest planet from the sun and the sun revolves around it. After all, if the student were to overhear his favorite teacher utter this sentence, he would actively believe that the earth is the farthest planet from the sun and the sun revolves around it. And someone finding the purist's typed sentence, would actively believe that snow is white under some circumstances. Yet, Schiffer argues, it is not true that in these cases the purist meant that snow is white or that the teacher meant that the sun is the farthest planet from the sun and the sun revolves around it. To avoid this undesirable consequence of adopting Grice's way of dealing with counterexamples (c) through (e), Schiffer proposes the following alternative: in such cases (silent thinking, writing notes to oneself, soliloquies, and the like) we should say that there *is* an intended audience, *viz.*, the speaker himself. In these cases the speaker intends by his utterance to produce a certain cognitive response *in himself*. Strictly speaking, then, there aren't any cases in which the speaker has no intended audience at all.[59]

Schiffer's way of dealing with the second sort of counterexamples has the added advantage that it accommodates Harman's counterexample (10) above. The misleading thing about Harman's case is that there appears to be an audience present. The speaker, however, does not really address his utterance to those present. Indeed, as Harman explains, the speaker says what he does in these circumstances to uphold his own personal dignity. If this is true, why not say that in such cases the speaker intends his audience to be himself, that he intends to strengthen his own belief, thereby strengthening his own view of himself. Accommodating Harman's counterexample in this way leaves us free to accept Schiffer's way of dealing with the earlier counterexamples (1) through (9).

Counterexamples designed to show that the analysis is not necessary for speaker meaning are a rather mixed lot. Looking over them, we can classify them into two broad categories: the first type of counterexample puts pressure on the specification of the audience's intended response; the second type puts pressure on the requirement that an audience be present. Accommodating these counterexamples has in some cases led to alterations in the proposed analysis; in other cases the counterexample itself is rejected. on the whole, we can see from this section that although at first glance there appear to be a great number of counterexamples to the necessity of the analysis, little alteration of the analysis is in fact required to accommodate them.

As with the question of sufficiency I propose that we remain optimistic about the prospects for an analysis that is necessary for speaker meaning. Many critics of the analysis see the necessity of the conditions for speaker meaning as posing the greater threat to the ultimate success of the program. In *Linguistic Behaviour* Bennett suggests that once we strengthen the analysis to make it sufficient, we can strategically weaken it to make it necessary. Thus, in his work he relegates the task of establishing the necessity of the analysis to a "mop up operation" to be tackled only after firmly establishing that the analysis is sufficient.[60] In a more recent review of Davidson's work Bennett takes an even stronger line: "All the Gricean needs is to offer one-way conditionals of the form: if $R(x, S)$ then S as used by x means that p, where $R(x, S)$ is strong enough to make the conditional true but weak enough to allow it to be interesting and instructive, even if not weak enough to make its converse true as well. This one-way Gricean approach lets us get a theory of meaning launched for a given language, while leaving the door open for x to exploit his meaning for S in ways not captured by the relation R."[61]

Being content with sufficiency alone seems a curious position for a Gricean. Sufficiency alone with outstanding counterexamples to the necessity of the analysis is precisely what one would expect if the relation between the semantic and the psychological were one of supervenience. Yet any Gricean sees the relationship between the semantical and the psychological as stronger than supervienience. This is especially clear if we consider the reductive Gricean. Supervenience is a much weaker relation than reduction. It requires merely that if two individuals are alike in all psychological respects, they will also be alike in all semantic respects. Supervenience allows, whereas reduction disallows, the possibility that two individuals alike semantically may differ psychologically. Now it is precisely this possibility that is left open if the analysis fails to provide necessary conditions for speaker meaning. It would seem, then, that the reductionist cannot rest content to have established merely that the analysis is sufficient.

4 Timeless Meaning

Thus far the analysis purports to provide conditions sufficient and necessary for speaker meaning. As it stands in formulation (14), however, the analysis is insufficient to account for linguistic meaning. Although Griceans insist that the phenomenon they seek to analyze is found outside language as well as in it, their intention was always that the analysis should ultimately accommodate linguistic meaning. There are two salient features of linguistic meaning to which the analysis must address itself: meaning in language is timeless, and it is structured. In this section I will explain how the Gricean proposes to accommodate the first of these features into the analysis.

As with the analysis hitherto, we have different proposals for accommodating timeless meaning into the analysis in the writings of Grice and Schiffer. Schiffer's proposal has come to be viewed as standard, but Grice continues to distinguish his proposal from Schiffer's.[62] As in the previous two sections I shall present the proposals of both Grice and Schiffer.

In his 1957 paper Grice offers the following suggestive but very vague comment on timeless meaning. He says that " 'x means (timeless) that such and such' might be equated with some statement or disjunction of statements about what people intend to effect by x."[63] In his 1968 paper Grice sets about developing this idea. Beginning with the notion of timeless meaning for an ideolect, Grice suggests that what is required for an utterance—a hand wave (H-W), for example—to mean "I know the route" is the following: "For an utterer U, H-W means 'I know the route' $=_{df}$ it is U's policy (practice, habit) to utter H-W iff for some A, U intends A to think that U thinks U knows the route."[64] The suggestion is, however, neither necessary nor sufficient for timeless meaning. It is not sufficient since U may have other ways of getting his audience to think that he knows the route. It is not necessary since H-W may have a second meaning in U's ideolect. To avoid these problems, Grice replaces the idea of a policy, habit, or practice with that of "having a certain procedure in one's repertoire." Grice illustrates how this suggestion avoids the problems of the earlier suggestion thus: "A fairly eccentric lecturer might have in his repertoire the following procedure: if he sees an attractive girl in his audience, to pause for half a minute and then take a sedative. His having in his repertoire this procedure would not be incompatible with his also having two further procedures: (a) if he sees an attractive girl, to put on a pair of dark spectacles . . . ; (b) to pause and take a sedative when he sees in his audience not an attractive girl, but a particularly distinguished colleague."[65] We thus get: for an utterer U, H-W means or has as one of its meanings "I know the route" $=_{df}$ U has in his repertoire the following procedure: to utter H-W if U intends A to think that U thinks U knows the route. Now to have a procedure in one's repertoire is explained by Grice thus: "U has in his repertoire the procedure of . . . $=_{df}$ U has a standing readiness (willingness, preparedness) in some degree to . . . ." This account of having a procedure in one's repertoire won't do, however, because of the following sort of case:[66] Aunt Matilda is exceedingly prim. Now while it is true that for Aunt Matilda the sentence "He is a runt" means that he is an undersized person, it is quite false to say that Aunt Matilda is willing to *any* degree to utter that sentence in any circumstances whatever.

At this point Grice proposes to abandon the attempt to provide a definition, and to content himself with a few informal remarks.[67] The gist of these informal remarks is that in the case of an ideolect we must be careful to speak of U's practice to utter x in *such and such circumstances*. The problem posed by Aunt Matilda is more easily accommodated if we turn from ideolects to a *shared* language. In the case of a shared language an individual has a procedure for using certain utterances by being a member of a community of speakers members of which are willing or ready to use those utterances to procure certain beliefs in their audiences. As an account of the timeless meaning of an utterance in a shared language Grice suggests the following: "For group G, utterance-type x means 'p' $=_{df}$ At least some (?many) members of G have in their repertoires the procedure of uttering a token of x if, for some A, they intend A to think that p; the retention of this procedure being for them conditional on the assumption that at least some (other) members of G have, or have had, this procedure in their repertoires."[68]

Schiffer begins his discussion of the timeless meaning of non-composite utterances with the observation: "x means 'p' in G only if members of G are able to mean that p by uttering x in certain sorts of circumstances."[69] In other words, Schiffer notes a connection between an utterance's timeless meaning in G and what individual members of G do, would, or could mean by uttering x." Schiffer argues that this condition, though necessary, is insufficient for timeless meaning. The problem is that this condition can be fulfilled if members of G rely on some nonconventional *natural* feature of x. Schiffer suggests that a necessary condition of timeless meaning is the following: the relevant feature of x that the speaker relies on to communicate that p must not be one that is true of x independently of people meaning something by uttering x. In other words, the relevant feature must be nonnatural, or conventional. One reason for this condition is the following: any natural feature may be used to communicate several different things; the success of employing a natural feature to communicate depends heavily on context to specify the intended meaning. A nonnatural feature is much less dependent on context and, for that reason, is a much more secure means of communication.

Schiffer illustrates the need for a nonnatural feature in the account of timeless meaning with a story about how the sound "grr" might come timelessly to mean in a certain population "I am angry." Suppose that at time t there are two individuals, A and B, both without a language, and that A wants to communicate to B that he is angry. Being a rational individual, A will choose the best means available for making B understand that he is angry. A ingeniously chooses to make the sound "grr," which resembles the sound a dog makes when angry. A is here exploiting his knowledge that "grr" is the sound dogs make when angry; and that B's knowledge that "grr" is the sound dogs make when angry, together with B's knowledge of the situation he is in with A, is a very good reason for B to conclude that

A is angry. In such a case the existence of mutual knowledge about a natural feature that a certain sound has makes it possible for A to communicate his intentions to B.

Here we have a successful act of communication, but one whose success did not come easy. In order to understand that A was attempting to communicate his anger and not something else, e.g., that there were angry dogs in the vicinity, B had to take in quite a lot about the situation he and A were in. At this point we cannot yet say that "grr" means anything in the group of which A and B are members.

Let us continue the story. Assume that A was successful in communicating his anger to B, and that at some future time, t_2, B is angry with A and wants A to know this. Assume also that the last incident is still fresh in their minds. B, also a rational individual, wants to choose the best means to achieve his end. His memory of how A once communicated his anger and his belief that A most likely remembers this incident will lead B to choose the utterance "grr" to communicate his anger to A. B's choice of "grr" to communicate his anger at t_2 makes it even more likely that at future times anyone in A's and B's community who wishes to communicate his or her anger to another and who is aware of these incidents of communication will use the sound "grr." This sound will be chosen because speakers will choose the means of communication most likely to succeed, and its past uses in successful communications of anger give "grr" this status in this community. What makes "grr" the most likely candidate in these circumstances, then, is no longer the fact that this sound is naturally associated with anger in dogs but the fact that, *nota bene*, members of this community have successfully used this utterance in the past to communicate their intentions. As time passes and more and more members of the community have occasion to communicate their anger, it will become mutual knowledge among members of this particular community that "grr" is the sound to utter if one wants most successfully to communicate one's anger. It is "self perpetuating regularities" of this type which form the foundation of timeless meaning.[70]

Schiffer incorporates the observations about timeless meaning into his analysis in the following way:

> (15) A whole utterance x means (timeless) that p in a community C if and only if it is mutual knowledge among members of C that
> (a) if almost any member of C utters something M-intending[71] to produce in some other member of C the activated belief that p, what he utters might be x; and
> (b) if any member of C utters x M-intending to produce in

some other member of C the activated belief that p, he will intend the state of affairs E (which he intends to realize by uttering x) to include the fact that x is such that there is a precedent in C for uttering x and meaning thereby that p (or an agreement or a stipulation in C that x may be uttered to mean thereby that).[72]

This analysis of timeless meaning is formulated so as to allow that members of C might have other ways of communicating that p and that utterances of x may be used even for purposes other than communication. The reference in condition (a) to what a member of C might do to communicate, given what he knows, ensures that x does not mean that p in C simply because some member of C is aware of some precedent to use x to mean that p in some subgroup of C but would never himself use x to mean that p. The qualification "almost any" in condition (a) is intended to allow that there may be members of C who do not participate in the shared use of x for whatever reasons—they may be too young, too senile, or mentally retarded, for example. Finally, we should understand the reference to mutual knowledge in the definition as follows: every member of C knows that anyone who is a member of C knows that . . . (as opposed to: every member of C knows of each member of C that . . .).

Formulation (15), then, is Schiffer's account of timeless meaning. Schiffer has said that if x meets the conditions for timeless meaning in a community, x will be in that community a conventional means of communicating that p.[73] That is, the feature of x that forms the basis of the mutual knowledge lying at the heart of communication (according to Schiffer) will have a *conventional* association with the relevant communication intention. Assuming this connection between timeless meaning and convention, Schiffer proposes to extract his account of convention from his account of timeless meaning.

Schiffer's account of convention borrows from David Lewis, and both claim a debt to David Hume.[74] In his *Treatise of Human Nature* Hume writes that a convention is

a general sense of common interest; which sense all the members of the society express to one another and which induces them to regulate their conduct by certain rules. I observe, [e.g.,] that it will be for my interest to leave another in possession of his goods, *provided* he will act in the same manner with regard to me. He is sensible of a like interest in the regulation of his conduct. When this common sense of interest is mutually expressed, and is known to both, it produces a suitable resolution and behaviour. And this may properly enough be called a convention or agreement betwixt us, though without the interposition of a promise; since the actions of each of us have a reference to those of the other, and are performed upon the supposition that something is to be performed on the other part.[75]

Hume is here aware that a convention arises out of an interest common to members of a given community, and that this common interest alone—without the need of any promises—can provide the foundation for a convention. What Lewis adds to Hume, and Schiffer borrows from Lewis, is an account of the development and perpetuation of a convention that draws on an idea from the theory of games. Game theory is concerned with games of strategy (rather than those of skill or chance) involving situations where two or more people must choose a course of action and where the best course of action for each is dependent upon what each expects the others involved in that situation to do. Games thus present us with what has been called a "coordination problem." The solution to the problem has been dubbed a "coordination equilibrium."

I shall very briefly present an outline of convention. I shall present only one extremely simple example of a coordination problem and explain how coordination problems can give rise to conventions. The example is this. Two people, A and B, are cut off in the middle of a rather important telephone conversation. Each believes that each wants the connection restored and the conversation to continue and that neither cares who waits and who dials just so long as the line is restored. The problem is to decide who should dial and who should wait, since if they both dial, they will be frustrated in restoring the line, and if they both wait, the line will never be restored. In such a case a coordination equilibrium is achieved if both A and B succeed in adopting strategies which are such that no other combination of strategies would have made either party better off. In a situation where such an equilibrium is achieved, the parties interests perfectly coincide. How, in the telephone case, can A and B achieve such an equilibrium? Since both A and B know that each wants the conversation to continue, each will form expectations about what the other can expect him naturally to do. In this case the situation contains a clue that A and B can use to coordinate their strategies: the original caller clearly has the relevant telephone number. Exploiting this clue, the original caller redials while the original recipient waits.

The first instance of being cut off requires such conscious deliberation about the other's expectations, but the second time these people are cut off in the middle of a telephone conversation they both wish to continue, it is much clearer what the optimal thing to do is: the original caller calls again. What makes this the obvious thing to do in this situation is the fact that it worked before and is mutually known by both A and B to have done so (cf. the story of "grr" above). In this way recurring coordination problems give rise to conventions: in the telephone case the convention that the original caller returns the call if telephone lines are cut. A convention is "a regularity in the behavior of members of a group which constitutes a solution to a recurring coordination problem."[76] In this way Lewis explains just how it is that "common interest" (to use Hume's phrase) can give rise to conventions in the absence of a promise.

Schiffer disagrees with one aspect of Lewis's account of convention. Schiffer does not believe that all conventions arise out of solutions to recurring coordination problems. Some conventions, Schiffer argues, arise because those involved desire to achieve a certain end or goal. Schiffer claims that this is so for conventions of etiquette and the case we are interested in: linguistic conventions. In these cases a certain practice is adhered to, not because each participant aims to coordinate his activity with the activity of another, but because each participant has an interest in a certain end: in the case of language, communication.

Schiffer agrees with Lewis that conventions are explained in terms of participants' expectations about the other participants' actions; they disagree over the *reason* each gives to explain *why* such expectations give each participant a reason for doing one thing rather than another. Can Schiffer's reason for linguistic conventions be incorporated into the reason Lewis suggests? If we were to regard meaning conventions, for example, as solutions to coordination problems *over time*, we could say that the common goal achieved by such coordination is communication. Schiffer, however, explicitly rejects this suggestion, claiming that it involves a falsification of the facts.[77] It falsifies, according to Schiffer, the order of the speaker's intentions: S's intention in uttering x is *not* to coordinate his action with those of others in C in order to communicate among members of C. Rather, S's intention in uttering x is to communicate to A that p, and he can do this quickly and efficiently because of the existence of certain meaning conventions.

Schiffer offers the following account of convention. A convention to do some type of act or activity x (e.g., uttering "grr") prevails in C when (only when) doing y (e.g., communicating that one is angry) if and only if it is mutual knowledge among members of C that

(a) there is a precedent in C for doing x (or an agreement or stipulation that one will do x) when (only when) doing y;

(b) on the basis (at least in part) of (a), almost everyone in C expects almost everyone in C to do x when (only when) doing y; (c) because of (b) almost everyone in C does x when (only when) doing y.

Incorporating convention into the account of timeless meaning, Schiffer offers the following final account of timeless meaning:

(16) X (timeless) means that p in C (if and only if there prevails in C a convention or set of conventions Z such that any member of C acts in accordance with Z only if he utters x M-intending to produce in some other member of C the activated belief that p.[79]

Searle has said, "Meaning is more than a matter of intention, it is also at least sometimes a matter of convention."[80] This is precisely what Griceans like Schiffer recognize when they turn from giving an account of speaker meaning to giving an account of the timeless meaning of an utterance. The latter is a matter of convention as well as intention.

Once we have an analysis of timeless meaning, we can speak of what is sometimes referred to as the *autonomy* of meaning. This feature of meaning in language permits a sentence to be uttered and to have meaning even though the speaker's intention at that moment may not be in keeping with what a Gricean analysis of meaning requires. What gives the utterance its meaning in the community are the mutual expectations members of that community have about which intentions are generally associated with that utterance. These expectations allow two things to happen. One, though some members of a community may never utter certain sentences, these sentences retain their meaning in the language of that community. Two, though a member of a community may employ an utterance in a way that goes against the expectations of other members, the meaning of that utterance doesn't change in that community (consider cases of irony, sarcasm, and jokes, for example). Such expectations also explain why within a given community not just any string of marks or sounds can be used to mean a given proposition. At this point one can perhaps see that the Gricean account of speaker meaning on an occasion and timeless meaning of an utterance are the foundation of a general account of language use. Indeed, Grice claims to have his sights set on this wider program from early on. He writes, "The wider programme just mentioned arises out of a distinction which . . . I wish to make within the total signification of a remark: a distinction between what the speaker *said* (in a certain favoured, and maybe in some degree artificial, sense of 'said'), and what he has 'implicated' . . . taking into account the fact that what he has implicated may be either *conventionally* implicated . . . or *nonconventionally* implicated. . . ."[81]

5 Structure

"It is characteristic of sentences (a characteristic shared with phrases) that their standard meaning is consequential upon the meaning of the elements (words, lexical items) which enter into them."[82] All Griceans are aware of this, and each has attempted to adjust their analysis to reflect this characteristic. Grice builds upon his account of the timeless meaning of unstructured utterances, which appeals to the idea of having a procedure in one's repertoire, to suggest that the analysis accommodate structure by bringing in the notion of a "resultant procedure." Grice then gives the following rough explication of the notion of a resultant procedure: "A procedure for an utterance-type x will be a resultant procedure if it is determined by (its existence is inferable from) a knowledge of procedures (*a*) for particular utterance-types which are elements in x, and (*b*) for any sequence of utterance-types which exemplifies a particular ordering of syntactic categories (a particular syntactic form)."[83] Details of these more basic procedures then follow. Grice ends by pointing out an "as yet unsolved problem": what is the epistemological status of these procedures or rules? If what we are after is an explanation of our linguistic practice, we are led to suppose that "in some sense, 'implicitly', we *do* accept these rules," Grice writes.[84] The problem is to say in what sense this is true.

The same problem arises for the suggestion made by Loar and followed by Schiffer. To understand Loar's suggestion one must shift the discussion from a consideration of sentences and their meanings to a consideration of language. Following Lewis, we can say that a possible language $\mathscr{L}$ assigns meaning to certain strings of types of sounds or marks and so, is a function from certain strings of marks or sounds called sentences to meanings.[85] Thus defined, a possible language is an abstract entity that has yet to be related to speakers. The next step is to define a relation holding between $\mathscr{L}$ and members of some group who use $\mathscr{L}$. For the Gricean this relation will be specified in terms of conventions pertaining to speaker meaning. At this point the Gricean will also want to accommodate the fact that meaning in $\mathscr{L}$ is structured and recursive. One can do this by appealing to a grammar (once again following Lewis). Like a language, a grammar has a semantics; a grammar too is a function from the marks and sounds that are elementary constituents of sentences to meanings. Over and above this, a grammar consists of a number of combining operators that take elementary constituents to build up strings of interpreted sounds or marks. Grammars are finitely specifiable—they have finite lexicons and a finite set of operators—yet they determine languages that are infinite. Thus, we may deal with issues concerning both structure and learnability by appealing to a grammar. The only thing that remains is to specify the relation between speakers in a group and some grammar.[87] Loar proposes that we think of a group's use of a language as being grounded in some grammar Γ.[88] But what is it to "ground" a grammar? This takes us back to Grice's unsolved problem. For our purposes it is unnecessary to delve into the complexities raised by this problem. It is sufficient to see the direction the analysis can take in response to the matter of structure.

With this my presentation of a Gricean account of meaning is complete. Though I do not wish to suggest that the analysis of meaning that Griceans offer is without difficulties, I am optimistic that we can adjust the analysis to accommodate any outstanding problems. Moreover, the analysis provides much insight into the way language functions.

In an early work devoted to developing conditions necessary and sufficient for speaker meaning and timeless meaning, Loar writes: "So, in effect, what I hope to have shown . . . is that semantic facts, including facts about word meaning, are in a way psychological facts, facts about the communication practices of a group. For many, the general idea will be already obvious, but it is by no means a trivial question what kind of psychological fact a semantic fact is."[89] I think this very well summarizes the attitudes of many early Griceans: they assume that the approach must be the correct one and believe that the only work needing to be done is to explain which psychological states ought to figure on the right-hand side of the analytic biconditional. But if we look more closely at what Loar is saying, we find that his assumptions are by no means obvious and that to defend them, we need to do a great deal more work besides that of finding conditions necessary and sufficient for speaker meaning and timeless meaning. One of Loar's assumptions is that semantic facts "are in a way psychological facts." This amounts in effect to an assumption that the semantic can be reduced to the psychological. In chapters 3 and 4 I want to concentrate on this general idea that the semantic reduces to the psychological. I want to consider in some detail what more a Gricean needs to claim to maintain such a reduction, in addition to his analysis of *which* psychological facts semantic facts reduce to.

Chapter 3
Asymmetry

The problem is to give an adequate and illuminating account of the fact that certain noises and marks have significance for individuals. The philosopher's task is not that of explaining how or why this phenomenon arose. Rather, his job is to explain what is involved in our concept of meaning.

In chapter 1, section 2, I identified two main approaches philosophers have taken to the problem: the formal approach and the analytic approach. Those working in the former tradition are primarily concerned to build theories of meaning that exhibit the structure of sentences and the interrelations among them. Those working in the latter tradition aim to construct biconditionals whose right-hand sides give conditions necessary and sufficient for applying the concept on the left-hand side. A Gricean analysis by employing psychological terms on the right-hand side, aims primarily to exhibit the precise relationship certain marks and sounds have to their users. As we have seen, some theory builders have gone so far as to reject analysis as a method suited to our concept of meaning. Contrary to this, I have suggested that although the formal approach is clearly relevant to meaning—as opposed, perhaps, to some other concepts—and can shed much light on that concept, the method of analysis may *also* prove illuminating. Once analysis is recognized as a legitimate approach to understanding meaning, the way lies open for reconciling these two approaches.[1]

After we accept that the method of analysis may help us to understand meaning, it is very important that we understand how this method works. In chapter 1, section 3, I claimed that analyses come in two varieties, reductive and reciprocal. Drawing on the work of Wisdom and Moore, I suggested that analysis may clarify meaning for us either by revealing that the concept is less fundamental in our overall scheme of concepts than some other concept (a reductive analysis) or by revealing precisely how that concept is related to others in our overall scheme of concepts *without* implying that those other concepts are more fundamental or more basic (a reciprocal analysis). To say that there are two different *kinds* of analysis is not to be committed to a different procedure in each case. Rather, we interpret differently the same procedure of giving conditions necessary and sufficient for the concept we are interested in. Which interpretation is appropriate to a concept is not something that is necessarily revealed in the analysis itself; the biconditional may provide no clue as to the kind of analysis we are engaged in. Only when we consider what account is to be given of the concepts employed on the right-hand side of the analytic biconditional can we be sure of the kind of analysis we have.

In what follows I shall concentrate on the reductive interpretation of Grice's analysis of meaning.[2] My aim will be to expose the assumptions of that interpretation and to oppose them. As I explained in chapter 1, section 5, Schiffer and Loar have both written that the real interest in Grice's work lies in its viability as a reductive account of meaning. Both have suggested that a Gricean reduction of the semantic to the psychological is an indispensible part of a program that aims to give a physicalist account of both the semantic and the psychological. The other part of that program involves a functionalist reduction of the psychological. Such a program is clearly committed to there being a noncircular analysis of meaning in terms of speakers' psychological states.

Circularity can infect the analysis in either of two ways. We may find that we cannot give conditions necessary and sufficient for meaning in terms of the psychological alone and that we need an injection of straightforwardly semantic concepts on the right-hand side of the biconditional as the only way of completing the analysis. Alternatively, we may find that though we can come up with psychological concepts that together are necessary and sufficient for meaning, understanding these psychological concepts involves semantic concepts from the original analysis. Notice that neither sort of circularity would undermine the analysis under a reciprocal interpretation.

I shall take it that the first sort of circularity will not prove a grave stumbling block for the reductionist. (This was the point of chapter 2.) As I see it, the real issue is whether we can give an account of the psychological concepts in the analysans that does not appeal to the very semantic concepts we set out to analyze in the first place.

Of the two interpretations we can give of a Gricean analysis of meaning, the reductive interpretation makes the stronger claim. If successful, a reductive analysis would reveal that our concept of meaning is secondary to psychological concepts in our overall scheme of concepts. And importantly, such a reduction would pave the way for a further reduction of the semantic to the physical. Contrary to Schiffer and Loar, I want to argue that a reduction of the semantic to the psychological cannot work, that it is bound to run up against the second of the two circularities mentioned above. A consequence of this failure to reduce the semantic to the psychological may be to make any reduction of the psychological, in its turn, more difficult.

My criticism of the reductive interpretation of a Gricean analysis will be that it is based not only on a mistaken view of the relation between our concepts of the semantic and the psychological but also on a mistaken view of the psychological. I shall argue that a correct understanding of the psychological is forthcoming only after one has a proper understanding of the way in which our psychological and semantic concepts interrelate.

Earlier in chapter 1, section 3, I quoted Schiffer as discounting any view that held that psychological concepts required reference to public-language semantic concepts as part of their analyses. At the time, he could not prove such a view false. Since that time Schiffer has tried to defend the view that circularity will not prove an obstacle to his reductive program.[3] Loar has devoted an entire book to the attempt to give an account of the propositional attitudes that makes no reference to public-language semantic concepts.[4] As a result of such work the reductionist is in a much stronger position to defend his program. We have various proposals to account for the psychological, some that make reference to the semantic and others that attempt to avoid any such reference. Which of these proposals is correct? Which gives an account of the psychological that best squares with how we understand our concept of the psychological? To decide this we must dig deep; we must embark on an investigation into both our psychological and our semantic concepts. We must ask whether the proposals put forward by Schiffer and Loar are appropriate to these concepts. Whereas Schiffer and Loar have concentrated first on the analysis of speaker meaning in psychological terms and then on an account of the psychological free of public-language semantic concepts, I intend to concentrate on an assessment of their general approach. What do such reductive accounts presuppose about our semantic and psychological concepts? What conception of meaning and mind lies behind this approach? And having answered these questions, we need to consider whether what is revealed is a true conception of meaning and mind.

I propose to begin my assessment of the reductive approach by recalling Wisdom's idea of a "new-level analysis" (see chapter 1, section 3). When I first introduced Wisdom's talk of levels, I said that if our concepts are on different levels, the one concept or set of concepts is in some sense more basic or more fundamental than the other; if they are on the same level, no such priority can be established. The reductive Gricean clearly believes that psychological concepts are more fundamental and more basic in our overall scheme of concepts than semantic concepts, but what exactly does this mean? In what sense are psychological concepts more basic? Only once we have established an answer to this question can we assess the claim that psychological concepts *are* more basic than semantic ones.

Let us approach this matter by first rephrasing the question. Rather than ask, In what sense is the psychological more fundamental? I shall ask, What grounds are there for believing that there is an asymmetry between the concepts mentioned on either side of the Gricean biconditional? At first glance it seems that we have made little progress. What exactly is at issue when two sets of concepts are asymmetrical? In this chapter I shall propose several possible kinds of asymmetry and then ask which kind supports a reductive Gricean thesis. Once we have identified the relevant asymmetry, we can ask, Is there such an asymmetry between our semantic concepts and psychological concepts?

Where a reductive Gricean claims an asymmetry, his antireductive opponent asserts a symmetry: our semantic and psychological concepts are on a par; neither set is more basic or more fundamental than the other. Just as we need to understand what the reductive Gricean means when he claims asymmetry, so we need to understand what his opponent means when he claims symmetry between these concepts. Opposition to a Gricean reduction has been strong, and these opponents are often clearer about what they mean when they claim symmetry than Griceans have been about their proposed asymmetry. From here on I shall mean "reductive Gricean" by "Gricean" and shall often omit the qualifying adjective, unless, of course, I indicate otherwise. One might think that we can understand the Gricean claim of asymmetry by the simple process of taking the Gricean to deny the symmetry proposed by the antireductionist. I shall argue, however, that this does not work. I believe that some opponents of a Gricean reduction have missed their target: the sort of symmetry they support is not one the Gricean need deny. Starting with the errors of his opponents, I shall attempt to piece together an understanding of the reductive Gricean claim that there is an asymmetry between our semantic and psychological concepts.

It has been suggested to me that although Griceans have always been aware of this demand for an asymmetry, it need not be fulfilled at the start.[5] Here is an analogy to clarify the point. Consider the Charles-Boyle gas law. That law preexisted the reduction (if it is one) of thermodynamics to statistical mechanics. The relevant "asymmetry" (really a complex set of relations between macro and micro theories) was discovered later. What the Gricean has produced is the psycho-semantic equivalent of the gas laws in the faith that future science will lead to the desired reduction and thereby yield the relevant asymmetry. The objection is that by pointing out that Griceans have not yet established an asymmetry, I am imposing on them a demand far higher than any imposed on science.

This response misinterprets my demand. The objection appears to be that we take the original Gricean analysis to have a role in the overall reductive program similar to that of the Charles-Boyle gas law in the overall reduction of thermodynamics to statistical mechanics. If this means that we may propose an analysis in advance of working out the rest of the program, I agree. As I hope I have shown in chapter 1, the importance and utility of the Gricean analysis does not depend upon the discovery of the relevant reduction. My point is that if one has reductive ambitions, one must be prepared to defend some relevant asymmetry between the concepts mentioned on either side of the biconditional. What I find curious in the objection is the assumption that some future science will yield an asymmetry for a Gricean reduction. At this point the analogy between a Gricean reduction and reduction in the physical sciences breaks down. There is a real question of how far the reductive Gricean can model his ideas on examples drawn from the physical sciences. There is an assumption that the model is essentially similar to what is being modeled. This is an assumption I intend to challenge (see especially chapter 4). To assume that science will yield the required reduction is already to assume there *is* an asymmetry between semantic and psychological concepts. But this is the very point in dispute. I shall argue that what philosophical investigation into our concepts of the semantic and the psychological reveals is that an asymmetry of the type the Gricean is assuming is implausible. It follows that I believe the reductive interpretation of Grice's analysis is misguided. We need to think of that analysis in some other way.

The question we need to consider first, then, is this: How are we to understand the Gricean claim that there is an asymmetry between the semantic and the psychological? Or again, What sort of asymmetry may be thought to support a Gricean reduction? The asymmetry in question cannot be trivial nor anodyne; it must impress us as important enough to support such a weighty claim. So we should not accept the following, for example, as the asymmetry that supports a Gricean reduction: the psychological is less obscure than the semantic. Even if true,[6] this claimed asymmetry may beg the question: we may hold that the psychological is less obscure because more tractable from the viewpoint of physical theory. But this already assumes the further reduction of the psychological to the physical, which is perhaps only plausible on the assumption of the original semantic reduction. Perhaps the following is the asymmetry the Gricean has in mind: the psychological has greater generality than the semantic. As it stands, this suggestion is too vague. Firming it up will yield one important way to try and understand the reductive asymmetry. Here is one way to do this: a creature need not possess thoughts to be capable of language, although to be capable of language a creature must possess thoughts. I shall label this an "ontological asymmetry." Before considering this asymmetry, I want to propose another. I shall label this an "epistemological asymmetry" and shall formulate it initially and somewhat crudely as follows: for there to be knowledge of what another thinks, one need not know what his words and sentences mean, although to know what another's words and sentences mean, one needs to make assumptions about his propositional attitudes.

Many of those who have considered the Gricean reductive thesis believe that it involves a commitment either to an ontological or an epistemological asymmetry. Holdcroft writes: "A different question is raised if we ask whether the Gricean analysis is reductionist. Most would probably say 'yes'; but I want to urge that the matter is perhaps less clear than it looks. . . . What is needed is an argument that the right hand side of our biconditional is more secure, ontologically, or even epistemologically, than is the left hand side."[7] Holdcroft doesn't offer a view on what argument the reductionist would offer. Evans and McDowell consider the matter and conclude that the asymmetry in question is very likely ontological. They write:

> Reduction requires that there be some ground for claiming an asymmetry. Now it seems unlikely that an epistemological asymmetry holds in the case we are considering. . . . But it might be held that there is an asymmetry of a different kind. . . . It might be said, the concepts of the propositional attitudes as such are independent of the concepts of semantics: for there is no requirement, if we are to ascribe propositional attitudes to an organism, that it possess a language. And it might be argued that such an asymmetry, conceptual but not epistemological, is enough to justify the view that the further conditions we are looking for might be reductive.[8]

In this chapter I want to examine these proposed ontological and epistemological asymmetries in some detail and to ask which of these the Gricean commits himself to when he commits himself to a reduction of the semantic to the psychological.

1 Surface Epistemological Asymmetry

I would like to begin with the asymmetry that Evans and McDowell reject, the epistemological. How might we understand the claim that there is an epistemological asymmetry between the semantic and the psychological? Let us compare the reduction in which we are interested with another: the attempt by philosophers to reduce statements about individuals to statements about sense-data.[9] Proponents of this sort of reduction have been quite clear about the kind of asymmetry they see as supporting their claim of reduction. The asymmetry is epistemological: the claim is that statements about individuals are equivalent in meaning to statements about sense-data, and this equivalence is sought in order to find an epistemologically secure ground for statements concerning material objects. Proponents hold that from an epistemological point of view sense-data are much less of a problem than material objects. If everything said about the latter could be shown to be equivalent in meaning to something said about the former, material objects would be as epistemologically secure as sense-data.[10] The reduction of statements concerning material objects to statements concerning sense-data, then, is based on an alleged epistemological asymmetry. If we could show that statements about material objects are equivalent in meaning to statements about sense-data, the latter being known directly or without difficulty, we would have a justification of our knowledge of material objects. And the epistemological security that certain concepts have would justify our saying that they are more fundamental or more basic in our overall scheme of concepts.

The interest in considering phenomenalism is this: the phenomenalist is proposing a reduction, and he is explicit about what sort of asymmetry is intended. Illusions, hallucinations, dreams, and the possibility of an evil demon may shake our confidence in our knowledge claims concerning the external world. Faced with an illusion, etc., the following question comes into focus: How do we know that our experiences are of a world independent of us? Establishing a reduction along phenomenalist lines would provide a secure epistemological anchor for such claims. Despite the many differences between a phenomenalist reduction and a Gricean one, we may perhaps construct an asymmetry for the latter by drawing upon the claims of the former. We might begin by considering the question, How do we know what another's words and sentences mean? Now from a naive and unreflective point of view there does not appear to be a problem: either we assume that the other is like us (e.g., that he speaks English), or we rely on a translation from his language into ours. We may consider this assumption less natural, however, when we consider the case of the alien, someone who does not speak our language and for whose language no manual of translation exists. The question now comes into focus: How do we know what this alien means by his words and sentences? The Gricean may respond to this challenge by arguing that faced with a people who speak a radically alien language and the task of interpreting their language, we could proceed by trying to discern in the speakers the intentions and beliefs mentioned in the Gricean analysis. The thought behind this method of radical interpretation is that matters psychological are empirically more accessible than matters semantic, and Gricean analysis teaches us that the two are logically equivalent. The idea that the psychological is empirically more accessible than the semantic gives content to the idea that psychological concepts are more fundamental or more basic in our overall scheme of concepts. This asymmetry of accessibility provides us with one possible understanding of the claim that there is an epistemological asymmetry between our psychological and semantic concepts. I shall label this asymmetry of accessibility "surface epistemological asymmetry."

The thought prompted by considering the phenomenalist reduction is this: a Gricean reduction, like this phenomenalist reduction, is supported by a surface epistemological asymmetry. But it is not obvious that the problem of radical interpretation is solved by such a reduction. For whereas sense-data, if countenanced, may be epistemologically more basic than material objects, it is very doubtful that the psychological is empirically more accessible than the semantic.

Davidson makes much of this doubt. We thus find Davidson writing, "Radical interpretation cannot hope to take as evidence for the meaning of a sentence an account of the complex and delicately discriminated intentions with which the sentence is typically uttered."[11] In what does such a doubt consist? Is the failure of such an epistemological asymmetry an indication that the Gricean reduction is doomed to failure? If the Gricean accepts the failure of this asymmetry, what *other* asymmetry can be invoked to support his reductive claim? In the following sections I shall offer some answers to these questions.

2 The Davidsonian Doubt

The claim, then, that there is a surface epistemological asymmetry between the semantic and the psychological is the claim that when we are faced with an individual who speaks a language we do not understand, we can come to understand his language by first coming to know his beliefs and intentions. The Davidsonian doubt is that this will not be possible. Davidson writes, "My claim is . . . that making detailed sense of a person's intentions and beliefs cannot be independent of making sense of his utterances."[12] And in another place, "If this is right, we cannot make the full panoply of intentions and beliefs the evidential base for a theory of radical interpretation."[13] I now want to suggest a reason for this doubt.[14]

To see the force of this doubt, consider the following situation. Say you come upon a member of an alien community who is a lecturer at the alien university and who is writing a book about the relation between the semantic and the psychological. When you come upon her, she begins to talk to you about her book. As you do not speak her language, the noises she utters are for you impenetrable. Now if a Gricean analysis is a proposal for radical interpretation, you could come to understand what the lecturer is saying to you by first coming to know certain of her beliefs and intentions. In this case you would come to see that this person has, roughly, the intention to produce in you the belief that she is writing a book on the question of whether the semantic is reducible to the psychological. But, says the objector, how can you know this unless you already understand this person's language? Such intentions and beliefs are altogether too complex for another to come to know without the aid of language.

It seems hard to deny that the detection of such complex beliefs and intentions requires the interpreter to understand the alien's language. But perhaps epistemological asymmetry can be salvaged along the following lines. It is a mistake to think of interpretation as proceeding sentence by sentence; rather, the radical interpreter will have to consider long stretches of behavior—both linguistic and nonlinguistic—before he will be able to begin interpreting. So the interpreter may be able to work his way into the alien's language by starting with expressions of simple beliefs and intentions. Using the knowledge gained here, the interpreter may be able to work his way up to an understanding of more complex beliefs and intentions and thereby come to interpret more and more of the alien's language. We could call this the "stepwise procedure" of radical interpretation.

I don't know of any Gricean who has proposed such a procedure for radical interpretation in such an unqualified form. However, a modified version of the proposal does have adherents, as we shall soon see. We might think of the proposal as the epistemological version of a proposal Griceans *have* made to the objection that individuals cannot have complex thoughts in the absence of language. The standard reply to this objection is to say that some simple thoughts exist independent of language, and these are the foundation of a rudimentary language, which in turn makes possible more complex thoughts, which in their turn make possible more complex language.[15] Adapting this response to the objection from radical interpretation seems a natural move for the Gricean.

When Davidson voiced his doubt, he gave the following examples: "We sense well enough the absurdity in trying to learn without asking him whether someone believes there is a largest prime number, or whether he intends, by making certain noises, to get someone to stop smoking by that person's recognition that the noises were made with that intention."[16] Such examples lead one to think that it is *only* complex beliefs and intentions that provide the stumbling block for this suggested method of interpretation. One might thus see no reason to reject the method for less complex beliefs. This suggestion is based, I believe, on a misunderstanding of the doubt. Properly understood, it is the doubt that we can come to know *any* beliefs and intentions— even the simplest—prior to knowing the alien's language.

Remember: we are considering here the beliefs and intentions only of language users. Also, I am assuming that the possession of even the simplest language allows for a complexity of thought not possible but for that language. What the stepwise procedure of interpretation requires is that we make sense of a division among both the utterances and the propositional attitudes (especially beliefs and intentions) of a language user into the simple and the complex. The picture we are being asked to accept is this: There are simple linguistic expressions, which correspond to simple thoughts. The radical interpreter may come first to know these simple thoughts and thereby to work out the meaning of these simple utterances. Using the knowledge gained there, the interpreter is then in a position to work out the alien's more complex beliefs and intentions and hence to translate the alien's more complex utterances. The claim, then, is that there is a simple/complex distinction among utterances that corresponds to a similar distinction among an individual's beliefs and intentions.

Now that we have a clear idea of the assumptions of the stepwise procedure, consider something else Davidson has written about interpretation: "We cannot decide how to interpret his 'There's a whale' independently of how we interpret his 'There's a mammal', and words connected with these, without end. We must interpret the whole pattern."[17] For Davidson constructing a theory for another's language must proceed under an assumption of holism. According to the holistic method of interpretation there is no simple/complex distinction to be drawn among a language user's utterances corresponding to the interpreter's proposed route to understanding the user's language. If Davidson is correct in this claim, radical interpretation cannot proceed in a stepwise fashion.

Now it seems incontrovertible that there must be *some* body of interconnected sentences that must be translated all of a piece if interpretation is to be possible.[18] Yet Davidson may have gone too far in demanding that we interpret the whole pattern, words connected "without end" with those in which we are interested. Dummett has written, "Holism merely in respect of how one might, starting from scratch, arrive at a theory of meaning for a language . . . is, so far as I can see, unobjectionable and almost banal."[19] Nevertheless, Dummett does not agree with Davidson on this issue. Somewhat later in the same paper Dummett writes, "If we are trying to discover, from observation of someone's linguistic behaviour, the sense which he attaches to a certain word, we shall naturally pay attention to all the judgements of truth value which he makes in regard to sentences containing that word, since such judgements obviously display the propensity he has to employ that word in a certain manner."[20] Dummett's holism of interpretation is somewhat weaker than that espoused by Davidson. Dummett speaks of translating a class of sentences containing the word in question; Davidson, on the other hand, says that the class of relevant sentences extends roughly to cover the whole of language. Whether Dummett would find this stronger form of holism beyond reproach is another matter.

Despite their differences Davidson and Dummett both acknowledge that some body of interconnected sentences must be translated of a piece in the course of radical interpretation; they differ in how each identifies that body of sentences. Dummett is surely right to say that when we want to translate some particular expression in the alien's language, the class of sentences of concern must incorporate all other utterances the alien may make containing that expression. However, if we limit ourselves to this body of sentences, we will undoubtedly be leaving out sentences that may shed some light on our understanding of that expression, even though only indirectly related to sentences containing the expression of interest. It may also help to understand in what situations the expression in question would not be employed. One way to cover both desiderata is to say that we must translate the alien's words "without end"; we must go for the whole in the strong sense. Yet one may object, What does my utterance that there is a whale out at sea have to do with my utterance, say, that there are two books on the table before me? Though the class of interconnected sentences is very large, must it be all-encompassing? The reply to this is that we cannot be sure in advance that these sentences are *not* connected. We must adopt as a methodological constraint on our task of radical interpretation that all sentences are so interrelated. There does seem to be some reason, then, to favor the stronger form of interpretation holism.

However, whether Dummett or Davidson is right here makes little difference in allowing us to proceed stepwise in radical interpretation: holism of interpretation in both its strong and weak forms is in conflict with a stepwise procedure. The conflict here may be brought into sharper relief by considering what lies behind the doctrine of interpretation holism.

Holism of interpretation is a natural extension of another form of holism, the holism of the mental. In its epistemological form, the holism of the mental is the thesis that there can be no attribution of a simple mental state to an individual independent of the attribution of certain other mental states. The force of this thesis becomes particularly apparent when one considers the attribution of beliefs and desires to an individual on the basis of some bit of behavior. We cannot explain a man's action simply by assuming he had a certain desire; we must add that he had a certain belief. Similarly, attributing a belief serves little explanatory purpose without also attributing a certain desire. Accepting this particular interdependence of belief and desire automatically involves us in another sort of interdependence: no belief and desire attribution can be arrived at in isolation from consideration of a much larger set of beliefs and desires. When we see a man reach for a pack of cigarettes, we may say he believes that the pack contains cigarettes and he desires to smoke a cigarette. But such an attribution would be wholly inappropriate if we knew that the man had successfully given up cigarette smoking several months earlier. Perhaps, in light of what else we know about this man, it would be more appropriate to say that he wanted to inspect the brand of cigarettes in order to know whether he should pass them on to his cousin, who smokes only Benson and Hedges. In attributing some particular belief or desire to another, one must take into consideration a great deal that goes beyond that particular mental state; one must consider what other states one would attribute to that individual, states both of the same type and of different types.[21]

What one may fail to notice is that among the language user's other beliefs and desires that we will have to take into account, there are bound to be some fairly sophisticated ones. By "sophisticated" I mean beliefs and desires that can be neither possessed by the subject nor identified by the theorist without the presence and aid of language. Thus, in attributing even the simplest beliefs to a language-using individual, it will be necessary to take into account other, more sophisticated or complex beliefs. It is generally agreed that we cannot come to know an alien's complex beliefs in advance of understanding his language (this is what led to the suggested stepwise procedure in the first place). If the mental operates in a holistic manner, then since we can identify less complex beliefs only after identifying the more complex ones, we cannot identify *any* belief until we have at least some idea of the believer's language.

I must emphasize that I am only speaking about cases in which our subject possesses a language. I am not concerned here with the question of whether languageless creatures can have beliefs, or if they can, how we can know the content of these beliefs. My concern is only in identifying mental states—simple and complex—in language users. Also, though I stress the importance of language in identifying mental states, I am not advocating an inversion of priorities. I am not arguing that one must translate the alien's language *before* one can identify his beliefs and intentions. I mean only to say that one cannot first understand what beliefs or intentions the alien has, no matter how simple, and then work out the meanings of his words and sentences. The two go together.[22]

The holistic character of the mental points to the conclusions that we cannot identify simple beliefs prior to identifying more complex ones, and hence, that we cannot identify any belief before understanding the alien's language. From this it follows that we cannot translate utterances expressing simple beliefs and intentions before translating utterances expressing more complex beliefs and intentions. Holism of the mental necessitates holism of interpretation in the case of language users.

Understanding how holism of interpretation follows from holism of the mental will help one to see why it is misguided to think that one can proceed in radical interpretation in a stepwise fashion from simple to more complex utterances. For the stepwise procedure to be possible, we must be able to come to know the beliefs and intentions associated with supposedly simple expressions prior to understanding any of the alien's language. These simple expressions help us in understanding the more complex uses of language. The question is how we come to know the simple beliefs and intentions in the first place. We have learned that we cannot identify these simple beliefs and intentions independently of the larger whole. So understanding the subject's simple beliefs and intentions requires that we have some grasp of his language.

Despite all this, one may think that *some* sort of stepwise procedure must occur in radical interpretation. Given this, one may conclude that I have been unduly unsympathetic to the sort of stepwise procedure that evolves out of an interest in maintaining the claim that there is a surface epistemological asymmetry between the semantic and the psychological. Radical interpretation is obviously a piecemeal procedure, and it would be very odd indeed if in the early stages we were not concerned with the expressions of thought that are in some sense simpler than the expressions tackled in later stages. My point has not been to deny this, but rather, to emphasize that in these early stages of interpretation we must assume things about the alien's beliefs *and* the meanings of his utterances. My opponent, still keen to establish an epistemological asymmetry, may see an opportunity here. He may argue that what is implausible is not the stepwise procedure but another thesis, which can be disentangled from it: the thesis that the radical interpreter can discern a *complete* evidential base of beliefs and intentions before knowing anything about the subject's language. Shorn of this implausible thesis, the stepwise procedure of interpretation proceeds in something like the following way: the interpreter forms *hypotheses* about the simple beliefs and intentions of his alien subject. Working from these, he establishes hypotheses about what the alien's utterances mean, works up to hypotheses about the alien's more complex beliefs and intentions, and so on.[23] All hypotheses, in particular, those about simple beliefs and intentions, stand open to reevaluation in light of further work.

Understood in this way, the stepwise procedure is indeed more plausible. But a high price has been paid for plausibility. It is now being conceded that one cannot firmly identify a subject's simple beliefs and intentions without some assumptions about what his utterances mean. Furthermore, in the later stages of the interpretative process, in the light of which we revise earlier hypotheses, we deal with both belief *and* meaning. One who espouses this version of the stepwise procedure cannot claim that we can ascertain another's thoughts independently of knowing his language. Yet this is precisely what the reductive Gricean needs to maintain if he is to support his proposed reduction of the semantic to the psychological by appeal to what the radical interpreter can know.[24]

I conclude that we must accept the Davidsonian doubt. Faced with an alien speaker, we cannot come to understand his language by first coming to know what beliefs and intentions he has. The stepwise procedure of radical interpretation does not mitigate this thesis. What conclusions must we draw from all of this for the Gricean program of giving a reductive analysis of meaning? I take up this question in the next section.

3 Reduction and Surface Epistemological Asymmetry

Many philosophers who follow Davidson and who accept his doubt believe that the doubt calls into question the program that employs Grice's analysis of meaning to reduce the semantic to the psychological.

Mark Platts is one philosopher who believes that he can bring the entire Gricean approach to meaning into disrepute by emphasizing the Davidsonian doubt. Platts asks us to consider the following claims:

(1) The notion of sentence meaning can be defined in terms of the notion of utterers' intentions.

(2) The meaning of any particular sentence in a language can be determined by reference to the intentions with which it is uttered.[25]

Platts, in effect, relies on the failure of what I am calling a surface epistemological asymmetry in order to discredit claim (2). He then proceeds to link the discredited claim (2) with claim (1). He writes: "If the analytic definition that [(1)] gestures at is to be of any interest, it must have implications for the determination of meanings of particular sentences. What could these implications be but the kind of meaning-specification indicated by [(2)], the kind of specification we have seen to be inadequate? So the claim [(1)] is either wrong or uninteresting."[26] Platts does not distinguish between reductive and nonreductive interpretations of Grice's work; he simply concludes that Grice's proposed analysis of meaning is either uninteresting or mistaken on the basis of the failure of what I am calling a surface epistemological asymmetry.

It seems to me that Platts has overreacted. First of all, it is not clear that the Gricean without reductive ambitions is committed to claim (2), and there is much of interest in the analysis shorn of this reductive interpretation. Second, Platts assumes that claim (2) is important for accounts of meaning without explaining why one would hold this. Without a convincing defense of claim (2) the Gricean may simply deny its relevance to his account of meaning. A connected point is this: Platts is assuming that the Gricean must base his reduction on a surface epistemological asymmetry between the psychological and the semantic. But no Gricean, as far as I know, bases his reduction on this asymmetry. As will soon emerge, Griceans base their reduction on another asymmetry, which, they argue, can be divorced from a surface epistemological asymmetry. If these Griceans are right, there is much of profound interest in an analytic definition of meaning despite its failure to help the interpreter to determine the meaning of particular utterances by reference to the intentions with which they are uttered.

Christopher Peacocke too seemed at one time to equate the failure of surface epistemological asymmetry with the failure of a reductive interpretation of the Gricean analysis. Peacocke, however, is more cautious than Platts. Peacocke would agree with my claim that there is more of interest in the Gricean analysis apart from its implications for reduction. In a paper devoted largely to giving an analysis of the actual language relation, which employs psychological but no semantic vocabulary in its analysans, Peacocke considers the objection that such an analysis would constitute a reduction of the semantic to the psychological. In reply to this objection Peacocke writes:

> But the objection as stated is . . . importantly misleading in its suggestion that it is *only* a kind of reductionism that can motivate the search for an account of the actual language relation that does not use semantical vocabulary. This is false. For suppose we agreed that we could not ascribe very finely discriminated beliefs and desires to a creature prior to, in some sense, translating his language. Then the account . . . , though it uses finely discriminated propositional attitudes, would still be needed . . . as a specification of the constraints that exist on the joint, simultaneous ascriptions of propositional attitudes and sayings; to fulfill *these* roles it is not required that finely discriminated propositional attitudes be ascribable to a creature in advance of understanding his language.[27]

Peacocke here appears to associate the reductive claim with the thesis that there is a surface epistemological asymmetry between the psychological and the semantic. Once again, a rejection of this asymmetry is taken to suffice for a rejection of the reduction. If, however, a reduction requires only some asymmetry or other, the failure of *this* asymmetry would defeat the reduction only if no other asymmetry is in the offing. As I shall soon explain, a Gricean would not agree that failure of a surface epistemological asymmetry was enough to force him to abandon his reductive claim. In a later paper Peacocke acknowledges this when considering the point that one cannot ascribe detailed intentions to a language-using agent before interpreting much of his language. He writes, "This point of course shows that Gricean intentions cannot be used as an evidential base in the enterprise of radical interpretation, and not that the Gricean reductions are not true."[28] Peacocke does not, however, indicate what he now thinks *would* have to hold in order for a Gricean reduction of meaning to be true.

It is, of course, always open to the Gricean to defend a surface epistemological asymmetry. I shall assume, however, that the Gricean does not want to deal with the problem this way.[29] In what follows I shall understand such an asymmetry as subject to the objections considered in section 2. The question I want to consider now is: How might the Gricean support a reductive interpretation in the absence of surface epistemological asymmetry?

4 Deep Epistemological Asymmetry

Let us grant for the moment that the reductive Gricean can accept the failure of surface epistemological asymmetry: from the point of view of radical interpretation at least, there is no asymmetry between the psychological and the semantic. The Gricean may insist that the interpretation of an alien's words and sentences was never part of his project. His task is to understand what constitutes meaning. Indeed, the Gricean may hold that if we should find that we *do* have a way of determining the meaning of an alien's utterances, we would not *ipso facto* have achieved our goal as theorists of meaning. That goal is to arrive at an adequate and illuminating account of meaning. Radical interpretation gives us an understanding of *speakers*. We would still need some way of moving from our understanding of speakers to an understanding of what meaning is. Perhaps we can achieve the latter, original goal without also coming up with a method of radical interpretation.[30]

Our goal, then, is to give an account of what constitutes meaning. Achieving this goal may or may not yield a method of radical interpretation. Achieving this goal, we might add, is separable also from a method of interpretation in the home case. It is important to recognize this point, as the reductive Gricean interpretation of the analysis has also been criticized on the ground that it requires the *audience* to discern certain of the speaker's intentions and beliefs prior to understanding the meanings of the speaker's utterances. We thus find Platts, for example, writing: "*If* uptake is required as part of the Gricean ascent from utterers' meaning to sentence-meaning, we shall need an *explanation* of *how* this uptake is achieved by the audience. Utterers' intentions are not recognized by unfailing intuition, nor do Acts of God figure large."[31] Platts is right in making a conditional assertion here. A Gricean might simply reply that there is no reason to think such uptake is required by the analysis. His is not meant to be an account of how communication occurs, an account that will match the phenomenology of communication.[32] Rather, the Gricean analysis is simply an account of what constitutes meaning, and this is separable from *any* method of interpretation.

John Biro has put the point well in a paper in which he discusses the Gricean account of meaning. Having considered a series of epistemological objections to the Gricean analysis, Biro has the Gricean claim the following: "The theory of meaning . . . was never intended to be a theory of a hearer's [and, I would add, an interpreter's] coming to know the meaning of an utterance, but only of what it is for an utterance to have that meaning. Constituting the meaning of an utterance is one thing, it may be said, betraying it is another."[33] I want to adopt the latter part of what Biro says here as a slogan for the reductive Gricean who acknowledges that there is no surface epistemological asymmetry between the semantic and the psychological: "Constituting the meaning of an utterance is one thing, betraying it is another."

The Gricean who commits himself to this distinction between constituting meaning and betraying it must reason in the following manner: As a matter of empirical, contingent fact there may be no knowing what beliefs and intentions a language-user has independently of understanding his language, but this need not be reflected in our account of what meaning *is*. An account of meaning is one thing, the account of what it is to know meaning is another. Now the Gricean account of meaning is that it is just a certain configuration of beliefs and intentions. So the Gricean position is that as a matter of empirical, contingent fact it may not be possible to come to know what another person intends and believes independently of understanding his language, but this need not be reflected in our theory of what these propositional attitudes are.

The Gricean thus appears to reject the suggestion that he is relying on an epistemological asymmetry to support his claim of reduction. With this distinction between constituting meaning and betraying it, the Gricean clearly intends to distance himself from what I have been calling surface epistemological asymmetry. However, there is a distinction between surface epistemological asymmetry and that of another kind, which I shall label "deep epistemological asymmetry." I want to suggest that the Gricean conception of what constitutes meaning may be linked with an epistemological asymmetry of this deep kind. The Gricean may agree that the radical interpreter cannot know an individual's Gricean beliefs and intentions before knowing his language yet propose a conception of beliefs and intentions that allows us in principle to come to know another's beliefs and intentions without any understanding of his language. That is, if we could but transcend the empirical limitations that constrain us to access another's thoughts through his language, we could know another's propositional attitudes purely, without first understanding his language.

But the Gricean may still object to the epistemological slant being given to his constitutive claim. His claim, theoretically at least, goes beyond even this epistemological claim. In theory another's beliefs and intentions may be the kind of thing that it is impossible even in principle to know without first understanding the other's language. As I shall soon explain, neither Loar nor Schiffer are in a position to deny this theoretical epistemological asymmetry, but this is due not to their Griceanism but to their physicalism. A reductive Gricean who was prepared to reject physicalism *could* deny even this epistemological asymmetry. Nevertheless, owing to his conception of the psychological, such a Gricean would still have to accept the following: if, per impossible, one could know another's beliefs and intentions purely, one would understand that language was not constitutive of these attitudes. In other words, beliefs and intentions are the kind of things that are essentially (that is, in their essence) knowable independently of language. This conception of mind, then, does have an epistemological consequence, albeit counterfactual or counterpossible. I shall use the expression "deep epistemological asymmetry" to capture this. The Gricean who wants to introduce a distinction between constituting meaning and betraying it cannot avoid a commitment to a deep epistemological asymmetry. And divorcing deep epistemological asymmetry from surface epistemological asymmetry both marks the reductive Gricean program and helps us to understand what his conception of mind is.

I want to suggest that the asymmetry that the Gricean relies on to support his claim of reduction *is* epistemological. But unless we distinguish kinds of epistemological asymmetry, we may miss this. If we understand epistemological asymmetry along the lines of a surface epistemological claim, the Gricean will simply deny that he is claiming an epistemological asymmetry. We have to understand the way the Gricean aims to divorce a surface epistemological claim from a deeper one. A commitment to a deep epistemological asymmetry lies behind the reductive Gricean's claim that psychological concepts are more basic or more fundamental in our overall scheme of concepts than semantic ones. By distinguishing kinds of epistemological asymmetry, I am in a position to agree with Evans and McDowell that the asymmetry supporting a Gricean reduction is not epistemological (*surface* epistemological), and at the same time to disagree with their suggestion that the asymmetry is ontological. The asymmetry is epistemological, but not the kind of epistemological asymmetry Evans and McDowell had in mind; rather, it is a deep epistemological asymmetry.

It may, however, be thought that Evans and McDowell claim something undeniable when they suggest that the Gricean is committed to an ontological asymmetry. An ontological asymmetry seems to be the most obvious asymmetry to which the Gricean is committed. Nevertheless, the best way to understand the reductive Gricean position is not, I believe, as a commitment to an ontological asymmetry. It is important to the characterization of the Gricean position that anyone who rejects the reduction of the semantic to the psychological must reject the characterization. Now I shall soon argue that the antireductionist need not deny thoughts to those who lack language. If this is correct and if the Gricean is also committed to thoughts in the absence of language, then we have not yet located the main source of opposition between the antireductionist and the Gricean. To do this, we must characterize the Gricean position as committed to a deep epistemological asymmetry. This is how we must understand the claimed conceptual asymmetry. Such an asymmetry and the conception of mind it embodies are things no antireductionist can accept. The antireductionist position is that there is no deep epistemological asymmetry between the psychological and the semantic.

Characterizing the antireductionist position in this way allows that the antireductionist and the reductionist may *agree* on the failure of surface epistemological asymmetry: from the point of view of radical interpretation there is an epistemological *symmetry* between the semantic and the psychological. The antireductionist who denies merely surface epistemological asymmetry, then, has missed his target. Or rather, he has missed his target if his point is *merely* to establish a surface epistemological symmetry between the semantic and the psychological. Davidson is one antireductionist who, I believe, has not missed the mark. Although he says very little in explicit support of his claim, Davidson does say that his doubt is not meant to present merely a practical obstacle to the reductionist. In one place he formulates his doubt in the following way: "There is a principled, and not merely practical, obstacle to verifying the existence of detailed, general, and abstract non-linguistic beliefs and intentions, while not being able to tell what a speaker's words mean."[34] Here Davidson makes clear that he seeks to establish more than that a certain method of radical interpretation is bound to fail. He tells us that there is a deep obstacle to a radical interpretation that aims first to establish the alien's beliefs and intentions.

Although Davidson claims that there is an obstacle in principle to such a radical interpretation, he nowhere develops the point. At least one way to develop it is to appeal to holism of interpretation and holism of the mental (see section 2). I believe that implicit in this holistic model of interpretation is a denial of a deep epistemological asymmetry between the psychological and the semantic. We should understand the theoretical difficulty that faces the Gricean in this way: in the field we cannot come to know a language user's beliefs and intentions independently of understanding his language, and this difficulty cannot be overcome by appealing to counterfactual circumstances in which these problems do not exist. There is no situation, actual or possible, in which the beliefs and intentions of a language user are accessible independently of an understanding of the believer's utterances. This, I believe, is the full force of the Davidsonian doubt.

The Davidsonian doubt is thus more than a doubt that a certain method of radical interpretation is possible. This doubt that there is any surface epistemological asymmetry indicates another, more profound doubt: that there is any deep epistemological asymmetry between the semantic and the psychological. The argument against a surface epistemological asymmetry that appeals to holism of interpretation and holism of the mental must be understood to run deep, otherwise the Gricean will simply accept it in stride.[35] The Davidsonian doubt is a doubt that we can divorce observations at the surface from deeper possibilities. It is a doubt that we can divorce what constitutes meaning from what betrays it.

If the Davidsonian doubt is to have any real impact on the reductive Gricean, it must be understood as a rejection of both a surface and of a deep epistemological asymmetry. But the arguments of section 2, if unsupplemented, are insufficient to establish the doubt at the deepest level. This is why the Gricean can agree with his opponent at that stage. Two things still need to be established in order to decide between reductionism and antireductionism. First, the reductionist must give some reason to think a deep epistemological asymmetry *is* true of the semantic and the psychological, and on the other side the antireductionist must explain why he rejects such an asymmetry. Second and relatedly, the reductionist must defend his position that divorces a surface epistemological asymmetry from a deeper one and rejects the former while maintaining the latter, and on the other side the antireductionist must give some reason for denying a divorce between a surface and a deep epistemological asymmetry.

John Biro has suggested a reason for why the Gricean cannot divide what constitutes meaning from what betrays it. There is, claims Biro, a crucial test of adequacy that any theory purporting to be a theory of meaning must meet.[36] The test is this: a theory of meaning must give some account of how hearers understand utterances. This is something Biro extracts from Dummett's statement that a theory of meaning is a theory of understanding.[37]

But Biro does not go deep enough in his diagnosis of the Gricean's mistake. The Gricean may simply question the slogan by asking why we should hold that a theory of meaning is a theory of understanding. A defence of Dummett's statement will also be a defence of a thoroughgoing Davidsonian doubt. Whether we go along with the reductionist or the antireductionist at this point will depend upon our conception of mind. The Gricean who holds a deep epistemological asymmetry in effect embraces a certain picture of mind, and the antireductionist denies this picture. Exactly what these alternative pictures amount to will emerge later in this chapter and in chapter 4.

In what remains of this section I want to develop further our understanding of the antireductionist claim that there can be no reduction of the semantic to the psychological, by comparing and contrasting it with another antireductionist claim made by Davidson, Nagel, and others to the effect that there can be no reduction of the psychological to the physical. I turn now to a discussion of this latter reduction.

5 The Reduction of the Psychological to the Physical

A physicalist is one who holds that a physical theory of the world is adequate for understanding all there is. In particular, he believes that such a physical theory can provide an understanding of all that goes under the title "psychological." A very clear statement of such a position is found in the writings of Hartry Field:

> Any interesting version of materialism requires not only that there be no irreducibly mental *objects*, but also that there be no irreducibly mental *properties*: the idea that although people and certain higher animals do not contain any immaterial substance, nonetheless they have certain mental properties that are completely unexplainable in physical terms, is an idea that very few people who regard themselves as materialists would find satisfying.[38]

Field is here rejecting not only Cartesian dualism (a dualism of substance) but property dualism as well. He and others countenance neither irreducible mental substances and events nor irreducible mental properties in their view of the world. Such a full-blooded reductionist must hold that we can at least in principle look at the physical features of an individual (and, possibly, his environment[39]) and read off from this what that individual believes, desires, intends, and the like. This will, of course, involve extensive knowledge of the brain and its function, as well as established correlations between this and the mental; but once this knowledge and these correlations are established, they must be generalizable, or we have no reduction.[40]

There are those who are less severe than Field. While they agree with him that mental substances are unacceptable, they insist that we must embrace some kind of property dualism. All substances or events are physical, but there are both physical and irreducible mental properties.[41] Admitting irreducible mental properties into our picture of the world alters the expectations we may have about what a physical theory of the world may achieve. If all substances and events are physical, then no doubt in some sense our physical theory will be a theory of all things; if, however, there are irreducibly mental as well as physical properties, then the scope of physical theory will be less. For one thing, if the antireductionist is correct, any correlations between the mental and the physical will *not* be generalizable. If we want to know what a person believes, intends, etc., it won't help us only to look at his physical features and environment. It follows from this that arguments against reduction are also arguments against a weaker claim, the claim that there are lawlike correlations between the mental and the physical. These arguments aim to show that an understanding of the physical basis of things will not suffice for a complete understanding of the psychological. In particular, we cannot establish what a person believes, desires, intends, and the like from our understanding of this physical basis.

I now want to outline some of the arguments that antireductionists have advanced in this area. The first thing one notices when encountering these arguments is that each argument tends to concentrate on one or another aspect of our mental lives; that is, they aim to show either that propositional attitudes are not reducible to the physical or that sensations and experiences are not so reducible. Some have thought that the former are more susceptible of reduction than the latter. I, however, believe that the arguments against the reduction of propositional attitudes and those against the reduction of sensation and experience are strikingly similar and that they are similarly effective against the reductionist. I will present these two sorts of arguments in a way that, I hope, reveals their similarity.

The argument I shall present against the possibility of reducing sensation or experience to the physical is due to Thomas Nagel. Nagel claims: (1) subjective experience is part of the world, (2) an objective view tells us nothing about the subjective point of view, and therefore, (3) the objective view is an incomplete view of reality.[42] I want to say something similar about propositional attitudes:[43] (1a) particular beliefs, intentions, and the like are part of the world, (2a) knowledge of the physical realm does not suffice for knowledge of these propositional attitudes, and therefore, (3a) knowledge of the physical realm is incomplete knowledge of the world. I turn now to a defence of these claims.

Nagel calls the acceptance of (1) "realism" and says this about it: "Ordinary mental states like thought, feeling, emotion, sensation, or desire are not physical properties of the organism. . . . Nevertheless, *they are properties of the organism*, since there is no soul, and they are not properties of nothing at all" (my emphasis).[44] What Nagel says here about realism is tied up with his denial of reduction, but the message is clear: subjective experience cannot be denied, even if it cannot be reduced to or identified with the organism's physical properties. In short, Nagel appeals to the obviousness of (1). I want to make a similiar appeal in favour of (1a). I take it as undeniable that particular beliefs, intentions, and the like are part of the world, and that we must continue to accept this even though we may learn that these thoughts do not reduce to anything more basic. Jerry Fodor puts the case for realism here well when he writes: "The simple facticity of at least *some* ascriptions of propositional attitudes had seemed to be among life's little certainties. . . . The burden of proof lies, surely, upon those who want to say that it is not the case that one believes even what one is strongly disposed to believe that one believes [i.e., that truths about mental states are on a par with truths about ordinary items like tables and chairs]."[45]

So much for what some, at least, have thought we could not deny.[46] Now for the support for (2) and (2a). Claims (2) and (2a) are in effect a statement of the antireductionist position. I will begin with Nagel's support for (2). Nagel claims that if an organism has conscious experience at all, then "there is something it is like to *be* that organism—something it is like *for* that organism."[47] To have experience, according to Nagel, is to have a particular point of view on the world. Although this point of view is particular to an individual, it has various general features shared by other individuals of the same kind. We can say, then, that there is something it is like to be a certain *kind* of organism. Nagel claims that a creature that exhibits a range of activity and possesses a sensory apparatus both very different from our own, like a bat or a Martian, is *ipso facto* a creature whose subjective experiences differ radically from ours. Now if we are presented with an individual whose subjective experience is of the *same* kind as ours and we want to understand what this individual is experiencing in some given situation, we have to take up his point of view. This is

possible, since he is a creature similar to us, and therefore, his particular point of view will share general features with ours. Only by
taking up his point of view in this way, Nagel argues, can we be in a
position to understand what he is experiencing. If, however, we are
presented with an alien creature, we cannot adopt his point of view,
since it is not of the same *kind* as ours. In this way, then, our understanding of the conscious experience of another is more or less se-
verely limited.[48]

Yet one may think that we are only so limited in our understanding
of the alien because we have not yet explored all the avenues potentially available to us. The reductionist argues that one such avenue is
opened up by a study of the brain. If we want to understand a Martian's experiences (or if he wanted to understand ours), we should
study the seat of consciousness (i.e., the brain or its analogue). Nagel
argues, however, that to accept that this kind of study could yield an
understanding of those experiences would be to abandon the point of
view distinctive of the Martian's (or our) experience. This point of
view is inherently *subjective* and won't fit within a physical theory
whose general aim is to achieve greater and greater *objectivity*. Physical theory aims to transcend the particular point of view; an objective
description of the world should in principle be accessible to *any* individual, Martian or human, with the intelligence to comprehend it.
But, and this is Nagel's point, to transcend the particular, species-
specific point of view is to leave behind what we sought to understand, namely, conscious experience. For that experience is just the
experience of the world from a particular, and particular kind of,
point of view. To put the matter in a slightly different way: the modes
of understanding in the physical and the mental realms are radically
different. An understanding of a creature's subjective experience will
not result from even a complete understanding of the physical realm,
since that mode of understanding is not the sort that can yield an
understanding of subjective experience. To understand the mental
realm a quite different approach is needed. While reductionists hold
out the hope that greater understanding of the physical will eventually lead to a further understanding of the mental, Nagel's argument, if correct, shows that greater understanding of the objective
world of brain and body yield no progress in understanding the subjective world of experience.[49]

An argument offered in support of (2a) is strikingly similar to this
argument of Nagel's. This argument is due to Davidson.[50] Davidson
begins with the observation that the mental is a holistic realm.[51] As he
puts it in one place, "Beliefs and desires issue in behavior only as
mediated and modified by further beliefs and desires, attitudes, and

attendings without limit."[52] In another place he presents a corollary idea: "It is only against a background of . . . a pattern that we can identify thoughts."[53] Some have understood Davidson to be saying that this observation alone is sufficient to rule out any reduction of the mental to the physical. But Davidson admits that this is only *part* of the story, a part shared with the physical realm as well. Duhem's thesis, that observations confirm theories as a whole and not one sentence at a time, expresses a similar observation about the prevalence of holism in the physical realm.[54] According to Davidson, the real argument comes when we notice that the constraining ideals in the two holistic realms are very different. Davidson writes: "The point is rather that when we use the concepts of belief, desire, and the rest, we stand prepared, as the evidence accumulates, to adjust our theory in the light of considerations of overall cogency; the constitutive idea of rationality partly controls each phase in the evolution of what must be an evolving theory."[55] Rationality, then, is the ideal governing the propositional attitudes. A principle of rationality so described clearly has no part to play in the physical realm. This allegiance to radically different governing ideals separates the mental from the physical and guarantees that our method of understanding the one must be and remain quite different from our method of understanding the other. Physical theory alone will never suffice for understanding the mental; the psychological does not reduce to the physical.

According to Davidson, to understand what another believes, intends, and the like, we must look not to the brain but to behavior. And we must keep in mind that the more behavioral evidence we accumulate, the better our chances of achieving a correct understanding of our subject. This means that our project of understanding another is dynamic, open to reevaluation and revision as new evidence becomes available. But more important, we must understand that as each new piece of evidence is brought to our attention, we must seek to integrate it with what we already know about our subject so as to make the subject appear rational to our eyes. This leads to two further observations. The first is that we must be open to the possibility that some future behavior of our subject may force us substantially to revise some attribution to him. The other, related observation is that it may very well prove impossible to find a single best interpretation of our subject; rather, we may have to rest content with several equally good yet mutually incompatible interpretations of his behavior. And because of the *sui generis* nature of the mental, we may have no grounds for choosing between these alternatives.[56]

Rationality, according to Davidson, is for the propositional attitudes what the single subjective point of view, according to Nagel, is for conscious experience. Together these form the hallmark of the mental. Reduction fails in both cases because of the distinctive methods of understanding each requires. Together with the view that these attitudes and experiences really exist, these antireductionist arguments lead us to conclude (3) that the objective view is an incomplete view of reality and (3a) that knowledge of the physical realm is incomplete knowledge of the world. The objective view omits the subjective point of view, and knowledge of the physical realm leaves us relatively ignorant of the propositional attitudes.[57] If we want to know what another individual believes, desires, intends, and the like, we must observe his behavior and interpret it so as to make him appear rational to us; if we want to know what another's conscious experiences are, we must look at things from his point of view.

We can supplement Davidson's view to make the parallel with Nagel's even more striking.[58] According to Davidson, in attributing beliefs and propositional attitudes to a subject, we should assess his behavior along the dimension of rationality. Supplementing this, we could say that the rational interpretation of another's behavior involves us in projecting ourselves into his frame of mind. Quine, for example, has said that propositional-attitude idiom is essentially "dramatic." He describes it as working thus: "We project ourselves into what, from his remarks and other indications, we imagine the speaker's state of mind to have been, and then say what, in our language, is natural and relevant for us in the state thus feigned. . . . Correspondingly for the other propositional attitudes.[59] Following Nagel, we could say that such a projection is possible only for creatures whose behavior and sensory apparatus is roughly of the same kind as our own, that is, whose reactions to the world share general features with ours.

I should note one important difference between the arguments of Davidson and Nagel. Whereas Davidson takes his to be an a priori argument against the possibility of any type identity theory, Nagel is less pessimistic about this possibility. Nagel leaves it open that there may be developments that will allow a reduction. The developments Nagel envisages, however, are radical. They involve on the one side the development of what he calls an "objective phenomenology"[60] and on the other side new concepts in the physical sciences. Nagel is still more pessimistic than many, however. We can say without any distortion of his views that Nagel gives an a priori argument against the possibility of reducing the mental to the physical on current conceptions of both the mental and the physical.

Finally, I want to comment on how these arguments relate to the semantic. Davidson holds that it is not possible for languageless creatures to possess thoughts.[61] As a result of this and his adherence to holism, Davidson holds that we must observe both linguistic and nonlinguistic behavior when attributing propositional attitudes to another. Nagel, in contrast, pays little attention to the role played by language, partly because he concentrates on experiential states. My rejection of the reduction of the semantic to the psychological is in part based on my belief that we cannot reduce the psychological to the physical. I want to show the importance of the semantic in understanding the psychological, and paradoxical as this may sound, I want to do this so as to allow the attribution of thoughts to the languageless. In the next section I will explain how the project of reducing the psychological to the physical is related to the project I want to reject, that of reducing the semantic to the psychological.

6 Deep Epistemological Asymmetry Continued

The arguments I presented in the previous section seek to cast doubt on a physicalist reduction of the psychological on the ground that the physical basis of things cannot reveal the kind of experience an individual is having or what he believes, intends, and the like. The argument is not just that there is at present no physical theory capable of revealing these things, for that conclusion is compatible with the claim that the brain sciences are in their infancy. Nor is it that the physical scientist is for some reason limited in what he can know about the physical universe. Neither a developed neuroscience nor a superscientist can get around Nagel's and Davidson's objections, if they are correct. It is not a question of expanding our physical theory of the world.[62] Their point is that certain kinds of things fall outside the scope of that science. Our mental life by its very nature is not the kind of thing open to that sort of investigation. Davidson and Nagel are proposing in effect that we think of our concepts of the psychological and the physical as too unlike one another to permit the reduction of the former to the latter. This observation, backed by an argument to show that the psychological *is* radically different in its essential nature from the physical, leads the antireductionist to claim not only that there is nothing physical we already know that could reveal another's mental life to us but also that there is nothing physical we could come to know that would reveal it to us.

Let us now consider a reduction of the semantic to the psychological. I claim that this reductionist is committed to what I am calling a deep epistemological asymmetry, and that opposition to the reduction must take the form of opposition to this claimed asymmetry. In other words, the antireductionist must hold that we cannot know another's beliefs and intentions prior to understanding his language and that this point runs deep. Here the epistemological consequence of what constitutes meaning reveals something rather different from the epistemological consequence advanced by Davidson and Nagel: here an inability to know another's intentions and beliefs prior to understanding his language shows that the concepts of semantics stand close to those of psychology.[63] The closeness of these concepts gets in the way of reducing the semantic to the psychological. Where we seek a reduction the concepts involved must be neither too distant nor too close.

A question that the antireductionist faces is this: What reasons do we have for the conclusion that the semantic and the psychological *are* too close to permit reducing the former to the latter? In other words, what reason is there for believing not only that there is a surface epistemological asymmetry between the semantic and the psychological but that this is a reflection of a deeper epistemological symmetry? The answer to this question will emerge if we look more closely at what a denial of this symmetry amounts to. I want next to give two interpretations of the reductive Gricean's claim that there is a deep epistemological asymmetry between the semantic and the psychological.

One thing I can imagine a reductionist to say is the following. Of course there isn't a method *now* available to the interpreter that would allow him independent access to an alien's beliefs and intentions, and there never will be so long as the interpreter insists on remaining in the field. One day, however, neurophysiology will open doors through which even radical interpreters can pass.[64] (Even if it is not possible in practice for the neurosciences to proceed to this point, owing to the brain's complexity and our limited capacities for knowledge, it is still possible in principle for a physical theory to yield that knowledge—to a Martian superscientist perhaps.)

Loar is one Gricean who argues in favor of reduction along the lines just indicated. In his book Loar discusses the attribution of specific and rather fine-grained beliefs to some alien Alpha-Centaurian creatures. He writes, "Given only the *non-linguistic* behavioral and environmental evidence . . . , it is difficult to see how we could ascribe to [the Alpha-Centaurians] specific theoretical beliefs as a better explanation of their feats than any other possible ascriptions."[65] To make these attributions, according to Loar, we need to observe the Alpha-Centaurian's *linguistic* behavior. In effect, then, Loar is here acknowledging that there can be no surface epistemological asymmetry between the semantic and the psychological. Yet despite his acknowledgment, Loar believes that there is room to claim a reduction. This is revealed by a parenthetical remark Loar adds in the course of making the claim quoted above. The full quotation reads:

> Given only the *non-linguistic* behavioural and environmental evidence (without further evidence about the Alpha-Centaurian's internal organization), it is difficult to see how we could ascribe to them specific theoretical beliefs as a better explanation of their feats than any other possible ascription.

Thus, according to Loar, if we remain at the level of what he calls "ordinary evidence,"[66] evidence offered by the Alpha-Centaurian's linguistic and nonlinguistic behavior and his environment, we will never be in a position to ascribe certain psychological states to him without the evidence of his linguistic behavior. But Loar's point is that we are not confined to ordinary evidence. Further evidence at least in principle is available to us, evidence about the Alpha-Centaurian's internal organization. This evidence, Loar believes, will enable us to ascribe rather sophisticated beliefs and intentions to the Alpha-Centaurian *without* needing to appeal to the *linguistic evidence.* In other words, once this further, internal evidence is available, we shall be able to ascribe even the most complex beliefs to the alien without having to know what his words mean. This amounts to a claim that there is a deep epistemological asymmetry between the semantic and the psychological.

Loar seeks to highlight two things in his discussion of Alpha-Centaurians. The first is that at the level of the ordinary evidence there is a crucial interdependence of belief and meaning. In other words, there is a surface epistemological *symmetry.* We may conclude from this, says Loar, that our "ordinary non-linguistic evidence is simply deficient," it is "more rudimentary" than the linguistic evidence.[67] The second point is that the scientist's evidence concerning the alien's internal organization provides us with a way of bypassing ordinary evidence when we want to attribute even the most sophisticated beliefs and intentions to the alien. These two observations together lead Loar to say of the first (i.e., the observation that at the level of the ordinary evidence there is a crucial interdependence of belief and meaning) that "there is nothing constitutive of belief-ascription in this."[68] Notice that because Loar rejects the constitutive claim at the surface level, he is in a position to accept a deep epistemological asymmetry between the psychological and the semantic. For Loar this asymmetry rests upon the belief that science will one day uncover features of a believer's internal organization that will enable one to attribute to him even the most sophisticated beliefs.

Loar is committed to the following interpretation of the deep epistemological thesis: we can in principle know the beliefs and intentions of language users prior to understanding their language. This possibility becomes apparent when we move from "ordinary" evidence to evidence on a "new level" (a neurophysiologico-functional level).[69] The reason Loar must accept this formulation of the thesis can be traced back to his naturalism. Harboring the aim of providing a physicalist theory of mind and meaning, Loar must allow that we can at least in principle develop this new route to the understanding of another's mind. This need not be true of all interpretations of the deep epistemological thesis, as we shall soon see.

Reductive physicalism, then, is one way and nowadays the most common way for the reductionist to give substance to his claim that there is a deep epistemological asymmetry between the psychological and the semantic.[70] There is another way. We can invoke a much older tradition in philosophy to support this asymmetry. I will identify this tradition as Cartesian, although I do not mean to imply by this that Descartes was the first or the only philosopher tempted to hold these views.

A Cartesian holds that just as there are physical or material objects and events in the world, so there are mental or immaterial objects and events.[71] Moreover, he is likely to hold the following epistemological corollary to his metaphysical doctrine: whereas material objects and events are directly accessible to all, immaterial objects and events are directly accessible only to the individual having that mental life.[72] The point may be put in this way: material objects and events are directly accessible from a third-person perspective, while immaterial or mental objects and events are directly accessible only from a first-person perspective. To say that mental objects and events are directly accessible only from the subject's perspective is not to deny *any* access to the observer of the subject; it is to differentiate the *kind* of access the observer may have from the kind the subject himself has. The observer may only have *indirect* access to another's mental life; that is, he may know what another is experiencing or thinking only by observing his behavior. Now if the subject is a language user, we must observe linguistic as well as nonlinguistic behavior (recall the argument from holism outlined in section 2).[73] We could say that on the Cartesian picture of things there is no surface epistemological asymmetry between the psychological and the semantic; if we want to know what another individual believes and intends, we must interpret both what he says and what he does.

If we consider the metaphysical doctrine of the Cartesian in conjunction with the epistemological corollary I have just outlined, we notice the following. The metaphysical thesis that there are two kinds of substance, one physical and one mental, does not require that epistemological access be as it is with us. The difference between first- and third-person access to the mental may be a contingent matter, contingent upon human capacities. In other words, an individual with powers superior to ours may have direct access onto this mental realm along with the subject himself. It just so happens that for us only the subject can have this direct access; the rest of us need to study his behavior. But if the mental is in some sense *there* in a realm separable from but on an ontological par with the physical, then nothing in principle prevents some individual distinct from the subject from having direct access. A godlike individual, for example, could have direct access to this mental realm.[74] But if a godlike individual could have such direct access, he could know what some subject was believing or intending without appeal to that subject's linguistic or other behavior. Such access is for us not possible; we can only make sense of it by appealing to something like a god's perspective. Nevertheless, if we believe that such a perspective would yield knowledge of a subject's beliefs and intentions, we could maintain, despite *our* epistemological situation, that there is a deep epistemological asymmetry between the psychological and the semantic.

The Cartesian, however, may protest that appeal to a godlike perspective misrepresents his position. Indeed, by noting this misrepresentation, the Cartesian may attempt to duck any commitment to what I have been calling a deep epistemological asymmetry. The reductive Gricean who adopts Cartesianism may claim that no epistemological asymmetry is entailed by his envisaged reduction. The Cartesian, unlike Loar, has no commitment to physicalism. He holds out no prospects for a knowledge of mind gained by advances in the physical sciences. He may dig in his heels and insist that such godlike individuals cannot even in principle know the immaterial substance that is our mind. He is committed to a realism that escapes the reach of such a theoretical epistemological thesis. To forestall such a move I formulated the deep epistemological thesis so as to cover more than the theoretical possibility of such knowledge. Owing to his metaphysics of mind the Cartesian is committed to allowing that if, *per impossibile*, one could know this immaterial realm, one could know another's beliefs and intentions without having to understand his language. The deep epistemological thesis is meant to cover this position. The Cartesian, then, like the physicalist, is committed to the thesis that there is a deep epistemological asymmetry between the semantic and the psychological. For ease of exposition I shall continue to speak of the Cartesian position as allowing that godlike individuals have direct access to the mental.[75]

Both Cartesianism and reductive physicalism, then, give us an interpretation of the claim that there is a deep epistemological asymmetry between the semantic and the psychological. It follows that both Cartesianism and reductive physicalism give us a way of understanding the Gricean's claim that there is an asymmetry between our concepts of the semantic and the psychological. I want to suggest that ultimately, the Davidsonian doubt amounts to a denial of both Cartesianism and reductive physicalism.

However, before getting involved in a discussion of this aspect of the Davidsonian doubt, I want to return for a moment to Davidson's and Nagel's arguments against the reduction of the psychological to the physical. Once we see the way both Cartesianism and reductive physicalism can ground a deep epistemological asymmetry between the semantic and the psychological, it is tempting to look back on the arguments of Davidson and Nagel and see them as arguments against a Cartesian, as well as a reductive physicalist, view of the psychological. This will become apparent if we return to consider the conclusions of those arguments. The conclusion of the arguments of both Davidson and Nagel is that because the methods of understanding the mental and the physical are radically different, the psychological cannot be reduced to the physical. According to Nagel, if we want to understand another's subjective experience, we must take up, to the extent possible, the other's point of view on the world. According to Davidson, if we want to understand another's propositional attitudes, we must observe his behavior with an eye to making him appear rational. Both Nagel and Davidson explicitly contrast these ways of understanding with those adopted in the physical realm: the neurophysiologist's perspective on the brain is not an appropriate perspective on the mind. Nagel's and Davidson's positive pronouncements on the correct way to understand the thoughts and experiences of another are in sharp contrast with not only the perspective of the reductive physicalist but the Cartesian perspective as well. Access to an immaterial realm, if it could be achieved, would obviate the need to observe behavior. The Cartesian, like the physicalist, makes the mind out to be something objective (though nonnatural), something open to anyone with the power to perceive it. According to Nagel and Davidson, however, there is no way around the fact that we have to put ourselves in our subject's place or observe his behavior (or both) if we want to understand his thoughts and feelings. If the reductive physicalist is mistaken about the psychological, for the reasons Nagel and Davidson give, the Cartesian is no nearer to a correct account of it.[76]

Let me return now to the reductive Gricean. By asking what kind of asymmetry supports a claim of reduction, I arrived at the conclusion that a reductive Gricean may be either a reductive physicalist or a Cartesian.[77] Loar, as we have seen, chooses a kind of reductive physicalism, but he gives evidence that he is aware of the Cartesian alternative available to the Gricean reductionist. He writes:

> Theories that take attitudes as the foundation of semantic description have been greeted by many with amazed incredulity. One reason has been a strong intuition, central in modern empiricist philosophy, that thoughts, beliefs, intentions, are in large part linguistic states and that, consequently, concepts of the content of such states cannot be invoked non-circularly in explicating linguistic meaning. That intuition has stemmed largely from laudable naturalistic tendencies—a rejection of the Platonic-Cartesian-Brentanian conception of thought.[78]

Loar thinks one can avoid Cartesianism and at the same time avoid the position that beliefs, intentions, and the like are essentially linguistic states. He continues, "My theory of beliefs, their functional semantic properties and truth conditions, would show that these concepts *can* be explicated without bringing in language and within a naturalist framework."[79] A kind of reductive physicalism is Loar's alternative to Cartesianism. Loar wants the advantages that a Cartesian metaphysic can offer a reductionist; he does not want its ontological excesses.

Loar seems to understand the rejection of Cartesianism as motivated chiefly by the rejection of what he calls nonnaturalism. Clearly, it is nonnaturalism that bothers Loar most about Cartesianism, hence the physico-functionalist alternative he develops so carefully in his book. But those who harbor the intuition that beliefs, intentions, and the like are in large part linguistic states may reject more than nonnaturalism. Cartesianism presents another source of concern: the picture of mind it embodies. A Cartesian metaphysic takes mind to be accessible independently of any ordinary evidence, i.e., the evidence offered by the subject's linguistic and nonlinguistic behavior. Ordinary evidence may be circumvented by one who wants to understand the mental life of another even if no individual with human powers can circumvent it. This concern one may and *should* have with Cartesianism is simply brushed aside by Loar when he takes up naturalism. Indeed, as I hope to show in chapter 4, reductive physicalism inherits its picture of mind from Cartesianism; its only improvement is that it makes the mind out to be an essentially natural phenomenon.

Cartesianism and reductive physicalism are guilty of the same error, since, as I shall argue below, no perspective—god's or the super neurophysiologist's—can reveal an individual's mental life to us without observation of his behavior. This, I suggest, is what the Davidsonian doubt amounts to. But this anticipates the work of the next chapter. For now it is sufficient to see that Cartesianism and reductive physicalism are two ways in which a Gricean can ground his claim that there is a deep epistemological asymmetry between the semantic and the psychological, and to see how one can maintain such a claim even in the face of evidence that there is a surface epistemological asymmetry here.

7 Ontological Asymmetry

That belief and desire and their content can be explicated without presupposing anything about natural language semantics will, to many, be implausible; the idea runs the risk of suggesting a picture of thought without language.[80]

I have been arguing that the asymmetry the Gricean relies on to support his reductive claim is epistemological, but that this is a deep claim and does not necessarily reflect the surface of things. Now this deep epistemological asymmetry may be thought to entail and be entailed by another asymmetry, ontological asymmetry. The reductive Gricean thus "runs the risk of suggesting a picture of thought without language." Here we surely do have the possibility of an asymmetry, since one may hold that there can be thought without language, whereas the converse of language without thought would, I take it, be denied by all.

The idea that an ontological asymmetry supports the Gricean reduction is widely held. The belief that the Gricean is committed to an ontological asymmetry encourages one to think that it is precisely this asymmetry that the antireductionist must be in the business of denying. Thus, the line of thought goes, anyone opposing a Gricean reduction of the semantic to the psychological must be committed to the thesis that there can be no thought in the absence of language. Evans and McDowell, who explicitly deny that the Gricean is relying on an epistemological asymmetry, also present the antireductionist as having to embrace the conclusion that there can be no thought without language.

Yet both the reductionist and the antireductionist can complain about this characterization of their position. Griceans, on the one hand, may and do deny that they are committed to attributing thoughts to the languageless. Their thesis is compatible with denying thoughts to the languageless. The antireductionist, on the other hand, may feel uncomfortable with the implausible thesis of denying thoughts to the languageless.[81]

The way out for both the reductionist and his opponent is to accept that their difference turns not on the issue of ontological symmetry versus asymmetry but on the issue of epistemological symmetry versus asymmetry. This is only apparent after we identify two kinds of epistemological asymmetry, surface and deep. And yet the ontological issue seems to be at the heart of the matter. My deep epistemological thesis, one might argue, has ontological implications. Surely if there is a deep epistemological asymmetry, there must be an ontological asymmetry.[82] Using this conditional, one might argue as follows. The antireductionist rejects the antecedent of the conditional, so he must reject the consequent as well. Hence, the antireductionist is committed to an ontological symmetry. The reductionist, on the other hand, may assume an ontological asymmetry (as many have thought he must). This assumption appears to force his commitment to an epistemological asymmetry. It appears, then, that the opposition between the reductionist and the antireductionist is over the issue of ontological symmetry, versus asymmetry. The reductionist must accept that the languageless can have thoughts; the antireductionist must deny thoughts in the absence of language. But the fallacies in the two arguments just presented are obvious.[83]

Formal fallacies aside, how can an antireductionist, someone who accepts a deep epistemological symmetry between the semantic and the psychological, accept the attribution of thoughts to the languageless? What exactly is the relationship between an epistemological asymmetry and an ontological asymmetry? In the following sections I shall discuss this relationship. Yet the full story will only emerge in chapter 4.

8 Does a Deep Epistemological Asymmetry Entail Ontological Asymmetry?

First let us take up entailment in the direction of a deep epistemological asymmetry to an ontological asymmetry. Prima facie it seems that the Gricean cannot consistently both accept a reduction and agree that only those endowed with language can have thoughts. The idea that supports this is the following. To be a reductionist, the Gricean must hold that there is a deep epistemological asymmetry between the semantic and the psychological, or so I have argued. The Gricean holds that another's beliefs, intentions, and the like of whatever degree of complexity are accessible independently of his linguistic behavior. Part of this picture of mental states seems to be that linguistic behavior is only contingently related to mental states. Linguistic behavior is, one might say, merely a vehicle for communicating and expressing these thoughts, a vehicle that we imperfect beings must rely on. As this picture of mind gets filled in, it becomes quite clear that one who holds it must also hold that individuals without language may still have thoughts. After all, if language is *merely* a vehicle, only contingently related to the thought it expresses, then taking away the language may frustrate communication but should not affect thought. This is why the reductive Gricean's conceptual thesis seems to imply that the languageless have thoughts.

This much, so stated, we must agree with: deep epistemological asymmetry does entail that thought without language is at least conceptually possible. Nevertheless, the Gricean can maintain that in actual fact the languageless cannot possess thoughts. The Gricean must only agree that our concepts of the semantic and the psychological, allow for the presence of thought in the absence of language; he may want to argue that there can be no such creatures for reasons having nothing to do with our concepts of the semantic or the psychological.

This is the distinction Schiffer is relying on, I take it, when he replies to an objection Hartry Field puts to the reductive Gricean. Field builds up to his objection in the following way:

> This Gricean approach presupposes that one can explain what it is to believe that Caesar is egotistical *without relying at any point on the semantical features of the sentence "Caesar was egotistical" in one's spoken or written language:* for if one relied on the semantical features of the spoken or written sentence in one's account of the belief, then to explain the meaning of the sentence in terms of the belief would involve a circularity. So the crucial question is whether that presupposition is correct.[84]

Field's own reply to this crucial question is this:

> I am inclined to doubt however that the presupposition is true. My *guess* is that in a typical case, *part of* what makes a symbol in my system of internal representation a symbol that stands for Caesar is that this symbol acquired its role in my system of representation as a result of my acquisition of a name that stands for

Caesar in the public language. If something of this sort is true, it would appear to defeat the above approach to the theory of meaning for a public language.[85]

In other words, Field is using the observation that there can be no inner language (thought) without public language in order to bring the charge of circularity to bear on the Gricean program of reduction. Schiffer replies to Field thus:

> In fact, there is no incompatibility and nothing is defeated. Intention-based semantics does not require that one have propositional attitudes *prior* to one's having acquired a public language; it is perfectly compatible with the hypothesis that one's ability to have beliefs and desires . . . proceeds *pari passu* with one's acquisition of a public language. . . . Perhaps it will help to put the point thus. We need to distinguish two claims: (*i*) the meaning of [sentence] σ *consists* in its having a certain meaning$_o$ . . . ; (*ii*) the meaning$_i$ of σ is (causally or otherwise) *dependent* upon its having a certain meaning$_o$. . . . The intention-based theorist is committed to denying (*i*), but he need not deny (*ii*); he must claim only that the meaning of σ consists in facts—no doubt mostly causal facts—which are specifiable without reference to anything semantical$_o$.[86]

The point is echoed by Loar who writes, "Moreover, the strong thesis under consideration [i.e., reduction] is compatible with its being *empirically* necessary for complex propositional attitudes that one have undergone language learning processes."[87] Another Gricean, David Armstrong, also denies that a suggestion such as Field's can weaken a Gricean reduction. Armstrong puts the point like this: "It seems to me a matter of fact that systems of abstract belief (and thought) and the attempt to express such beliefs (and thoughts) linguistically developed hand in hand. . . . All that has been argued is that there is no logical link between possessing such beliefs and having the corresponding linguistic competence."[88] Yet on reflection we find that Schiffer, Loar, and Armstrong are not quite saying the same thing: Loar's claim is weaker than Schiffer's; Armstrong's is stronger.[89] Against Loar one could argue that the reduction would stand even if the reasons that thought requires language are not empirical or contingent but conceptual. The causal dependence thought may have on language may be a deep, conceptual dependence. Thus, it may turn out (following Armstrong) that the development of thought goes hand in hand with the development of language and that the two *are* logically linked. The point is that if thought is *causally* dependent on language, the reductive Gricean need not be concerned. We can conclude that Armstrong's claim is too strong if the Gricean analysis is compatible with a logical link between possessing beliefs and possessing language. The point is best formulated by Schiffer: the Gricean reductionist need not worry so long as the inner meaning of a sentence does not *consist in* its having an outer, or public meaning.

Properly understood, the Gricean thesis that there is an asymmetry between the semantic and the psychological is compatible even with the thesis that the languageless cannot have thoughts. Yet this inability must result either from contingent factors or from conceptual factors unrelated to our concepts of the semantic and the psychological. Another way to put the point is this: if there is a deep epistemological asymmetry between the semantic and the psychological, thoughts are possible in the absence of language; nevertheless, this possibility may be canceled either by the empirical facts of this world or by conceptual facts unconnected with the concepts at issue.

When philosophers claim that the languageless cannot think, their claim is crucially incomplete. Whether this claim conflicts with a Gricean reduction depends upon how it is completed. The claim poses a threat to the reductive Gricean only if it is conceptually related to our concepts of the semantic and the psychological. Davidson does attempt to support the claim in this way.[90] Davidson claims to have an argument showing that our psychological concepts cannot be instantiated if our semantic concepts are not, just because we cannot grasp the former concepts without at the same time grasping the latter concepts. Schiffer's point is that our psychological concepts may not be instantiated when our semantic concepts are not, even though we *can* grasp the former concepts independently of the latter.

If all this is right, the mere intuition that there is and indeed can be no thought without language will not suffice to support an antireductionist claim. What matters is whether we can support this intuition with conceptual considerations related to our concepts of the semantic and the psychological. Once again we find that what the antireductionist must argue is that the reductionist's claim of a deep epistemological asymmetry between the semantic and the psychological is ill founded.

9 Does an Ontological Asymmetry Entail Deep Epistemological Asymmetry?

Having considered whether epistemological asymmetry entails ontological asymmetry, I now want to consider whether ontological asymmetry entails deep epistemological asymmetry. If we can defend the entailment in this direction, then anyone who holds that there can be thought without language is *eo ipso* committed to a deep epistemological asymmetry. Exploiting this entailment, the Gricean can try to gain support for his reduction simply by arguing for such an ontological asymmetry. Indeed, the Gricean may urge that in the absence of any argument to the contrary it is implausible to deny thought to the languageless merely because they lack language.[91] It would then follow that a conceptual asymmetry between the semantic and the psychological is plausible.

Such an entailment has repercussions for the antireductionist in another way. Consider the contrapositive of the entailment: failure of a deep epistemological asymmetry entails failure of an ontological asymmetry. Since the antireductionist argues that a deep epistemological asymmetry fails, he must also hold that ontological asymmetry fails. In other words, if the entailment holds, the antireductionist must deny thoughts to the languageless.

A strong intuition supports the claim that ontological asymmetry entails a deep epistemological asymmetry. One way to bring out that intuition is as follows. Suppose we attribute thoughts to the languageless. In other words, suppose that psychological concepts may be instantiated prior to and independently of the concept of meaning. From this it seems to follow that our grasp of the concepts of the propositional attitudes is independent of our grasp of the concept of meaning. How else can we make sense of the claim that the one set of concepts may be instantiated independently of the other? Now if our grasp of the concepts of the propositional attitudes is independent of our grasp of the concept of meaning, we have precisely the conceptual asymmetry that the Gricean reductionist urges us to accept. Thus, a plausible ontological thesis seems to support the conceptual asymmetry that the Gricean needs to maintain his reduction. The entailment we are considering in this section can be reformulated thus: the thesis (1) that one set of concepts can be instantiated independently of another entails the thesis (2) that our grasp of the one set of concepts is independent of our grasp of the other.

We further reinforce the plausibility of such an entailment if once again we consider the contrapositive. The *anti*reductionist denies that we can have a grasp of our concepts of propositional attitudes independently of a grasp of the semantic concept of linguistic meaning, and rejecting this appears to involve the antireductionist in a rejection of the thesis that one can have thought without language. The intuition here is this: when we admit that one can have thought without language, we seem thereby to admit that we *can* grasp what thought is without recourse to the concept of linguistic meaning. This latter idea is precisely what the antireductionist wants to deny. Thus, if the antireductionist denies thesis (2), he seems to commit himself to denying thesis (1) as well.

There thus seems to be a quite strong intuition that ontological asymmetry entails deep epistemological asymmetry. Despite this admittedly strong intuition I want to deny the entailment. The denial will come in two stages. In this section I will present a reason for believing that ontological and deep epistemological asymmetries can come apart. This argument is meant merely to prepare one to see this separation of issues. In chapter 4, section 5 I develop my reasons for thinking that these issues *must* come apart. That argument comes at the end of a much longer one explaining why I believe that the reductionist is wrong to maintain a deep epistemological asymmetry between the psychological and the semantic. As I have already stated, if we can maintain a separation between ontological and deep epistemological asymmetries, it will have notable consequences for both the reductionist and the antireductionist. The reductionist will no longer be able to support his thesis by insisting on the implausibility of denying thoughts to the languageless. The antireductionist will no longer need to accept the perhaps implausible thesis that only those endowed with language can have thoughts.

My strategy in this section is to argue that a certain kind of semantic analysis of the propositional attitudes is evidence that ontological asymmetry does not entail conceptual asymmetry. The evidence works to deny this entailment by threatening the contrapositive: if one denies a deep epistemological asymmetry, one thereby denies ontological asymmetry as well.

One way the antireductionist may deny an alleged deep epistemological asymmetry between the semantic and the psychological is by maintaining that propositional attitudes require a *semantic* analysis. One such semantic analysis he may offer to support his claim is that belief, for example, is a relation to a sentence with meaning in the theorist's language. Quine makes the following observation about such an analysis: "Taking the objects of propositional attitudes as sentences does not require the subject to speak the language of the object sentence—or any. A mouse's fear of a cat is counted as his fearing true a certain English sentence."[92] Quine's point is that taking this line on propositional attitudes does not mean that the attitude holder speaks the same language as the theorist, or indeed speaks any language at all. Adopting this analysis ensures that propositional-attitude concepts depend on semantic concepts, but by making attitudes relations to sentences in the *theorist's* language, we are free to see the attitude holder as languageless.

An important distinction that such an analysis draws is that between theorist and subject. This distinction is brought in to allow that theorist and subject do not speak the same language. But as an additional advantage it allows that the subject may have *no* language at all. In such a case the theorist is one who has a language and thinks; the subject is one about whom the theorist wonders whether he has thoughts even though he has no language.

The distinction that this semantic analysis of propositional attitudes introduces can help us to see that although the antireductionist denies a deep epistemological asymmetry between the psychological and the semantic, he need not deny ontological asymmetry as well. This is because the semantic analysis of propositional attitudes he uses to support his rejection of a deep epistemological asymmetry allows that the attitude holder may have no language of his own. The analysis of propositional attitudes as relations to sentences with meaning in the theorist's language guarantees that such attitudes are to be understood with reference to language. At the same time it shows that this conceptual requirement can be fulfilled even when the attitude holder has no language: the theorist can understand the attribution of thought to his languageless subject with reference to his own language.

I claim only that a certain sort of semantic analysis of propositional attitudes is evidence that ontological asymmetry does not entail deep epistemological asymmetry. I admit that at this point such an analysis is only evidence that the entailment fails. Such evidence may be open to reinterpretation. Indeed, the reductionist may want to point to the intuition presented at the beginning of this section and argue that this intuition is itself evidence in *favor* of the mooted entailment. He may argue that the plausibility of this intuition should alert us to the possibility that something is fundamentally mistaken in an analysis of propositional attitudes that takes them to be relations to sentences in the theorist's language. But the reductionist need not reject this analysis of the propositional attitudes altogether; he has an even more powerful argument at his disposal. Drawing on the distinctions I introduced in the previous section, the reductionist can argue that the semantic analysis under consideration is only a reflection of either empirical, contingent facts or causal, conceptual facts. In other words, he may deny that this analysis is a reflection of conceptual facts related to our concepts of the semantic and the psychological. In this way the reductionist may appear to accommodate the analysis while maintaining his reduction.

I want to argue, however, that the analysis we give of propositional attitudes does reflect our concepts of the semantic and the psychological. In chapter 4 I shall argue that to deny the relationship between this kind of analysis and such conceptual reflections is in effect to commit oneself to an unsatisfactory picture of mind. I shall further argue that after we develop a better picture of the psychological and its relation to the semantic, we shall see that a deep epistemological *symmetry* is compatible with ontological *asymmetry*. That is, we shall see how an antireductionist picture of mind leaves room for the attribution of thoughts to the languageless. With some idea of the antireductionist picture of mind we shall be in a position to explain away the intuition the reductionist relies on to support his picture of mind. Thus, if we accept the analysis that makes propositional attitudes out to be relations to sentences in the theorist's language, and if the analysis reflects our concepts of the semantic and the psychological, we can deny that ontological asymmetry entails a deep epistemological asymmetry.

10 Davidson's Argument

The conclusion of the previous section is that under certain assumptions commitment to an ontological asymmetry does not entail commitment to a deep epistemological asymmetry. One of the consequences of this conclusion is that the antireductionist need not deny thoughts to the languageless. At least one antireductionist, however, does not try to make his position compatible with ontological asymmetry. Indeed, Davidson has argued that a conceptual symmetry between the semantic and the psychological entails an ontological symmetry.[93] I want to conclude this chapter by explaining why I think Davidson's argument, as it stands, does not succeed.

Davidson begins his discussion with the following observation about belief: "Belief is central to all kinds of thought. . . . The system of [endless interlocked] beliefs identifies a thought by locating it in a logical and epistemic space."[94] This said, Davidson uses the notion of belief to argue that there can be no thought where there is no language. The argument has two main steps: (1) a creature can have a belief only if it has the concept of belief, and (2) a creature can have the concept of belief only if it is a member of a speech community. Davidson adds an important qualification to the first step of his argument, namely, that to have a belief, the creature in question must be capable of having the concept of some belief or other, but it need not have the concept of any particular belief.[95] To support the first step of his argument, Davidson writes, "Someone cannot have a belief unless he understands the possibility of being mistaken, and this requires grasping the contrast between truth and error—true belief and

false belief."[96] In support of the second step of his argument Davidson writes, "But this contrast . . . can emerge only in the context of
interpretation, which alone forces us to the idea of an objective public
truth."[97] We can refute this argument by arguing either that one need
not have the concept of belief to have a belief,[98] or that being a member of a speech community is not the only way to come to have the
concept of belief.

To support the first step of this argument, Davidson invokes the
notion of surprise. About this notion Davidson writes, "Clearly
enough I could not be surprised . . . if I did not have belief in the first
place."[99] Let me explain how Davidson uses the notion of surprise in
his argument. Davidson begins by observing that to attribute a belief
to a creature we must be able to distinguish between some subjective
state of that creature and the world so that we can say that the creature's state is a true or false representation of the world. This distinction, then, is a necessary condition of belief. It is clearly not a
sufficient condition. We approach sufficient conditions, according to
Davidson, when we add that the creature must be *aware* of this distinction between his subjective state and the objective state of the
world. Only if the creature has such an awareness, says Davidson,
can it exhibit the surprise so crucial to believing. Being aware of the
subjective/objective distinction just is what Davidson means when he
talks about having the concept of belief. Let me tell the following
story to illustrate the thought. Say a creature has the belief that there
is food in the kitchen. And say that this belief does *not* correctly
represent the world. Now when this creature realizes his mistake, he
will be surprised. Surprise is the result of the creature's registering
discord between his subjective state and the objective state of the
world. In one place Davidson writes, "Surprise requires that I am
aware of a contrast between what I did believe and what I come to
believe."[100] In summary, then, to have belief requires that a creature
be capable of exhibiting surprise, and a creature is only capable of
exhibiting surprise if it has the concept of belief. With the notion of
surprise Davidson hopes to make a case for the first step in his argument that will at the same time provide a bridge to the second.

The helpfulness that introducing this notion of surprise brings to
the discussion in this highly obscure area is diminished by something
else Davidson says in the course of his discussion of the relationship
between having beliefs and being surprised. He writes, "Clearly
enough I could not be surprised (*though I could be startled*) if I did not
have beliefs in the first place" (my emphasis). Davidson is working
here with a very tightly connected set of concepts. Someone who has
a belief will exhibit surprise when he realizes that his belief is false.

But we must be very careful not to confuse being surprised with being startled. It would seem, then, that observing another's behavior cannot help us to decide whether someone is exhibiting surprise or is just startled; we must *first* decide whether the creature has beliefs. Introducing this element of surprise into the discussion, then, cannot help us to distinguish believers from nonbelievers, as one may have thought. We must establish whether someone is a believer before we can describe him as surprised.[101]

Whether or not we invoke the notion of surprise, Davidson is obviously right that it is never sufficient for belief merely that there be a distinction between a creature's subjective state and the objective state of the world. Bennett has made a similar point using the notion of registration. Bennett defines "registration" as a "theoretical term, standing for whatever-it-is about the given animal which validates predictions of its behaviour from facts about its environment."[102] Registration is necessary for belief, but it quite clearly is not sufficient. We see this if we consider the behavior of self-regulating heat-seeking missiles. It may be that the missile registers where its target is and adjusts accordingly, but it is, at the very least, extravagent to attribute beliefs to these missiles. We approach sufficient conditions, Bennett thinks, if we add being educable to the notion of registering. Being educable is roughly being capable of learning from one's mistakes.[103] Whether educability alone is sufficient for belief, it is clearly necessary. Davidson, in contrast to Bennett, rejects this way of approaching sufficient conditions.[104] Davidson insists that for a creature to have a belief the creature must be aware of the distinction between his subjective state and the objective world.

One may have the following reaction to Davidson's argument thus far. One may agree that having a belief requires an awareness of a subjective/objective distinction and that a creature has registered this when it exhibits surprise, but we may disagree with Davidson that awareness of this distinction just is having the concept of belief. Davidson writes, "Such awareness . . . is a belief about a belief."[105] This may be disputed. As Davidson characterizes them, the state of being startled is nothing more than stimulus and response, and the state of being surprised involves having the concept of belief. Surely there is room in between. Having *some* awareness of a distinction between one's own subjective state and the objective state of the world very likely allows for the educability and inquisitiveness that Bennett refers to. Of course, Davidson rejects Bennett's way of achieving sufficient conditions because Davidson's understanding of the condition of awareness is very strong.

One can interpret this objection to Davidson in different ways. One may agree with Davidson that a creature has the concept of belief just in case it is aware of a distinction between what is subjective and what is objective but then disagree with Davidson over the conditions for having this concept or making this distinction. This in effect would be a rejection of the second step in Davidson's argument. Yet one may also view this as a disagreement over the first step in Davidson's argument. One might agree that belief requires some awareness of a subjective/objective distinction but argue that one can have this without having the concept of belief. I want to oppose Davidson by opposing the first step of his argument.

If we consider various concepts other than that of belief, we find that the conditions required for instantiating the concept are quite different from those required for having the concept. Consider, for instance, our concept of swimming or of having an arm. Clearly, what is required of one who instantiates the concepts of swimming or having an arm is quite different from what is required of one who has the concepts. Obviously, one can have an arm or be a swimmer without having the concept of having an arm or the concept of swimming. One may be tempted to generalize the point: the conditions for having the concept ϕ are different from the conditions for instantiating ϕ. Having done this, one might expect that the conditions for having the concept of belief will be different from those for having the belief.

But belief may be an exception to this general rule. There may even be reasons for thinking that these conditions coincide where the concept in question is mental. One way of looking at Davidson's argument is as an argument to the effect that belief is just such an exception. The reasoning would rely on accepting the idea that an awareness of a subjective/objective distinction is a necessary condition of believing. Davidson thinks that one becomes aware of this distinction in coming to have the concept of intersubjective truth and that this latter concept is one we come to have in linguistic communication. Interpreting others requires that we have a grasp of the concept of intersubjective truth. Thus, it is the connection between belief and intersubjective truth that conspires to make the concept of belief an exception to the rule presented above. In the case of belief, to instantiate the concept one must have the concept, and this because one cannot instantiate the concept unless one grasps the concept of intersubjective truth. Now I do not want to deny that linguistic communication depends upon the notion of intersubjective truth, nor do I want to deny that having the notion of intersubjective truth entails an awareness of the subjective/objective distinction. What I want to argue is that there is another way of satisfying the condition of having an awareness of the subjective/objective distinction, a way that non-linguistic creatures are able to satisfy.[106] A creature that has the concept of intersubjective truth is clearly aware of a distinction between what is subjective and what is objective. But what of the creature that responds to its mistakes by perservering, that exhibits an interest in getting things right, that learns from its mistakes? Doesn't such a creature exhibit some awareness of the distinction between his subjective states and the way the world is? Consider a dumb animal that has been tricked: it may continue to search around for the food it believed to be by the kitchen table. Such an animal exhibits an awareness that something has gone wrong, that the world is not, we might say, as the animal believed it to be. We might say that such a creature is surprised (and not merely startled). And not only surprised, but puzzled as well. Only a creature that exhibited such behavior would be in a position to learn. Learning requires some awareness of a distinction between what is correct and what is incorrect. Here we have a way of seeing that a creature who is aware of the subjective/ objective distinction need not have the concept of truth. This way allows that nonlinguistic creatures may have some awareness of the subjective/objective distinction, an awareness exhibited in their behavior of surprise and puzzlement. In essence, this is a return to Bennett's notion of being educable (and perhaps the notion of being inquisitive). Bennett's picture is now filled out: we can say that it is an awareness of a subjective/objective distinction that gives rise to the behavior required for a creature to be in a position to *learn*. Having such an awareness may involve anything from exhibiting an urge to get things right (involving the creature and its environment) to possessing the concept of intersubjective truth (which involves the creature in a linguistic commitment to other creatures). We may thus attribute belief, which essentially involves an awareness of a subjective/objective distinction, to nonlinguistic as well as to linguistic creatures. To be sure, languageless creatures must be capable of acting in the world. This interacting with the world gives rise to the creature's awareness.

Davidson writes: "To make the distinction [between having any propositional attitudes and having none] so strong, and to make it depend on language, invites an accusation of anthropocentrism. The complaint is just, but it ought not to be levelled against me. I merely describe a feature of certain concepts."[107] Thus, according to Davidson our concepts of the semantic and the psychological are interdependent. For us this amounts to a rejection of conceptual asymmetry, but for Davidson it is a rejection of an ontological asymmetry as well. An implication of Davidson's argument is that rejection of ontological asymmetry just follows from a rejection of conceptual asymmetry. However, I do not think that Davidson's argument, as it stands, is correct.[108] I want to maintain, contrary to Davidson, that just because the antireductionist rejects a conceptual asymmetry between the semantic and the psychological, he need not deny ontological asymmetry as well. As we have seen, Davidson is committed to the entailment from deep epistemological asymmetry to ontological asymmetry at least in part because he refuses to draw a distinction between having a belief and having the concept of belief. I have argued that Davidson gives no good reason for holding that having belief requires having the concept of belief, and I have suggested independent reasons for thinking this requirement implausible. Once a distinction is drawn between having belief and having the concept of belief, one is free to embrace antireductionism and also to accept that there may be thought where there is no language. It is this position that I shall develop in chapter 4.

In this section I hope I have provided considerations that divorce ontological asymmetry from a deep epistemological asymmetry. In section 8 I suggested that one could be a reductionist and still agree that there is and perhaps even can be no thought where there is no language. The discussion there was meant to show that the fact (if it is one) that there is no thought without language alone is never sufficient to establish an antireductionist claim. A reductionist can accept that fact. What the reductionist *cannot* accept is that the support for that fact rests upon deep conceptual facts about the nature of our concepts of the semantic and the psychological. Thus we see that certain deep epistemological matters, and not ontological ones alone, divide the reductionist from his opponent. In section 9 I brought evidence to suggest that one could oppose reduction and still agree that some languageless creatures can have thoughts. The discussion there was meant to show that the fact (if it is one) that there may be thought without language neither supports the reductionist position nor weakens the antireductionist one. The antireductionist is making a conceptual point, namely, that we cannot fully understand our concept of thought without reference to language. This point holds even if it should prove possible for the languageless to think. The conclusion of the section does not agree with a claim made by Davidson. Davidson holds that there can be no thought without language, and he suggests that this follows from an acceptance of a conceptual *symmetry* between the semantic and the psychological. I considered Davidson's argument for this in the last section and suggested some reasons for thinking it does not succeed.

I conclude that what ultimately divides the reductionist from his antireductionist opponent is not a disagreement about whether there is an ontological asymmetry between the semantic and the psychological. Suitably understood, an ontological symmetry may be accepted by both, and both may accept an ontological asymmetry. The division runs deep over the issue of whether there is a certain sort of epistemological asymmetry between the semantic and the psychological. It now remains for me to explain the picture of mind to which one who holds a deep epistemological asymmetry is committed, and to say why I think it is unsatisfactory.

Chapter 4
Meaning and Mind

In the previous chapter I advanced two claims. The first was this: commitment to a deep epistemological asymmetry is a commitment to a certain false picture of mind. Second, I claimed that the conceptual thesis that there is a *symmetry* between our semantic and psychological concepts does not necessarily involve a commitment to an ontological symmetry. In this chapter I propose to defend these claims.

The reductive Gricean, as we have learned, proposes to divorce the thesis that propositional attitudes have a nature that is essentially nonsemantic (that is, public-language semantics) from the issue of whether having an outer or public language is causally necessary for possessing thoughts and the issue of whether human beings can in fact come to know another language user's thoughts in advance of understanding his language. By proposing this divorce the Gricean unmoors his understanding of the essential nature of thought and meaning from surface observations concerning both epistemological and ontological dependence. I suggest that the Gricean makes his mistake in the way he understands the epistemological issues. In proposing to divorce surface epistemological observations from deep epistemological issues the Gricean commits himself to a view of mind and meaning that, I shall argue, is mistaken. Before I say any more about what this Gricean picture of mind and meaning is, and what I take to be wrong with it, I want to consider a certain reply a Gricean might make to the objection that one cannot come to know another's beliefs and intentions in advance of knowing his language.[1] The reply is this: *Of course* one can't know the beliefs and intentions of another without knowing his language. The Gricean claim is that semantic concepts are logically equivalent to certain psychological concepts, and it follows from this that in coming to know certain of a person's psychological states one is *eo ipso* coming to know the meaning of his words and sentences. It seems to me that this remark addresses itself to the letter, but not the spirit, of the objection.

In effect, the Gricean is here trading on a distinction between what I am calling a surface and a deep epistemological asymmetry. Under the guise of agreeing with his objector about the plight of the radical interpreter (agreeing, that is, that there is a surface epistemological symmetry), the Gricean asserts what amounts to a deep epistemological *asymmetry* between our semantic and psychological concepts. He concludes that if our concepts *are* asymmetrical and if the Gricean analysis is correct, there is a sense in which one cannot know what is represented by the right-hand side of the biconditional in advance of knowing what is represented by the left-hand side: the one just is the other. But this, I believe, misrepresents the objection. As I understand him, the objector makes this claim about the situation of the radical interpreter because he believes that there is a deep epistemological symmetry between our semantic and psychological concepts, despite the correctness of the Gricean analysis.

The observation of a surface epistemological symmetry may be variously interpreted. The Gricean reductionist takes the observation to be an inessential part of our theory of propositional attitudes. A surface epistemological symmetry does not reflect the true nature of the concepts with which we are concerned. Indeed, the Gricean must hold that this surface observation is mistaken and misleading as to the true nature of the semantic and the psychological. Although there is the appearance of two equal and equally important sets of concepts (an appearance revealed in this surface epistemological symmetry), the fact is that one set of concepts is dominant and in certain configurations (represented by the right-hand side of the Gricean biconditional) can be used to explain and understand the other. We might sum up the Gricean position thus: the antireductionist is right about the way we in fact must come to know another's propositional attitudes, the reductionist is right about what the propositional attitudes are.

I think that the Gricean owes us some explanation of why he denies that a surface epistemological symmetry between the semantic and the psychological can be taken as a reflection of what the propositional attitudes are like in themselves. In the absence of some *other* guide to understanding what is involved in the true nature of our concepts, one may be tempted to take this symmetry as an indication of the way our concepts of the semantic and the psychological work. I believe that some reductive Griceans propose to divorce their view of the true nature of these concepts from the observation that there is a surface epistemological symmetry between these sets of concepts because of their *prior* commitment to some form of reductive physicalism. Their prior commitment to reductive physicalism, in combination with the belief that such physicalism for the entire mental realm can be attained only if we first reduce the semantic to the psychological, leads some reductive Griceans to reject this observation when it comes to saying what is involved in our concepts of the semantic and the psychological. More important than this, however, is the picture of mind with which the reductive physicalist works. It is this picture which, I believe, explains the Gricean's willingness to embrace this divorce.

Contrary to this, I want to argue that the surface epistemological symmetry between our semantic and psychological concepts is an indication that there is a deeper epistemological symmetry as well; it is a reflection of the true nature of these concepts. I want to argue that denying this is the result of having adopted a false picture of mind. In chapter 3 I suggested that the reductive Gricean claim that there is a deep epistemological asymmetry between the semantic and the psychological can be supported by an appeal either to reductive physicalism or to Cartesianism. I want now to add that it is the picture of mind common to these two theories that grips the reductive Gricean and tempts him to deny that this surface epistemological symmetry is a reflection of the true nature of our semantic and psychological concepts. The reductive Gricean adopts this picture of mind as his guide in understanding our concepts of the semantic and the psychological in *lieu* of adopting this observation of symmetry.

The reductionist may argue, however, that I associate the "mistaken" picture of mind with theories proposing a reduction of the semantic to the psychological only because I concentrate my attentions on Cartesianism and reductive physicalism. A functionalist theory of the psychological, on the other hand, is a theory of mind that looks as if it can combine a reduction of the semantic to the psychological with many of the elements that I identify with the "correct" picture of mind. And functionalism is the theory of mind that has been favored by reductive Griceans such as Loar and Schiffer. In section 3 I shall argue that functionalism only *appears* to be able to incorporate a correct picture of mind. When we look more closely at the theory, we see that it shares its conception of mind with Cartesianism and reductive physicalism.

What my consideration of functionalism should reveal is that my discussions of Cartesianism and reductive physicalism help us to see just what this mistaken picture of mind is. In the end, it is this picture—not Cartesianism or reductive physicalism—to which all reductive Griceans are committed. I believe that in adopting this conception of mind, the reductive Gricean makes his mistake. I won't fully establish that the Gricean *is* committed by his reduction to a mistaken conception of mind until the end of this chapter.

Finally, in section 5 I shall explain how the correct picture of mind requires that we think of the semantic as conceptually on a par with the psychological. Having done all this, I will be in a position to defend the other rather substantial claim of chapter 3, that a deep epistemological *symmetry* between our concepts of the semantic and the psychological does not entail ontological symmetry, *pace* Davidson. I shall explain why one who rejects a reduction of the semantic to the psychological can nevertheless accept that languageless creatures may have thoughts.

1 The Objective Conception of Mind

In chapter 3 I suggested that an appeal either to reductive physicalism or to Cartesianism may be used to give backing to the claim that there is a deep epistemological asymmetry between the semantic and the psychological. In this chapter I have suggested that introducing a divorce between surface and deep epistemological issues is the mark of a mistaken conception of mind and that this mistaken picture is shared by reductive physicalists and Cartesians. I want now to explain how this mistaken conception of mind may be thought to arise.

The mistaken conception of mind makes the mind out to be an objective phenomenon.[2] There are two ways of understanding this: either we can establish what it is for a phenomenon to be objective, or we can contrast this conception with another conception of mind, one that makes the mind out to be an essentially subjective phenomenon. I shall say little about the subjective conception until section 4; in this section I shall concentrate in the main on describing the objective conception of mind.

As these terms have come down to us in modern times, what is subjective pertains to the subject of consciousness, whereas what is objective is, by opposition, what lies outside the conscious subject and is presented to it. Charles Taylor has identified this tradition as having its roots in the seventeenth-century view of man and his relation to nature.[3] What characterizes this tradition is the idea that the subject is the locus of all meaning in contradistinction to a world of things thought of as devoid of intrinsic meaning. The emptying of all intrinsic meaning is, for Taylor, the objectifying move. An objective understanding marked modern seventeenth-century science. This science viewed things as mechanistic, atomistic, and tending towards homogeneity. That is, it tended to explain apparently distinct things as constructions out of the same basic constituents by appealing to the same basic principles.

Thomas Nagel has described the objective conception as one that is both centerless and featureless.[4] An objective phenomenon, one for which the objective conception suffices, need not be understood from any particular point of view. Contrary to this, a subjective phenomenon, one for which there must be a subjective conception, is essentially tied to a particular point of view.[5] The being of an objective phenomenon is independent of its appearing in this or that way to a perceiving, sentient creature. This is why we can say of any objective phenomenon that it can be characterized independently of any subject and can be thought of simply as part of what is there anyway. Thus, it is natural to associate what is objective and only what is objective with what is real. Furthermore, with this characterization of the objective we can understand the tendency to take physical objects as the model of the objective.

The natural, modern applications of the terms "subjective" and "objective" are respectively the conscious subject and what lies outside the subject and is presented to it. However, this distinction was no sooner drawn than it became blurred: the very consciousness of the subject came to be viewed as an objective phenomenon. Let me now sketch one seminal source of this idea.

We can trace to Descartes much contemporary discussion of the problem of mind and its relation to body. Notoriously, Descartes sought to regain the world, and banish the sceptic, using the Archimedean point of his own consciousness. Descartes used this first-person standpoint, the standpoint of consciousness, both to establish the existence of an external world of bodies and to establish that world as essentially distinct from mind. Both conclusions can be traced to an act of introspection. From this act of introspection Descartes concluded that one can doubt the existence of the entire world, including one's own body, and also that from this very act of doubting one can establish that the doubter exists. Descartes concluded from this that mind and body have distinct essences: the essence of mind is to think; the essence of body is to be extended. In the *Principles of Philosophy* Descartes writes, "We can conclude that two substances are really distinct one from the other from the sole fact that we can conceive the one clearly and distinctly without the other."[6] Hence, Descartes's thought experiment led him ultimately to the view that there exist both physical substance and mental substance.

At the point at which the distinctness of mind is located in the distinctness of a certain kind of substance, we have the beginning of a shift to an objective conception of mind. The world of mental things and events is placed alongside of, but essentially modeled on, the world of physical things and events. The important idea for Descartes was the distinctness of these two kinds of substance; our *conception* of each kind of substance was less of a concern to him. Thus, Descartes begins by observing that the subject of consciousness bears a particular and peculiar relationship to his own mental life. Descartes claimed that indubitability was the mark of this special relationship. We might say that what is special about the subject's relation to his own mental life is that all aspects of that life are presented to the subject in a subjective form, that is, from a point of view or with a certain phenomenological quality. However we describe it, it is undeniable that some sort of special relationship exists. It is part and parcel of what it means to say that the mind is an essentially subjective phenomenon. However, Descartes no sooner makes this observation than he misinterprets it, and in doing so, he moves from having a subjective conception of mind to embracing an objective conception of it.

Noting the peculiarly intimate nature of the relation the subject bears to the contents of his own mind, Descartes moves to a conception of mind as a substance with an essence distinct from physical substance.[7] Having posited this new kind of substance, one is tempted to reinterpret the originally observed relation between subject and mind as a subject's special, privileged access to this mental substance. Introspection comes to be understood as a rather special form of perception trained on objects of this immaterial realm. We come to think of this subject as having direct access to this substance constituting his mind.[8]

Let us now turn for a moment from this Cartesian, first-person point of view on the mind and consider the third-person point of view on another's mind.[9] Pretheoretically, what we observe here is that while a mental life is present to the subject in a rather particular way, it is also presented in a particular way to persons other than the subject. Of all the ways the mind could be present to another, it is in fact present through behavior. We look to the behavior of another when determining that he is a subject of experience and when determining what those experiences are. We naturally conclude from this that there is a certain asymmetry of first- and third-person perspectives on the mind: the former does not rely on behavior, while the latter has no immediate perspective or experiential qualities attached to it.

The Cartesian conception of mind as an immaterial substance has repercussions for our understanding of the third-person perspective as well as the subject's perspective on the mind. Where the subject has privileged or direct access to this immaterial substance, persons other than the subject have only the indirect access afforded by the subject's behavior. The subject's behavior, on this conception of things, is seen as the intermediary between the immaterial substance that is the mind and individuals other than the subject. This is how the Cartesian understands the asymmetry of first- and third-person perspectives.

But such understanding in effect leads to the loss of any real asymmetry of perspectives, and at the same time it loses everything that qualifies the mind as an essentially subjective phenomenon. As I explained in chapter 3, the Cartesian metaphysic allows us to say that the difference between the first- and third-person perspectives on the mind is an essentially contingent matter. Certain special godlike individuals could have the powers to detect this mind substance directly, that is, without relying on the behavior that interposes itself between one mind and another in the human sphere. One can imagine these godlike individuals as able to observe directly the workings of this immaterial substance. The mind, for such individuals, lies open to impersonal investigation.[10] If introspection is understood as a special kind of perception, then these imagined individuals can match it in the way they perceive others' minds.[11] If this is right, there is nothing special about the subject's perspective after all. Once we envisage the possibility of individuals with these special godlike powers, the perspective of the subject turns out to be merely one among many. The subject's own direct perspective is then one that can be shared. And once we see this, we have to admit that there is nothing special about the subject's perspective after all. The subject's perspective is only privileged when considered in contrast with the perspective of other human beings. That privilege ceases once these godlike individuals are introduced.

But now we have slipped into an objective conception of the mind. We are understanding the mind as something that can be essentially and completely apprehended from a third-person perspective. This conception is of something that is there anyway and need not be understood from a particular point of view. All this is a consequence of interpreting the subject's particular and peculiar relation to his own mind in the way the Cartesian does. The irony is that in seeking to explain this special relation, the Cartesian loses sight of it. Once this special relation is interpreted as a special access to a special object, its special quality fades away. The special nature of it is seen to be relative to kinds of perceivers. But to say this is to imply that the mind is objective and hence to be committed to the loss of this special nature.

The consideration of godlike creatures with the power to detect immaterial substance with the ease with which humans detect material substance provides a vivid way to see the point. Once we consider an immaterial mental substance as directly presented to individuals other than the subject himself even if only in a thought experiment, we see that the introduction of this special substance in itself does nothing to help us understand what is distinctive of mind.[12] And this thought experiment also helps us to see *why* the introduction of an immaterial mental substance cannot help us here. The reason is that we are trying to understand an essentially subjective phenomenon on the model of an essentially objective phenomenon. It is not enough that this objective phenomenon is immaterial rather than material.

To avoid conceiving the mind as an objective phenomenon we must understand the particular relation the subject bears to his own mental life as unique, not just unique at the moment and relative to a certain kind of individual, but unique, period. We must understand the asymmetry between first- and third-person perspectives on the mind as essential to our understanding of the kind of thing the mind is, not as something we can do away with by a thought experiment. On the Cartesian conception of mind, coming to understand the true nature of mind is associated not with our ordinary mode of access to another's mind but with some possible or counterpossible mode of access afforded to individuals with godlike powers. That is, the conception of mind as an objective phenomenon is marked by the fact that it introduces a divorce between our ordinary mode of access to another's mental life, behavior, and our theory of what these states are in themselves. Denying such a divorce is the mark of a subjective conception of mind.

In the centuries since Descartes philosophers have grown suspicious of this immaterial realm. Among other things, there persists the problem of accounting for the interaction of this immaterial substance and material, or physical, substance.[13] To avoid this, some philosophers have come to think of the mind as nothing over and above the body. Thus, in this century we have various reductive physicalist theories of mind claiming that mental states and events are nothing but physical states and events and that mental properties are nothing over and above physical ones. In this way much that is thought to be unpalatable and difficult about Cartesianism is avoided. But one thing may be said to remain the same in this radical shift of theory about the mind: the objectification of the mind introduced by Descartes continues to be a feature of the new reductive physicalist picture of mind. On this picture the mind is both real and objective; it is also straightforwardly *physical*.

The shift to a physically objective conception of the mind highlights even more starkly the impoverishment of the an objective conception of mind. By emphasizing the difficulties and implausibilities involved in positing an immaterial realm, the physicalist ignores the original and important insight of Descartes: the subject bears a strikingly particular and peculiar relationship to his own mental life. The Cartesian starting point is reversed: instead of emphasizing the first-person perspective on the mind, the third-person perspective is now brought into prominence. Indeed, the first-person perspective may now be thought to be submerged, overwhelmed by the perspective of the other. By losing touch with this perspective, the physicalist can be seen more readily than the Cartesian to have lost touch with the essentially subjective nature of mind.

A telling point of contact between the reductive physicalist and the Cartesian comes in the way they understand the third-person perspective. It is when one looks at how the reductive physicalist understands this perspective that the objective conception of the mind, a conception that the reductive physicalist shares with the Cartesian, comes into sharp focus. Like the Cartesian the reductive physicalist notes that in the ordinary course of things (i.e., for ordinary human observers) a subject's linguistic and nonlinguistic behavior makes his mind available to others. And like the Cartesian the reductive physicalist ignores this in his theory of the mind. On the reductive physicalist picture, however, there is no need to bring in godlike individuals with special powers to make the point. A god's perspective on the immaterial mind is replaced by a neurophysiologist's perspective on the material mind. The crucial point is that once this perspective has been achieved, the observer need no longer rely on the interpretation of another's behavior to know what another's thoughts and feelings are. The reductive physicalist envisages that with the development of the brain sciences we can in principle, at least, achieve this perspective on the mind of another. As the Cartesian, the reductive physicalist thinks of behavior as incidental to understanding what mental states are in themselves. Our theory of those states need make no mention of behavior.[14] Once again we have a conception of the mind as an objective phenomenon; a conception of it as something that may be thought of as simply there, independent of its being there for someone; a conception of something that may be fully comprehended from an external and impersonal point of view. The impersonality of this conception is even more clearly evident on the reductive physicalist conception of mind once one notices the emphasis in this conception on the third-person perspective.[15]

It is not farfetched to assume that the objective conception of mind is a feature of Cartesian theorizing about the mind inherited by the reductive physicalist. Once we conceive of the mind as an objective phenomenon, we are in a position to reject our ordinary, everyday perspective of the mind of another as revealing of the true nature of mind. The thoughts and feelings of a subject can be thought of as lying behind the behavior, requiring us to achieve either a god's or a neurophysiologist's perspective in order properly to theorize about them.

Adopting a kind of reductive physicalist theory of mind, Loar writes: "Among the important evidence for beliefs is linguistic behaviour; we expect ascriptions of beliefs to fit linguistic dispositions. But while language must have a central place in the full picture of attitudes, it is not necessary to introduce it in the foundation of the theory of attitudes."[16] According to Loar the "ordinary evidence" for the ascription of propositional attitudes to another is his behavior, and essential to this evidence is linguistic behavior. From this we can conclude that at the level of the ordinary evidence there is a surface epistemological symmetry between the semantic and the psychological. Despite this, however, Loar insists that language is *not* an essential feature of "the foundation of the theory of attitudes." In other words when we construct our theory of what propositional attitudes are in themselves, the semantic need play no part. If this is right, the reductive Gricean can maintain that there is after all an asymmetry between our concepts of the semantic and the psychological: although it may not be possible to construct a theory of the semantic without reference to the psychological, it *is* possible to construct a theory of the psychological that makes no mention of the semantic. The ordinary evidence is merely evidence concerning what I have been calling a surface epistemological symmetry; it is not evidence concerning the very nature of the concepts in question. The reductive Gricean who accepts reductive physicalism or Cartesianism is in a position to make this divorce between the ordinary evidence for the attribution of propositional attitudes to another and the foundations of the theory of attitudes (Loar), or between surface epistemological matters and deep epistemological matters (my way of putting it), because of the picture of mind he adopts. The reductive Gricean is working with an objective conception of mind, and this paves the way for such a divorce. I shall further argue that *only* if one objectifies the mind in this way will one be tempted to reduce the semantic to the psychological.

Having discovered what I think lies behind the Gricean claim to reduce the semantic to the psychological, I want to oppose that reduction by arguing that it is a mistake to think of the mind as an objective phenomenon. I want to offer an alternative conception of mind, one that acknowledges the mind as a subjective phenomenon. I shall argue that once one ceases to conceive of the mind as an objective phenomenon one can no longer keep conceptual matters separate from surface epistemological ones or maintain a divorce between our account of what mental states are in themselves and our ordinary evidence concerning them. Once we deny this divorce, we find that we must take seriously the idea that the semantic and the psychological are equal and equally important concepts, that they cannot be reduced one to the other.

Before I begin my sketch of what I take to be the correct picture of mind, let me consider something else Loar has written: "The epistemology of belief-desire ascriptions must be kept distinct from their explication; not doing so perpetuates the methodology of the positivists' inevitable, noble, failures of phenomenalism, behaviourism, and semantic instrumentalism about science. It is difficult to imagine this tendency not to be equally disastrous in the theory of attitudes."[17] There is something curious about Loar's reference to positivism here. Positivism in the other cases Loar mentions leads to reduction. In the present case positivism, if that label is apt, is invoked to warn *against* reduction. But Loar sees no problem with the reductive tendencies of phenomenalism and behaviorism. The positivist mistake, according to Loar, was to try to explicate truth conditions in terms of evidence conditions. He writes, "It is then curious that it is precisely because Gricean theories block a priori constitutive connections between attitude-ascriptions and linguistic evidence that such opponents have objected to them."[18] In other words, if Loar's view of the positivist mistake is correct, we are in danger of repeating that mistake *unless* we follow the reductive Gricean program.

Now "a priori constitutive connections between attitude ascriptions and linguistic evidence" is precisely what I am proposing.[19] Also, I have proposed that we *not* keep the epistemology of belief-desire ascription separate from their explication. Am I then, as Loar claims, falling into the positivist trap? I believe not. Rather, Loar is mistaken, I would say, in thinking that *only* a form of positivism can lead one to an account of the psychological intimately related to the semantic. It is a question of our conception of both meaning and mind.

2 A Mistaken Picture of Mind

The conclusion of the previous section may be summarized as follows: since certain philosophers tend to view the mind as an objective phenomenon, they are inclined to reduce the semantic to the psychological. Yet I aim to establish a still stronger conclusion. I hold that if the Gricean wants to maintain a reduction of the semantic to the psychological, he is committed to conceiving the mind as an objective phenomenon. Establishing this conclusion will occupy the rest of this chapter.

I shall begin by summarizing the line of thought leading from an objective conception of mind to a reduction of the semantic to the psychological.

If we see the mind as part of the objective order, we can in principle disregard our ordinary modes of access to it and contemplate alternative modes of access.[20] The ordinary mode of access to the mind of another is his linguistic and nonlinguistic behavior. The alternative modes of access envisaged by Cartesians and reductive physicalists are those available to a godlike observer of the mind and a neurophysiologist observer of the brain respectively. The theorist who objectifies the mind is then in a position to introduce a distinction between our ordinary mode of access to another's thoughts and the theory of what those attitudes are in themselves. He can admit that in the ordinary course of things when one wants to know what another individual believes, intends, and the like, one must look at his behavior, and that if the other is a language user, the behavior one must observe will include *linguistic* behavior. However, such a theorist can argue that this behavior need not be introduced into one's theory of the propositional attitudes. From the ordinary, everyday perspective the semantic and psychological appear to be interdependent, but this appearance disappears once we achieve the perspective on the mind that the alternative modes of access provide. From these new perspectives one can argue that the semantic is not really important to our understanding of the psychological. It is only thought to be so if one thinks that the ordinary perspective on the mind of another cannot in principle be replaced by other perspectives. Abandoning the ordinary perspective, then, leaves us free to entertain the possibility that the semantic reduces to the psychological.

I have repeatedly stressed that a proper assessment of the Gricean reductive analysis of meaning must involve an investigation of our semantic and psychological concepts. I now add that in order correctly to understand our semantic concepts, we must first correctly understand our psychological concepts.[21] It is because the reductive

Gricean adopts an objective conception of the propositional attitudes that he is in a position to contemplate reducing the semantic to the psychological. Altering that conception will have repercussions for that reduction.

Now what, if anything, is wrong with a conception of mind that leads one to think that ordinary, behavioral evidence for what another is thinking is not essential to our understanding of what propositional attitudes are in themselves, and that holds out hope for a reduction of the semantic to the psychological? One problem for such a picture of mind is that it has difficulty in accounting for how ordinary, behavioral evidence can be evidence, however indirect, for what another is thinking. The question one needs to ask is: How, on this picture of mind, does behavior, which when interpreted by another yields access to the subject's beliefs, intentions, and the like, come to have the relationship it does to that subject's thoughts? The question can be broken into two separate ones: the first concerning how nonlinguistic behavior comes to have the relationship it does to the subject's simple thoughts, the second concerning how linguistic behavior comes to have its associations with the subject's thoughts. The question is not a new one. Nor is criticism of a picture of mind that makes the relationship between thoughts and related behavior merely contingent. What is interesting is the way in which we can see this misguided picture of mind to lie behind the Gricean proposal to view the semantic as reducible to the psychological. Any problem faced by this view of mind, then, will also face this reductionist proposal.

The question I am here posing to the reductive Gricean is one many philosophers have asked of ideational theorists of meaning.[22] According to ideational theorists, linguistic behavior is merely a means whereby an individual makes his thoughts available to another. If we want to know in what the meaning of an utterance consists, we must look to the thought of which it is the "external sign."[23] Clearly, then, the ideational theorist of meaning must hold that the ordinary evidence afforded by the language user's linguistic and nonlinguistic behavior is not essential to our understanding of what meaning is, behavior is only contingently related to the thought it expresses. According to the ideational theorist we can imagine human beings so constituted as to allow telepathic communication of thoughts, thus making the work of behavior unnecessary or redundant. According to this theory the *ordinary* evidence for what another thinks or means is something we can in principle ignore. Hence, the theory of what thinking or meaning is need make no mention of behavior.

The similarity between the ideational theorist's conception of the

semantic and the psychological and the reductive Gricean's is striking. As we have seen, the reductive Gricean also denies that the
ordinary evidence is essential to our understanding the nature of
meaning and mind; he too offers a theory of the propositional attitudes that makes no essential reference to this evidence. Both the
ideational theorist and the reductive Gricean associate the understanding of linguistic behavior with something *else*, namely, the
speaker's thoughts; and both hold that the account we give of these
thoughts need make no essential reference to that behavior.[24] This
similarity between the reductive Gricean and the ideational theorist of
meaning enables me to approach my criticism of the former by rehearsing some of the arguments that have been brought against the
latter.

One can see criticism of ideational theories as having been initiated
by Bishop Berkeley in the eighteenth century. Berkeley sought to
expose the mistake of other empiricists (notably Locke) who held that
the mind "hath the power of framing abstract ideas."[25] Their mistake
was holding the opinion that "language has no other end but the
communicating of our ideas, and that every significant name stands
for an idea." Such an assumption quite naturally leads to the thought
that generality in language is the expression of generality in thought.
Deny this assumption, however, and one is free of the need to
claim such powers of abstraction for the mind. Berkeley denied the
assumption:

> And a little attention will discover that it is not necessary (even in
> the strictest readings) singular names which stand for ideas
> should, every time they are used, excite in the understanding the
> ideas they are made to stand for. . . . Besides, the communicating
> of ideas marked by words is not the chief and only end of lan-
> guage, as is commonly supposed. There are other ends, as the
> raising of some passion, the exciting to or deterring from an
> action, the putting the mind in some particular disposition.

Berkeley, then, can be said to have loosened the grip the ideational
theory of meaning had on philosophers; however, it was over another century before such theories were exposed as radically misguided. Dummett writes, "The whole analytic school of philosophy is
founded on the rejection of this [ideational] conception, first clearly
repudiated by Frege."[26] Frege's rejection of the suggestion that an
utterance's meaning is to be explained in terms of the speaker's ideas
is made clear when Frege introduces the distinction between sense
and reference. To solve the puzzle of identity statements involving
proper names Frege suggests that we draw a distinction between a

sign's sense and its reference; he also argues that "the reference and the sense of a sign are to be distinguished from the associated idea."[27] Frege argues in particular that "an essential distinction between the idea and the sign's sense" is that the latter may be the common property of many while the former is a part or mode of an individual mind.[28] Very roughly, for Frege sense is public, while ideas are private. This observation led Frege to characterize senses as abstract entities, items of what he calls "a third realm."[29] Items of this realm exist eternally and require no bearer for their existence. For Frege senses are essentially public entities, while ideas are subject dependent and essentially private entities. The private and subject-dependent character of ideas makes them unsuited to explain meaning, according to Frege.

Wittgenstein can be seen to have taken Frege's criticism of ideational theories one step further. As I have just explained, Frege allows for private subject-dependent ideas; his point is merely that sense is not to be confused with these. According to Frege two people may associate different private ideas with the same word. To say that these ideas are private is just to say that it is undiscoverable which idea the speaker in fact associates with his word. This is why ideas are unsuited to explain the public meaning of utterances. One of the things Wittgenstein questioned is the coherence of allowing that there may be some undiscoverable thing left over once communication has been achieved. In other words, Wittgenstein questioned the notion of such a private realm of ideas. According to Wittgenstein we should reject not only the view that the meaning of an utterance is to be identified with the ideas that lie behind it, but also the view that ideas exist undiscoverable behind the utterance. According to Wittgenstein we can have no coherent conception of such a realm.[30]

More recently Dummett offered an argument designed to show that the ideational theory of meaning (he labels it the "code conception of meaning") is radically misguided.[31] The argument is intended to show that the significance of an utterance is not explained by appeal to speakers' thoughts, where those thoughts are conceived without reference to language. Dummett's criticism of ideational theories of meaning is in effect a criticism of the conception of thought they embody. I shall begin my criticism of the conception of mind that lies behind the reductive Gricean account of meaning with Dummett's argument. This argument, as I understand it, embodies a criticism of the conception of thought that lies behind the ideational account of meaning.

The real problem with the ideational, or code, conception of meaning is that it models someone's mastery of his mother tongue on his mastery of a second language. Why this is the model the ideational theorist must be working with is easy to explain. The ideational theorist attempts to account for the significance of utterances by appeal to thoughts. Thoughts are taken to have a significance that simply gets transferred to the utterance. How thoughts come by their significance is not something these theorists spend much time on. Similarly, when the speaker of one language learns another, we think of him as beginning with a firm grasp of his native tongue and devising translations between this and the new language that confronts him. His understanding of the *first* language is taken for granted; it does not present a problem for us. We explain his understanding of the new language by reference to his understanding of the old one.

What is open to question is whether the model of learning a *second* language is the correct model for a theorist of meaning to be working with. We may break down the process of coming to acquire a second language into two abilities: the ability to understand one's native tongue and the ability to translate sentences of the new language into sentences of the old. These two abilities are in principle separable. We can imagine a rather complex computer being programmed to match sentences of one language with sentences of another without *understanding* either. What this observation teaches us is that the ability to translate does not by itself presuppose an understanding of the second language like the understanding someone has of his mother tongue. When we consider the process of learning a second language, we need only presuppose an understanding of the first, or native language. The problem of how we understand that first language need not arise if what we seek to explain is how we learn *another* language. However, no such presupposition can be made if what we seek to explain is the understanding we have of our mother tongue. But the ideational theorist just is in the business of explaining our understanding of our first language, and so the model of learning a *second* language is inappropriate. To assume an understanding of concepts and thoughts is merely to push the problem back one step. Once we do that, we seem to be at a loss to explain what we set out to explain, namely, our understanding of our mother tongue. As it stands, the ideational theory of meaning is either circular or incomplete.

The question then arises whether the ideational theory can be completed in a satisfactory manner. It is Dummett's contention that we can complete the ideational theory with a move which renders the theory itself unnecessary. If we return to the model of learning a second language, we notice that translation consists in matching a word or sentence of the new language with a word or sentence of one's native tongue. Perhaps, then, the problem with using this model to help us to understand our native language in terms of already existing thoughts and concepts is that we lack representations of thoughts and concepts to match with our sentences and words. If this is the problem, we need only posit mental representations (images or ideas), which can serve to match or link concepts and thoughts to words and sentences. But again we are left with the question: What is it to associate a concept or thought with such a representation? The question of *understanding* has not been answered until we can give some explanation of this.[32]

At this point Dummett suggests that we step back from our problem for a moment and ask a slightly different question, namely, what is it to grasp the concept of, say, square? And he gives the following reply: "At the very least, it is to be able to discriminate between things that are square and those that are not." He continues:

> Such an ability can be ascribed only to one who will, on occasion, treat square things differently from things that are not square; one way, among other possible ways, of doing this is to apply the word "square" to square things and not to others. And it can only be by reference to some such use of the word "square" . . . that we can explain what it is to associate the concept square with that word. An ability to use the word in such a way . . . would, by itself, suffice as a manifestation of a grasp of that concept.[33]

Once we realize that the correct use of a word would suffice as a manifestation of a grasp of a certain concept, we no longer need to ask how a concept or thought comes to be associated with a word or sentence. Nor do we need to ask what it is to associate a concept or thought with a representation. Indeed, we can now see that the conception of a thought as something that lies behind the utterance and gets communicated with the help of the utterance gives rise to the problems in the first place. That model only postpones the question of what understanding consists in, and it provides no hints for an answer. Alternatively, if we take thought to be essentially bound up with linguistic behavior and not conceivable in isolation from it, the problem of how to associate thought with behavior cannot arise.

I want to note three things about this argument of Dummett's. First, the argument does not show ideational theories to be irreparable. What it does is to point to a major incompleteness in the theory. It suggests a more complete picture and notes that this picture has no need to make reference to anything beyond language and its use. It remains open to the ideational theorist to propose a way of completing his picture. I agree that the burden of argument now rests on the ideational theorist, and that the burden looks to be intolerable, but the possibility still remains. Second, note that although Dummett moves from the question, What is it to associate a concept or thought with a word or sentence? to the question, What is it to grasp a concept or thought? he could just as well have begun by presenting the ideational theorist with *both* questions. Until both questions are given a satisfactory reply, the ideational theory of meaning is only marking time. And third, it strikes me that Dummett has missed the opportunity to develop his picture of what it is to grasp a thought or concept so that it includes attributing concepts and thoughts to the languageless. I now want to propose such an extension.

Dummett asks what it is to associate a concept or thought with a bit of linguistic behavior. Difficulty in giving an answer to this question leads him to ask a slightly different one: What is it to grasp a thought or concept in the first place? The answer he offers to the latter question is such that it is no longer necessary to think of concepts and thoughts as existing in independence from their expression in language. A proper understanding of what it is to grasp a concept or thought leaves no room for the question, What is it to associate a concept or thought with a bit of language? But what about the thoughts of the languageless? If we accept that the languageless can have thoughts,[34] how are we to understand these thoughts? We might agree that when we ordinarily attribute thoughts to a languageless individual, we do so on the basis of its behavior. If we accept the picture of thought that the ideational theorist is working with—the picture of thought as essentially independent of behavior—we might ask how the behavior we use to attribute thoughts to another comes to have the relationship it does to those thoughts. Failing to see a direct way to answer this question, we may ask what it is to grasp the thought or concept said to be associated with this nonlinguistic behavior. We may model a reply to this question on Dummett's reply to the parallel question concerning our grasp of the thoughts and concepts that we associate with linguistic behavior. We could say that the ability to perform intentional *actions* would suffice as a manifestation of certain concepts and thoughts.[35]

Once we realize that the ability to perform actions in the world would suffice as a manifestation of a concept or thought, we have no need to ask how a particular concept or thought gets associated with a piece of nonlinguistic behavior. Once again we see that the problem we had in answering this question arises from a certain conception of thought, a conception of thought as something lying behind behavior and characterizable in independence of it. To understand what it is to grasp a nonlinguistic thought is to understand what it is to manifest such a thought in nonlinguistic behavior. The notion of a thought characterizable in independence of behavior finds no place here.[36]

What this argument and Dummett's original one show is that postulating concepts and thoughts that bear no essential relation to linguistic or nonlinguistic behavior gives rise to problems that have yet to be addressed adequately. The ideational theorist of meaning speaks of utterances as "external signs" of thought, and this metaphor can be extended to the relationship thought has to nonlinguistic behavior. But at some point the metaphor must be abandoned and the relationship between thought and behavior addressed; the metaphor only serves to mask the problem. Once we begin to face the problem, we soon realize that not only is the relationship between thought and behavior problematic; there is the prior problem of accounting for thought itself. It seems that we do better to abandon the conception of thought that gives rise to these problems. In other words, we do better to rid ourselves of a conception of thought that takes it to be something accessible in independence of the ordinary, behavioral evidence.

Dummett suggests that we cease picturing language as a code for thought and accept that "the only effective means of studying thought is by the study of language which is its vehicle".[37] Once we do this, says Dummett, we see that the philosophy of language is a particularly significant part of philosophy because it is part of the study of thought itself. Without wishing to contradict this, I would add that the study of thought involves us in the study of behavior quite generally—nonlinguistic as well as linguistic. Trying to understand thought without taking into account the thinker's behavior is like traveling down a blind alley.

Now it strikes me that the reductive Gricean has been tempted down the same blind alley as the ideational theorist. The Gricean who aims to reduce the semantic to the psychological is committed to giving an account of the psychological that has no recourse to the semantic. It follows that the Gricean sees the psychological as conceivable in independence of its manifestation in linguistic behavior. The reductive Gricean, then, is faced with the same problems as the ideational theorist.

However, as I noted earlier, Dummett's argument does not show that ideational theories are irreparable. It remains open to the ideational theorist to propose a way of completing his picture. The same can be said for the reductive Gricean. Now my aim is not simply to point out that the reductive Gricean has more work to do.[38] Rather, I want to show that, in addition to having to address the problems raised by the Dummettian argument, the reductive Gricean is committed to an objective conception of mind. This commitment arises in the following way. The Gricean, in order to maintain his reduction, is committed to some sort of asymmetry between the semantic and the psychological. In the face of evidence of a surface epistemological symmetry, the Gricean retreats to the claim that there is a deep epistemological asymmetry between the semantic and the psychological and argues that observations at the surface can be divorced from these deeper matters. It is this deep asymmetry alone that needs to be reflected in one's theory of what the propositional attitudes are in themselves. In other words, to maintain a reduction of the semantic to the psychological, the Gricean must divorce his theory of the propositional attitudes from their manifestation in linguistic behavior. Linguistic behavior, he holds, is only contingently related to those attitudes. In this chapter and the previous one I argued that denying that mind is manifest in linguistic behavior is common to both Cartesian and reductive physicalist theories of mind. I also argued that these theories embody a conception of mind as an objective phenomenon. I now want to say that *any* theory that denies that mind is manifest in linguistic behavior—that is, any theory that makes the relation between mind and linguistic behavior merely contingent— embodies an objective conception of mind. And since the Gricean is committed by his reductionism to holding that the mind is only contingently related to linguistic behavior, he is *ipso facto* committed to an objective conception of mind. If I am right, then the Gricean faces not only the problems facing any account of mind that aims to divorce mind from any essential connection with ordinary evidence but also he faces the problem that his conception of mind is inconsistent with the essentially subjective nature of mind.

I shall soon give my reasons for saying that any theory, and so any reductive Gricean theory, that divorces mind from any essential links with linguistic behavior embodies a mistaken conception of mind. But before I do, I want to consider an objection. It is this. By concentrating my efforts on Cartesianism and reductive physicalism, I have obscured a more plausible account of mind, the one most often appealed to by reductive Griceans. The theory I have overlooked is functionalism. Functionalism is particularly appealing to the Gricean because it extends the possibility that we can account for the propositional attitudes without making essential reference to linguistic behavior, while at the same time it makes reference to behavior (nonlinguistically characterized) an essential element of the proposed account of mind. The hope, then, is that functionalism affords the Gricean a way of reconciling his reduction of the semantic to the psychological with an account of the latter that does justice to the ordinary evidence. My objector will point out that if reference to behavior in one's theory of mind is what characterizes a subjective conception of mind, as opposed to an objective conception of mind, a functionalist theory of mind gives us a subjective conception of mind. If the Gricean is a functionalist, rather than a Cartesian or a reductive physicalist, he can avoid the mistaken picture of mind. Furthermore, given the way the functionalist brings behavior into his account of mind, the Gricean can avoid the problems posed by Dummett's argument. I turn now to a brief discussion of the functionalist account of mind.

3 Functionalism

One way of characterizing functionalism is this: according to functionalism "each type of mental state is a state consisting of a disposition to act in certain ways and to have certain mental states, given certain sensory outputs and certain mental states."[39] It is sometimes claimed that such an account of mental states is a substantial advance over both behaviorist and certain physicalist accounts and that it avoids many of the problems encountered by these earlier accounts. Functionalism, then, may be seen to be the heir to these two reductive accounts of mind.

One reason that functionalism is thought to be an advance over behaviorism is that in contrast to behaviorism it does not deny that mental states may be a real part of the causal explanatory order. In fact, functionalism attempts to say what mental states *are*. And this advance is related to another one. The behaviorist attempts to analyze mental states in terms of dispositions to behavior. Thus, for example, a behaviorist might claim that a desire to listen to music is a disposition to play a record. However, the desire to listen to music may also be a disposition to go to a concert or to ask a friend to sing. Indeed, it seems that mental states, if they are dispositions at all, are dispositions to a wide range of behavior; they are what Ryle called "multi-traced dispositions." However, the move from single to multitracked dispositions does not solve all the behaviorist's problems. For example, Susie's desire to listen to music will dispose her to go to a concert only if she believes that there is a concert on offer and she has no objection to traveling to the concert hall. In other words, we cannot attribute a particular mental disposition without reference to *other* mental states of the individual. There seems to be no way of eliminating such outright reference to other mental states. This problem is sometimes summed up by saying that behaviorism fails to account for the holism of the mental. Functionalism, on the other hand, is specifically designed to take account of the holistic nature of the mental: mental states are defined not only with reference to their perceptual inputs and behavioral outputs but also with reference to other internal states of the organism.

By thus identifying mental states functionalism proves also to be an advance over an early form of physicalism sometimes referred to as central-state materialism.[40] Central-state materialists are type physicalists.[41] They hold that mental states and events are reducible to physical states and events. Once such a reduction has been established, it has the effect of denying mentality to creatures lacking a certain physical state-type. Functionalism, in contrast, is not restrictive in this way. It allows for what has been termed a "variable realization" of the mental by identifying mentality not with a first-order property of systems (as central state materialism does) but with a second-order property of systems.[42] A functional property is a property of a property. In this way functionalism allows what central-state materialism does not: that creatures without brain stuff in their skulls may still qualify as sentient, cognitive beings.[43]

Functionalism can allow for the variable realization of the mental because it tacks the mental down not to a particular kind of stuff but to input, output, and other inner states of the organism. By appealing to working systems rather than to what realizes them, functionalism manages to preserve not only our intuition that no nontrivial first-order physical property is shared by all realizations of the mental but also our intuition that the mental must be characterized with reference to behavior. Precisely for this reason one may think that functionalism is a reductive account of mind that can avoid the conception of mind I have attributed to reductive physicalists and Cartesians.

I want to argue that despite explicit mention of behavior in the account of mental states, the functionalist picture of mind still embodies a conception of mind as something accessible in independence of the ordinary evidence. To see this, we must look more closely at the way functionalism brings reference to behavior into its account of mental states.

When introducing functionalism, I said that it has some claim to being a descendant of two reductive accounts of mind, behaviorism and central-state materialism. Functionalism too is a reductive view of mind, it "reduces mentality to input-output structures."[44] To serve as a reduction, the functionalist characterization of mental states must be careful, of course, not to make ineliminable reference to anything mental. But the characterization of functionalism that I mentioned at the outset of this section does not seem to meet this requirement of reduction. That characterization makes reference to input, output, and other *mental* states. The functionalist claims, however, that the requirement of reduction *can* be met by a more elaborate and careful characterization of functionalism. One example of this is a widely held version of functionalism offered by David Lewis.[45] Lewis proposes that we take mental terms to be theoretical terms and that we define our mental-theoretical terms by reference to the platitudes of a commonsense psychological theory. This cluster of platitudes will serve to define mental states by marking out their causal relations to stimuli, responses, and each other. Lewis suggests that we define mental-theoretical terms in the following way: Assemble the commonsense platitudes, and think of them as containing both theoretical terms (the psychological terms) and nontheoretical terms (whatever is left over once the psychological terms have been accounted for); convert each mental-theoretical predicate into a name; and replace all the nominalized mental-theoretical terms with free variables. We can then approach the original theory with the existential closure of the derived open formula and the additional demand that the theory have a unique realization. We can then say that the defining theory contains input and output terms but no specifically *mental* terminology. In this way the functionalist can avoid making ineliminable reference to the mental in his characterization of it.

All the weight of the functionalist characterization of the mental then falls on the characterization of input and output. How exactly are input and output to be characterized? Block has convincingly argued that in its characterization of input and output, functionalism falls into the trap of being either too liberal or too chauvinist. That is, either functionalism ends up attributing mental states to systems that don't truly warrant such ascriptions (liberalism), or it falsely restricts the attribution of mental states to systems that share some characteristic deemed important (chauvinism). Let me explain why this is so. First consider chauvinism. If we return for a moment to Lewis's theoretical definition of mental states, we find Lewis suggesting the following as the *form* of our commonsense platitudes, "When someone is in so & so combination of mental states and receives sensory stimuli of so & so kind, he tends with so & so probability to be caused thereby to go into so & so mental states and produce so & so motor responses."[46] This, according to Lewis, gets filled out in accordance with commonsense psychological theory by mentioning objects present in the vicinity of the organism on the input side and movements of arms and legs on the output side. But such a characterization is clearly species specific: one can imagine a snakelike creature with no arms or legs suffering pain, for example; and there may be creatures with minds who communicate and manipulate by emitting strong magnetic fields. Perhaps we should abandon our commonsense platitudes in our characterization of mental states and define mental states by reference to the most current scientific theory. This would yield, say, a neural characterization of input and output. But this proposal makes us no better off. Such a characterization is equally species specific.

Not only do the proffered characterizations of input and output incur the charge of chauvinism, but Block offers an argument designed to show that *any physical* characterization of inputs and outputs will yield a version of functionalism that is inevitably either chauvinist or liberal. The argument is as follows. Imagine that your body has been seriously injured and that your best way to communicate is by modulating your EEG pattern in Morse code. It works like this: you find that thinking certain exciting thoughts produces a pattern your audience can interpret as a dot, while thinking a dull thought produces a dash. Imagine the process reversed: others communicate with you in Morse code by producing bursts of electrical activity that affect your brain by causing long or short afterimages. In such an event we might say that the brain itself has become an essential part of your input and output devices. Earlier we noted that functionalism claimed to be an advance over a physicalism of the central-state materialist variety precisely because the former can allow for the variable realization of mental states, whereas the latter cannot. But, Block argues, "if this functionalist point against physicalism is right, *the same point applies to inputs and outputs,* since the physical realization of mental states can serve as an essential part of the input and output devices. That is, on any sense of 'physical' in which the functionalist criticism of physicalism is correct, *there will be no physical characterization that applies to all and only mental systems' inputs and outputs.*"[47] The conclusion of this argument is that *any physical* characterization of inputs and outputs will yield a version of functionalism that is either chauvinist or liberal.

At this point the functionalist may retreat from a physical characterization of inputs and outputs and say that all he needs to do is to enumerate inputs and outputs, characterizing them in no way other than as inputs and outputs. This move would certainly avoid the charge of chauvinism, but it seems unable to avoid the charge of liberalism. We would have no way of distinguishing between mental systems and, say, economic systems. The latter, like the former, have inputs and outputs and a rich variety of internal states. Block imagines that a wealthy shiek gains control of the economy of a small country like Bolivia and manipulates its financial system until it is functionally equivalent to himself.[48] Unless we have some way of restricting the characterization of input and output, it seems that the functionalist has to attribute a mind to the shiek's contrived system. But, Block writes, "if there are any fixed points when discussing the mind-body problem, one of them is that the economy of Bolivia could not have mental states, no matter how it is distorted by powerful hobbyists."[49]

There is one move remaining for the functionalist: characterize inputs and outputs in mental terms. This would avoid the chauvinism to which characterization in some specific physical terms leads, as well as the liberalism to which characterization in neutral terms leads. The problem with this move is that it is blatantly (i.e., viciously) circular. The problem is noted by Armstrong when he considers the reference to behavioral output in the functionalist characterization of mental states. He writes:

> We may distinguish between "physical behaviour", which refers to any merely physical action or passion of the body, and "behaviour proper" which implies relationship to the mind. . . . Now, if in our functionalist formula "behaviour" were to mean "behaviour proper", then we would be giving an account of mental concepts in terms of a concept which would be circular. So it is clear that in our formula, "behaviour" must mean "physical behaviour".[50]

To avoid the problem of circularity, Armstrong opts for a purely physical characterization of behavior, but if Block is right, this leads inevitably to either chauvinism or liberalism.

Block has touched on a substantial criticism of functionalism, reminiscent of the type of criticism aimed at its reductive predecessors. As Block admits, however, it is only a "burden of proof argument" and is not meant to be a conclusive argument against functionalism. Block has merely challenged the functionalist to come up with a characterization of input and output that is neither chauvinist nor liberal nor circular. It is clear that Block does not expect that the functionalist will be able to meet his challenge. I would like to press the point against the functionalist and suggest a reason why the functionalist *cannot* meet the challenge Block has presented. The reason is that the functionalist, with his reductionist inclinations, is bound to misinterpret the way in which behavior is relevant to the characterization of the mind.

In the previous section I argued that unless we take behavior to be the manifestation of our grasp of various concepts and thoughts, we run up against the dual problem of explaining in what our grasp of concepts and thoughts consists and how our concepts and thoughts are related to the behavior that makes them available to others. These problems arise whether we consider simple thoughts and their relation to nonlinguistic behavior or more complex thoughts and their relation to linguistic behavior. Dummett has claimed that the ability to use language would suffice for the manifestation of a grasp of a concept or thought; extending the point, I claimed that the ability to perform intentional actions would suffice for manifestation of a grasp of certain (simple) concepts and thoughts. I argued that to deny that mind is manifest in behavior is to place it behind behavior, as it were, and to contemplate a mode of access to another's mind alternative to the ordinary mode of access. I rejected the idea that only when we transcend the ordinary mode of access to the mind of another can we appreciate what the mind is in itself, can we appreciate the nature of pure mind. This attempt to find the mind in itself led Descartes to view mind as something utterly mysterious both in itself and in its relations with the body. Then in an attempt to naturalize the mind and demystify it and its relations, philosophers were led by this attempt to find the mind in itself to a view of mind as something purely physical.

I claimed that to divorce our theory of what the propositional attitudes are in themselves from how we ordinarily attribute them to another is in effect to objectify the mind. That is, by divorcing mind from behavior we suggest that mind is the sort of thing that can be studied from an external and impersonal point of view. I claimed also that the Cartesian and reductive physicalist both objectify the mind in this way and that because of this conception of mind they run into the problems outlined above.

In this section I have been considering the suggestion that a functionalist theory of mind can avoid both the problems and the conception of mind of the Cartesian and reductive physicalist theories. The functionalist claims to avoid an objective conception of mind by adverting to behavioral output in his characterization of mind. Furthermore, the functionalist is not open to the problems raised by Dummett's argument, since his theory cannot be accused of conceiving of mind as lying behind the behavior that makes it available to others. I now want to argue that despite appearances, the functionalist is working with an objective conception of mind and does face problems *parallel* to those faced by the Cartesian and reductive physicalist.

To understand that the functionalist is committed to an objective conception of mind, one must understand that the objective conception as I have characterized it is divorced from the *ordinary* evidence for attributing propositional attitudes. To avoid this conception, one's theory of mind must not simply bring in reference to behavior but must understand it as, in Armstrong's words, "behaviour proper." That is, the behavior that forms as essential part of the theory of mind must be behavior mentalistically characterized. As we have seen, however, the functionalist's characterization of the behavioral output that forms part of this definition of mind must be in terms of what Armstrong called "physical behaviour." If the functionalist were to characterize the output as behavior proper, it would make his definition blatantly and viciously circular. The reason for this is that the functionalist is in the business of constructing a *reductive* account of mind. My point is that if certain sorts of behavior manifest a grasp of certain concepts and thoughts, the relevant behavior is not physical behaviour. The behavior that manifests a grasp of certain concepts and thoughts is behavior infused with mentality; it is behavior proper. Of course, to say this is to be committed to a circular account of mental states and events, but the circle is not vicious if reduction is not one's goal. My reason for understanding the relevant behavior in this way is that by doing this, one can avoid an objective conception of mind. A theory of mind that characterizes mental states and events in terms of behavior proper represents the mind as a subjective phenomenon. (I will explain why this is so in the next section.)

The functionalist, then, cannot accept my insistence on the importance of behavior mentalistically or semantically characterized to our concept of thought. The functionalist who is also a Gricean would insist that we can characterize the psychological without reference to interpreted behavior (behavior proper), and he would insist that we can reconstruct the semantic in terms of the psychological, nonmentalistically characterized. But now he is committed, along with the Cartesian and reductive physicalist, to an objective conception of mind. The functionalist may try to gain some ground by pointing out that his view of mind can at least avoid the problems raised by Dummet's argument. Granted this point, he will argue that I cannot hold that *any* theory that embodies an objective conception of mind will run up against such problems.

I agree that the functionalist does not face the problems raised by Dummett's arguments in exactly the same form as does the Cartesian and reductive physicalist. Nevertheless, it takes only a slight modification of that argument to bring out a parallel problem for the functionalist. The problem for the functionalist is this: having committed himself to a nonmental characterization of inputs and outputs, the functionalist must say what distinguishes mental systems from other nonmental systems that share a similar functional organization.

The Cartesian tries to explain the significance of behavior by reference to hidden thought. This leads to such questions as, How does a thought come by *its* significance? and, How is this significance imparted to behavior? The central-state materialist too tries to conjure up significance from somewhere other than behavior itself. The advantage of his brand of physicalism over Cartesianism is that central-state materialism makes no reference to hidden or occult occurrences; the significance of the behavior comes from things potentially open to the objective view of humans. The functionalist also hopes to avoid a mystery: a thought's significance is understood by reference to such things as perceptual input and behavioral output nonmentalistically characterized. But the old question still remains for the functionalist: How do such physical systems come by their significance?

By characterizing behavior in this way, the functionalist, like the Cartesian and the central-state materialist, is divorcing his theory of what the propositional attitudes are in themselves from our ordinary evidence for what another believes, intends, and the like. The functionalist too envisages a mode of access to the mind of another alternative to the ordinary mode of access. In this way the functionalist objectifies the mind, makes it out to be something that can be observed and understood from an external and impersonal point of view. This is particularly apparent if we consider Loar's brand of functionalism. In one place Loar writes: "For on the functionalist interpretation of the belief-desire theory, scientific discoveries in psychology and physiology will be relevant and even telling. So the standard scheme does not contain all the principles via which belief-desire ascription could be confirmed, but rather those we normally rely on in our use of the theory."[51] The ordinary mode of access to the mind of another (the "standard scheme") involves interpreted behavior or behavior proper, but Loar foresees scientific discoveries that will enable us to bypass behavior so characterized. Once again, we find that the mind has been divorced from its manifestation in behavior, which we rely on only in commonsense theory. Loar is then faced with the problem of explaining how this uninterpreted functional system that science reveals relates to the interpreted subject of common sense.

Yet the functionalist, may still wish to press his case. True, Loar's version of functionalism relies on scientific discoveries in constructing a theory of propositional attitudes, but this is not true of all versions of functionalism. Earlier I mentioned such a version of functionalism, one that defines mental states by reference to the ordinary platitudes of common sense. Someone who holds this version of functionalism may argue that he can avoid the criticism that he has objectified the mind, since his theory of what the propositional attitudes are in themselves is *not* divorced from ordinary evidence. In reply to this I would point out that what I mean by "ordinary evidence" is behavior mentalistically characterized, and this no functionalist can accept without having to abandon his hope of *reducing* the mental to something else. As a reduction, a functional account of mind that makes reference to behavior mentalistically characterized is hopelessly circular, yet without falling into this circularity, the functionalist cannot incorporate what I have been calling the correct view of mind into his characterization of mentality.

At this point the functionalist may insist that the ordinary evidence for what another is thinking is ultimately not behavior mentalistically characterized. It may only seem to be so if we take as our model the everyday ascriptions of mental states to another whose language and culture is familiar to us. The functionalist may point out that in the case of radical interpretation our evidence for ascribing mental states to another is *not* mentalistically characterized. Here the evidence for what another is thinking is physical behavior. The radical interpreter uses physical behavior as the basis for his interpretation. Ultimately, the functionalist argues, the ordinary evidence for what another believes, intends, and the like is behavior nonmentalistically characterized. My mistake, according to the functionalist, can be summarized this way: By considering the ordinary evidence for attributing mental states to another, I am looking at only a superficial phenomenon. Upon closer inspection what we find is that the basis for ascribing mental states to another is behavior physically characterized. Once this is recognized, there can be no objection to a theory that incorporates this observation into its characterization of what the propositional attitudes are in themselves. Such a theory may be reductionist, but it does not divorce our theory of the propositional attitudes from facts about our ordinary evidence for ascribing mental states to another. The functionalist will point out that reduction itself is the only issue dividing us; we must ultimately agree on how the ordinary evidence should be characterized.

But I do not agree. I stand by my claim that the ordinary evidence must be mentalistically characterized. If the functionalist has properly characterized the case of radical interpretation, then radical interpretation, I would say, cannot be used as our model in the home case. The home case is the *ordinary* case, and there we do *not* begin with mere physical behavior and add to this an interpretation; rather, we begin with mentalistically characterized behavior. What we observe is behavior infused with mentality. And even in the radical case, I would argue, we do not begin with mere physical behavior. It is true that we are in the dark about what interpretation to give an alien's behavior, but we must assume that his behavior has *some interpretation or other*. Our task as radical interpreters is to discover which interpretation is appropriate, and this we do by becoming more familiar with our subject's ways. Thus, even in the case of radical interpretation it is inappropriate to say that our evidence for what another is thinking is mere physical behavior.

It seems to me that only by construing the evidence in the way I do can we avoid an objective conception of mind. I conclude, then, that Cartesianism and *all* forms of reductive physicalism are ultimately committed to what I have been calling a mistaken view of mind. These theories of mind are all committed to viewing the mind as an essentially objective phenomenon, something that can be contemplated and understood from an external and impersonal perspective. My reason for saying this is that all these theorists persist in divorcing their theory of what the propositional attitudes are in themselves from the ordinary evidence. In their theory of what the propositional attitudes are in themselves both Cartesians and central-state materialists fail to make reference to behavior; the functionalist makes reference to behavior in his theory of the propositional attitudes but fails to appreciate that the relevant behavior must be mentalistically characterized. In section 5 I shall explain how accepting that the ordinary evidence must form part of our theory of what the propositional attitudes are in themselves commits us as well to a symmetry between the semantic and the psychological. In the next section I shall explain how what I have been calling the correct view of mind, the view that takes mind to be essentially connected with the behavior that manifests it, can avoid an objective conception of mind and, more important, how this view of mind fits in with a subjective conception of mind.

4 A Subjective Conception of Mind

Let us begin with the essentially Cartesian observation that the subject bears a particular and peculiar relationship to his own mental life. I suggest that we understand this observation thus: the mind is manifest to the subject in a subjective form that either involves a point of view or has an experiential (or phenomenological) quality. This observation lies at the heart of a subjective conception of mind. The question is, How are we to understand this observation? In section 2 I argued that Cartesians misunderstand this observation by trying to explain it as the subject's having a special, direct relation to a special, immaterial substance. I claimed that this understanding leads to the following understanding of the third-person perspective on the mind of another: the immaterial substance of another's mind is by its very nature the sort of thing that can be observed directly, without the aid of intermediaries such as behavior. It is not something accessible to humans, but we may take it to be the prerogative of certain imagined individuals. Realizing this, I claimed, highlights the barrenness of the Cartesian understanding of the first-person perspective. The mind is thought to be essentially comprehensible from an impersonal, external point of view. It is conceived on the model of an objective phenomenon. I argued that this conception of mind is inherited by reductive physicalists and modern day functionalists.

By concentrating on the first-person perspective on mind, we may be mislead as to the true nature of mind. And this may be the case despite the fact that this perspective is crucial to a proper understanding of mind. I suggest that we begin, rather, with a third-person perspective. My discussion of Cartesianism, reductive physicalism, and functionalism reveals that we must be very careful how we understand this third-person perspective if we want to avoid an objective conception of mind. In particular, we must not conceive of the mind of another as lying "behind" his behavior, or as needing to be reconstructed from observations of physical behavior. What the interpreter begins with is not mere physical behavior; he observes behavior proper. Behavior proper is behavior infused with mentality, behavior mentalistically characterized. It is interpreted behavior.[52] If we understand matters this way, we are on the path of conceiving the mind as a subjective phenomenon.

Understanding the concept of behavior proper requires that we understand two things. First, we must understand that only a genuine subject, a subject of experiences and points of view, can exhibit behavior proper. Only the behavior of a subject qualifies as behavior proper, as distinct from mere physical behavior. Furthermore, one can appreciate behavior as behaviour proper only if one is oneself a subject of experiences and points of view. In other words, we can understand and interpret another's behavior only if we are sufficiently similar to our subject.[53] Being a subject of consciousness with experiences similar to the subject whose behaviour we are observing puts us in a position to see the world as our subject sees it, to experience the world as he experiences it, and thereby to appreciate the thoughts and feelings that his behavior manifests. This way of understanding the third-person perspective on the mind of another leaves no room for imagined godlike creatures or superneuroscientists. There is no room here for an impersonal and external point of view on the mind of another. Understanding another's mind is firmly tied to understanding it from a particular point of view. By correctly understanding the way behavior figures in our conception of mind, by understanding that a mind is manifest in and does not lie behind or beyond behavior, we understand both what it is to be a subject of experiences and points of view and what it is to appreciate others as subjects of experiences and points of view.

A correct understanding of the third-person perspective on the mind of another thus leads us to a conception of mind as a subjective phenomenon. With this perspective on the mind we can conclude that our concept of mind is the concept of something manifest to the subject in experience and points of view and manifest through behavior to others, who are themselves subjects of experiences and points of view. Our concept of mind thus unites first- and third-person perspectives and does so in such a way as to allow us to conclude that we are dealing with an essentially subjective phenomenon. The existence of this subjective phenomenon is bound up with its being manifest to, or appearing in this or that way to, a perceiving, sentient creature. We cannot think of it as simply there; rather, we must think of it as there *for someone.* A commitment to the idea that mind is manifest in behavior is a commitment to the idea that ordinary evidence cannot be ignored in one's theory of mind.

The conclusion of this discussion is that the view of mind that takes it to be manifest in behavior and that eschews all talk of contingent relations to behavior is a view of mind as a subjective phenomenon. The way all of this ties up with my discussion of the reductive Gricean is as follows. Because the Gricean, is committed to a reduction of the semantic to the psychological, he is forced to deny that mind is manifest in, specifically, linguistic behavior. This is simply part of the reductive Gricean's commitment to the idea that the ordinary evidence for the attribution of beliefs and intentions to others forms no part of the theory of what those propositional attitudes are in themselves. Furthermore, insofar as the Gricean is either a Cartesian, a reductive physicalist, or a functionalist, he is committed also to an objective conception of mind. Ultimately, I want to show that all reductive Griceans are committed to an objective conception of mind by their reduction, which forces them to deny that mind is manifest in linguistic behavior.[54] Thus far I have argued that a subjective conception of mind is consistent with the idea that mind is manifest in behavior. To establish that all reductive Griceans are committed to an objective conception of mind I must show not only that a subjective conception of mind is consistent with the idea that mind is manifest in behavior but that a subjective conception of mind is *inconsistent* with the idea that mind is only contingently related to behavior. Only if I can do this will I be able to say that *all* reductive Griceans, not just those who hold a Cartesian or reductive physicalist or functionalist account of mind, are working with an objective conception of mind.

My position is this: to deny that the mind is manifest in behavior is *ipso facto* to deny its essential subjectivity and to be committed to an objective conception. A possible objection to my position might be framed as follows. What is essential to a subjective conception of mind is that such a conception never lose sight of what I have called the particular and peculiar relation a subject bears to his own mental life. It is possible to construct such a conception without bringing in any essential reference to the subject's behavior. Another way to put the objection is this: so long as we firmly hold to the first-person perspective on mind, there is no need to make essential reference to the third-person perspective as well. Thus, claims the objector, we can form a properly subjective conception of mind and still *deny* that mind is manifest in behavior. There is, then, no route from the reductive Gricean's denial that mind is manifest in behavior to a commitment to an objective view of mind. In short, the objector holds that a properly subjective conception of mind is consistent with the idea that mind is only contingently related to behavior.

I confess that I am unable to prove this objection to be mistaken, but I nevertheless believe that the position just outlined is misguided. First, it is important to see that however compelling such a conception may appear, it is by no means the only available account of subjectivity. The point of my discussion in this section was to show that we can develop a subjective conception of mind that unites first- and third-person perspectives on mind. The existence of this alternative puts pressure on the objector to put forward some reason for thinking that his view of mind is the correct one.

Furthermore, we saw in section 2 that by divorcing mind from its manifestation in behavior, the theorist runs up against certain problems. I presented those problems through an argument most recently advanced by Dummett and then developed the argument so that we could see how it affects those who choose to divorce mind from not physical behavior but behavior proper. My objector's view of mind is open to these arguments and so is less attractive than a view of mind that can avoid these problems and still maintain an essentially subjective conception of mind.

Finally, I want to ask why my objector is so keen to stand by a view that is not necessary and that only leads to further, very difficult problems? I believe the answer is that this objector, like so many before him, has succumbed, however inadvertently, to an objective conception of mind. Of course this is not obvious, or he would not appear to have an objection to my conclusion concerning the reductive Gricean. Like the Cartesian, my objector insists that by concentrating on the first-person perspective on mind, he can come up with a purely subjective conception of the mind that involves no essential connections to behavior. But no real understanding of this first-person perspective has been advanced, and we have seen how one proposal to understand it, the Cartesian, runs straight into an objective conception of mind. I conclude that the theorist who aims to divorce the subjective conception of mind from any essential connection to behavior has illicitly assimilated his conception to an objective conception of mind. What stands in the way of our seeing this is the inchoate nature of the suggestion.[55]

One way to see that such an assimilation has occurred is to ask oneself *why* there is this temptation to divorce mind from its manifestation in behaviour. If one *begins* with an objective conception of mind, as the Cartesian and the reductive physicalist do, it will be very clear that minds are essentially independent of behavior. But the claim is that this objective conception has been dropped in favor of a subjective conception of mind. Why, then, maintain a feature so central to the discarded conception: essential independence from behavior? Freedom from the objective model should free us as well from this way of thinking of the relationship between mind and behavior.

5 The Semantic and the Psychological

My contention is that the reductive Gricean is committed to what I have been calling a mistaken view of mind. I argued first that the Gricean is not in a position to accept a view of the mind that takes it to be manifest in linguistic behavior and then that because of this, he is committed to an objective conception of mind. Many reductive Griceans explicitly commit themselves to an objective conception of mind by holding either a reductive physicalist or a functionalist theory of mind, that is, a theory that takes mind to be an objective phenomenon. As the result of my discussion in the previous section we may conclude that any Gricean who aims to reduce the semantic to the psychological is thereby committed to some objective conception of mind. One may reason that since he aims to reduce the semantic to the psychological, the Gricean is committed to an objective conception of the psychological, or one may say that since he is working with an objective conception of the psychological, the Gricean naturally aims to reduce the semantic to the psychological.

But the reductive Gricean may wish to dispute my claims concerning his commitments. He may want to argue that he can consistently maintain that there is an asymmetry between our concepts of the semantic and the psychological and at the same time embrace what I am calling the correct view of mind. He may point out that all I have said in section 2 is that the correct picture of mind takes it to be manifest in behavior; nothing I said there commits him to accepting that mind is manifest in specifically *linguistic* behaviour. The reductive Gricean may propose that we look at things in the following way: first, reconstruct the semantic in terms of the purely psychological (this is what the Gricean analysis is meant to do), and then give an account of the psychological concepts employed on the right-hand side of the biconditional which takes into account the way in which psychological states issue in behaviour proper (albeit nonlinguistic behavior proper). [56] In this way the Gricean claims to avoid commitment to what I am calling a mistaken view of mind.[57]

In this section I shall argue that the position envisaged by the reductive Gricean is not really plausible. As I see it, the correct picture of mind is incompatible with a reduction of the semantic to the psychological. I shall argue that when correctly understood, the picture of mind that the reductive Gricean is now so keen to embrace requires that we see our concepts of the semantic and the psychological as working together, neither fully understood without reference to the other. This rules out a reductive interpretation of the Gricean analysis.

I want to approach this matter by returning to an issue raised and discussed in chapter 3, the issue of ontological asymmetry. In that chapter I claimed that the observation that there is, or even can be, no thought without language does not ultimately divide the Gricean from his antireductionist opponents. In section 8 of chapter 3 I showed that the Gricean can accept thought without language so long as our concepts of the semantic and the psychological do not necessitate this acceptance. In section 9 of chapter 3 I suggested that one who denies a Gricean reduction is not thereby committed to denying thoughts to the languageless. In this final section I want to argue both that the antireductionist may attribute thoughts to the languageless and that on a correct view of mind there can be no reduction of the semantic to the psychological. The defence of these two claims is very closely related.

I shall begin by considering the position of the reductive Gricean who wants to allow that there may be *some* thoughts in the absence of language and who tries to gain support for his reductive program with this observation.[58] From their earliest writings Gricean have accepted that at least some propositional attitudes require that one possess a language.[59] Some of their early opponents pointed to this as evidence that we cannot analyze meaning in terms of psychological states that are semantically untainted.[60] The Gricean had a standard reply to this objection. He argued that so long as *some* thought does not require language, his reduction is free from the threat of circularity. We thus find Strawson writing: "All that the analysis requires is that we can explain the notion of conventions of communication in terms of the notion of pre-conventional communication at a rather basic level. Given that we can do this, then there is more than one way in which we can start pulling ourselves up by our own linguistic bootstraps."[61] This attempt to avoid circularity in the reductive analysis of meaning involves the Gricean in a number of complexities: first, he must make preconventional communication plausible; second, he must explain how we pull ourselves up by our own linguistic bootstraps.

In this connection Strawson offers us "a story of the analytic-genetic variety," a story echoed by Schiffer.[62] This is a story about the origin of language that needn't be true. The purpose of telling such a story is this: if such a story makes sense, if nothing about the concepts involved rules it out, we can accept the story as teaching us something about these concepts. The Gricean story is meant to teach us something about our concepts of the semantic and the psychological. It goes like this:

> There are certain propositional attitudes such that it is possible for agents to have them independently of having any language or other conventional means of communication, and such that once agents have these propositional attitudes, they will communicate with one another. Once agents begin to communicate with one another they will begin to develop a conventional system of communication. Once even a rudimentary "language" or conventional system of communication is possessed by a group of agents it will then become possible for them to have propositional attitudes which they could not otherwise have; and this will make it possible for them to communicate things which they could not otherwise communicate, which in turn will result in a more sophisticated "language", which in turn will make it possible for them to have propositional attitudes they could not otherwise have, and so on.[63]

Whether any actual language arose in this way is beside the point. The fact that it makes sense to tell the story, the fact that a language *could* have arisen in this way, helps us to see what is possible with respect to our concepts of thought and language. If such a story makes sense, the Gricean needn't be worried by the observation that some thoughts require a language.[64] This Gricean story is only *prima facie* evidence that our concepts of the semantic and the psychological are independent. What is telling is whether the Gricean can defend his story, and this involves showing that preconventional communication and a bootstrap method are plausible. The story, then, is merely an elaboration of the standard reply; it does not further the defence of that reply.

Preconventional communication does not present any real problem it seems to me. That there can be some sorts of communication in the absence of linguistic conventions need not be denied. What may be thought to introduce a problem, however, is the *Gricean* account of such communication. According to the Gricean, communication, whether preconventional or conventional, is the communication of certain beliefs and intentions: the speaker must have, and the audience must recognize, the speaker's intention to produce certain beliefs in the audience.[65] But it is a real question whether an individual can have such propositional attitudes in the absence of language.

At this point the Gricean may either change his story or set to work defending his claim that languageless individuals may possess the sophisticated beliefs and intentions required for the first acts of communication on this Gricean account of communication.[66] If he chooses the latter way, he will find himself faced with the problem of explaining how one pulls oneself up by the bootstraps from these prelinguistic Gricean intentions and beliefs to more sophisticated ones that require language. Given these problems, the Gricean may do best to change his story.

The story with which the Gricean began requires that he defend the claim that the languageless can have the beliefs and intentions required for the first acts of Gricean communication and that he defend as well a two-stage process of bootstrapping. The new story requires neither of these defences. According to the new story the Gricean need only defend the claim that an individual can have *some* thoughts in independence of language. These needn't be as complex as the beliefs and intentions required for the first acts of Gricean communication. The Gricean claim is that our psychological concepts are independent of our semantical concepts if there are any thoughts that do not depend upon language.[67]

One way of supporting this new story would be the following. Observe that it is *prima facie* implausible to deny thoughts to the languageless simply because they lack a language. This move will shift the burden of proof onto those who wish to withhold such attributions to such individuals. Next, check the arguments put forward to the effect that only those endowed with language can have thoughts, and show why they do not succeed.[68] Hold that until we are convinced to the contrary, we can make sense of the attribution of at least some thoughts to the languageless. This will suffice to show that our concepts of the semantic and the psychological are not symmetrical. We may then allow the reduction of the semantic to the psychological to stand.[69]

The Gricean's claim, then, is that the concepts of the semantic and the psychological are independent, and this is supported by the claim that some languageless creatures clearly do have some thoughts (albeit simple ones). If this story is plausible, he will gain his conceptual point by a simple ontological observation. If a theorist can make sense of the attribution of thoughts to the languageless, then it would seem that his concept of the psychological is not dependent upon that of the semantic. Moreover, it would seem that there is *prima facie* evidence that such attributions *do* make sense.

In chapter 3, section 9, I argued that the possibility of a certain kind of analysis of the propositional attitudes is evidence that there is no entailment from an ontological asymmetry to conceptual asymmetry. The analysis I had in mind was that propositional attitudes are relations to sentences with meaning in the theorist's language. I argued that such an analysis allows our concepts of the semantic and the psychological to be interdependent, while at the same time it allows for the attribution of thoughts to the languageless. The Gricean who follows the story just given would argue the reverse of this: the *apparent* entailment from ontological asymmetry to conceptual asymmetry should be taken as evidence that there is something fundamentally wrong with this kind of analysis of the propositional attitudes. The evidence for the apparent entailment is that if the theorist can make sense of the attribution of thoughts to the languageless, then it would seem that our psychological concepts are *not* dependent upon semantic ones in any way.[70]

Neither side of this dispute, it seems, has at this point anything more than *prima facie* evidence in favor of his position: the reductionist stresses the implausibility of withholding attributions of thoughts to the languageless and draws conceptual conclusions from this; the antireductionist points to a certain semantic analysis of the propositional attitudes as evidence that ontological asymmetry does not entail conceptual asymmetry. Notice that, if the antireductionist is right to interpret his semantic analysis of the propositional attitudes in the way I have suggested, he can maintain a conceptual symmetry without committing himself to an ontological symmetry as well. In other words, the antireductionist can *also* accept that there may be thought without language. Nevertheless, antireductionism does have one disadvantage even at this early stage. The antireductionist position has an air of paradox about it: how can one who holds that our psychological concepts and our semantic concepts are interdependent hold at the same time that we can make sense of the attribution of thoughts to the languageless? If such attribution makes sense, it would seem to tell against the alleged conceptual symmetry. The reductionist, then, seems to be at an advantage.

I think that we can dispel the air of paradox surrounding the anti-reductionist position and show that the Gricean strategy of trying to gain conceptual ground through ontological observations is misguided. To see this, let us begin by asking the Gricean on what grounds he is willing to allow the attribution of thoughts to the languageless. One way might be this: if this Gricean is also some sort of Cartesian who holds that mental substance is distinct from semantic substance, he could say that while some creatures possess both substances, others possess the former but not the latter.[71] Another way would be to hold that there is only one kind of immaterial substance, mental substance, that various combinations of this substance (perhaps one suggested by a Gricean analysis) yield the semantic, but that some individuals lack or have not sufficiently developed the combination required for meaning. Still another way would be to accept reductive physicalism or functionalism and to hold that neurophysiological or functional evidence will make it clear that an individual has thoughts despite his lack of language.[72]

But what about the reductive Gricean who rejects Cartesianism, reductive physicalism, and functionalism? And what about the Gricean who claims to renounce an objective conception of mind? On what grounds is such a reductive Gricean willing to attribute thoughts to the languageless? The Gricean I introduced at the beginning of this section is such a Gricean. This Gricean does not want to hold that the mental is independently accessible in the way I have argued that Cartesians, reductive physicalists, and functionalists must hold that it is; his only claim is that the mental is accessible in independence of the semantic. He could agree that mental states are manifest in behavior. His position is that the thoughts of the languageless are manifest in nonlinguistic behavior and that we can explain the thoughts of those endowed with language using this semantically untainted material. This reductive Gricean, then, claims to be in complete agreement with the thesis that behavioral manifestation is an essential ingredient of our psychological concepts.

I want to claim that a Gricean who accepts a reduction of the semantic to the psychological while at the same time maintaining that the psychological is manifest in behavior has achieved only a *partial* understanding of our psychological concepts. His position correctly reflects the way in which those concepts are bound up with behavior characterized in a certain way. He is right to observe that behavior can manifest the psychological even where there is no *linguistic* behavior. However, his position fails to recognize that after a certain point we must characterize the behavior that manifests thought *semantically*. Having more complex thoughts requires an individual to exhibit them in the more subtle manifestations that only language can provide. In acknowledging that the psychological is manifest in behavior, one must also acknowledge this last point.

My conclusion in section 2 of this chapter is not simply that our concept of the psychological is essentially bound up with behavior. That conclusion is part of a larger one: we cannot bypass or ignore the *ordinary* evidence in the attribution of mental states to another, and the ordinary evidence is linguistic as well as nonlinguistic. If I am right in thinking that the ordinary evidence is the only possible basis for the attribution of mental states to another, then we must conclude that our concepts of the semantic and the psychological are on a par. The reductive Gricean who rejects both Cartesianism and all forms of reductive physicalism *claims* to acknowledge the ordinary evidence, but his acknowledgement is only partial. He accepts that ordinary evidence is crucial to the characterization of some thoughts but claims that the more complex thoughts can be constructed on this semantically untainted base. But I would say that the attempt to construct the more complex thoughts out of the less complex is tantamount to denying the ordinary evidence.

That the psychological is an essential part of the semantic is an observation that Grice's original analysis of meaning exploits. Yet the reductive Gricean chooses to ignore the way in which the semantic is an essential part of the psychological. What can obscure this symmetry between the semantic and the psychological is the curious fact that despite the interdependence between these two sets of concepts, we can still make sense of the attribution of thoughts to the languageless. As we have seen, the Gricean can exploit this possibility to support his reduction: if we can make sense of the attribution of thoughts to the languageless, our concepts of the semantic and the psychological must not be essentially interdependent. What the reductive Gricean tends to overlook is this: we can make sense of the attribution of thoughts to the languageless because these thoughts may be manifest in behavior that forms a *part* of our concept of the psychological. When we acknowledge the importance of behavioral manifestations to our concept of the psychological, we must also acknowledge that at a certain point (one not reached by all creatures with a mental life) thought requires the subtle and sophisticated manifestation that only language can provide.

One might say, the more sophisticated the thought, the more sophisticated the expression of it. But this is not quite right. It is nearer the truth to say, the more sophisticated the expression, the more complex the thought. In this way we avoid the temptation to objectify the mind. Understanding thought and language to be interrelated in this way offers us a way of understanding the observation that language allows for the development of thought: the simplicity of certain thoughts is to be understood relative to the simplicity of their nonlinguistic behavioral manifestations, while the complexity of certain other thoughts is to be understood relative to the complexity of their linguistic manifestations. This explains why it is quite wrong to conclude from the fact that individuals with thoughts but no language preceded individuals endowed with language in history that we can understand or explain the thoughts of those endowed with language on the model of prelinguistic thoughts.

It is sometimes asked whether these states of the languageless are properly called "thoughts," or whether this term is best reserved for the states of those endowed with language. This question is sometimes asked in the following way: Are these states of the languageless different in kind or merely in degree from the states of those endowed with language? The latter is not a useful question. To answer that the states of the languageless are different in kind from those of the language-endowed is to miss the rather important way in which the two are alike; to say that they are merely different in degree is to miss the important way in which they are different. They are alike in that both states are manifest in behavior; they are different in that each is manifest in a substantially different kind of behavior, the one linguistic and the other nonlinguistic. We have to understand that our concept of the psychological is bound up with behaviour and that in many cases that behaviour is linguistic.

Once we properly understand the view of mind to which the antireductionist adheres, we can no longer expect to gain support for a Gricean reduction with the observation that there are some thoughts that the languageless may possess. The languageless *may* exhibit the behavioral manifestations that the antireductionist wants to say form part of our conception of the psychological. But in contrast to the reductive Gricean, the antireductionist insists that language completes the conception. In a sense, then, there is no semantically innocent conception of the psychological; the semantic is an essential part of our conception of the psychological. Our concepts of the psychological and the semantic are on a par, but our understanding of how they fit together also allows that the languageless may exhibit the behavior required for us to attribute thought to them.

The reductive Gricean who wishes to support his thesis with the observation that it is plausible to attribute some thoughts to the languageless must rethink his argument. It is no longer obvious that this observation supports his reduction. The observation is one that the antireductionist is also in a position to accept.

It is not over ontological matters that the reductive Gricean and his antireductionist opponent stand divided. They disagree over epistemological matters. The Gricean accepts, whereas his opponent rejects, a deep epistemological asymmetry between the semantic and the psychological. In his acceptance of this asymmetry the reductive Gricean commits himself to an objective conception of mind. In the end, my objection to the Gricean analysis of meaning under its reductive interpretation is to the picture of mind that it presupposes.

In chapter 3, section 4, I said that the following slogan captures both the Gricean's acceptance of a surface epistemological symmetry and his assertion in the face of this of a deep epistemological asymmetry: constituting the meaning of an utterance is one thing, betraying it another. In this way the reductive Gricean divorces his account of meaning from the interpretation and understanding of others. Here, I have argued, the reductive Gricean makes his mistake. This is what places his account at odds with a properly subjective conception of meaning and mind.

This reductive Gricean position may seem curious in light of the concerns of early Griceans (here I am using the term in its wider sense). One early Gricean concern was that purely formal accounts of meaning were deficient in a crucial respect: they omitted facts about language use from their account. However, at the point when the reductive Gricean proposes to divorce surface from deep epistemological matters, he too has left behind any real concern with interpretation and understanding. Facts about language use no longer guide the Gricean once reduction becomes his goal. Perhaps the final lesson the Gricean approach to meaning will teach us is that we must see our concepts of the semantic and the psychological as interdependent.

Reductive Griceans hope that questions in the philosophy of language receive their answers from work in the philosophy of mind. I have argued that answers to questions in the philosophy of mind ultimately lead us to the philosophy of language. My conclusion does not proceed from a general prejudice against reductions; rather, it has emerged from a consideration of our concepts of both meaning and mind.

Notes

Chapter 1

1. See also Grice 1968 and 1969.
2. Stevenson 1944. See also Morris 1946 and Ogden and Richards 1923.
3. Watson 1919.
4. Stevenson 1944, p. 43.
5. Stevenson 1944, p. 57. Several pages later Stevenson also adds, "provided that the disposition is rendered fixed, at least to a considerable degree, by linguistic rules" (p. 70).
6. Grice 1957, pp. 41–42. Stevenson uses the example of a cough (1944, p. 57).
7. I explain this sense in chapter 2, section 1. It is assumed that the dresser in this example has no special motivation in donning his coat.
8. Grice 1957, p. 43.
9. The label "ideational theory of meaning" comes from Alston 1964, chapter 1.
10. Locke 1690, book 3, chapter 1, section 1.
11. Locke 1690, book 3, chapter 2, section 1.
12. A notable exception to this empiricist conception of meaning is to be found in the writings of Bishop Berkeley (1710). (See chapter 4, section 2 for a discussion of the empiricist conception.)
13. The language of encoding is not Locke's, but has come to be associated with Locke's conception of language through the work of Michael Dummett. See, for example, Dummett 1978a.
14. One philosopher who attempts to develop Locke's suggestion that words serve as signs of ideas is D. M. Armstrong (1971). In that article Armstrong takes himself to be developing Locke's work in conjunction with Grice's. According to Armstrong, Grice's work should be understood as telling us "just what mental state of the utterer utterances are signs of" (p. 431).
15. Dummett 1978a, p. 5. See also Peter Hacker 1972.
16. Especially in Wittgenstein 1958. Of the two Wittgenstein's is the more thoroughgoing repudiation. See chapter 4, section 2.
17. In this chapter I am assuming a basic acquaintance with Grice's work. I present and discuss his account of meaning in some detail in chapter 2.
18. Prima facie it appears that conditions (1) and (2) are in direct conflict, and so are conditions (2) and (3). How these conflicts can be avoided is discussed by Dummett (1973, chapter 1), Davidson (1984i), and Wallace (1977), among others.
19. Davidson more recently stressed the same point. (See this chapter, section 2.) Davidson notes that some such condition *must* be satisfied if the theory of meaning is to serve as a model of language learning (see Davidson 1984a). The point has been made so much of in recent years that Quine has felt the need to write:

"There is disturbing evidence of a budding misconception that the 'lively appreci-
ation of the native speaker's ability to understand new sentences' is modern. It
has long been cited as what distinguishes genuine language from signal systems"
(1977, p. 225).

20. Searle 1971a, pp. 6–7.

21. Compare Stevenson's insistence on this point, which I mentioned at the beginning of this section.

22. Davidson 1984e, p. 155.

23. For this reason Grice uses the term "utterance" in "an artificially wide sense."
That is, nonlinguistic items and behavior may count as utterances. See Grice 1968,
p. 55.

24. A caveman's gestures may, of course, have structure, but it is not semantically
relevant structure. See chapter 2, footnote 11.

25. Brian Loar 1972, p. x.

26. Grice addresses the question of structure in his 1969 paper. Proposals for accommodating structure can also be found in Schiffer 1972, chapter 4; and Loar 1976
and 1981, chapter 9. Critics of the Gricean program sometimes overlook these
proposals. Such criticism perhaps compels Loar to write: "The theoretical utility
of Gricean intentions has little to do with non-linguistic or non-conventional
communication, and of course nothing to do with ignoring the compositionality
of linguistic meaning. . . . It is an interesting and satisfying feature of the Gricean
theories that they enable us to capture the analogies [between linguistic and
nonlinguistic performances]. But the focus of the communication intention theory
is *linguistic* meaning" (1981, p. 244). So long as we keep this in mind, we can
safely emphasize that the primary purpose of Grice's original work was to give an
account of the general phenomenon of meaning.

John McDowell has suggested to me that Grice's method of analysis is not
suited to concern with structure. If this is true, it shows that Grice's analysis *must*
be supplemented if it is to serve as an adequate account of linguistic meaning. Of
course, this would be another reason to see structure as of secondary concern to
the Gricean.

27. Strictly speaking, so-called use theorists are identified by two theses. The first is
that the philosophy of language falls within the scope of the philosophy of mind.
The second is that it is mistaken to think of meaning in terms of some core or
standard meaning, which gets modified in use. As I understand him, Grice would
agree with the first of these theses but would disagree with the second. See Grice
1968, p. 54.

28. Wiggins 1971a, p. 48.

29. Searle 1970, p. 18–19.

30. Dummett writes: "Davidson was, perhaps, the first to propose explicitly that the
philosophical problems concerning meaning ought to be investigated by enquir-
ing after the form which such a theory of meaning for a language should take"
(1976, p. 70).

31. Dummett 1975, p. 97.

32. Grice 1957, p. 43. See chapter 2 below for the details of this elucidation.

33. Consider, for example, the attempted analysis of knowledge as justified true
belief. See footnote 89 of this chapter.

34. Davidson, esp. 1984b; Tarski 1944 and 1956. Davidson was aware of the work that
needed to be done to accommodate Tarski's approach, developed for a formal
language, to natural languages. Notice that many of Davidson's requirements are
reminiscent of the work of earlier formal semanticists (see section 1 above).

35. Davidson 1984b, p. 24.
36. Dummett 1975, p. 97.
37. Dummett 1976, p. 69.
38. Dummett 1975, p. 99.
39. Dummett 1975, pp. 97–98.
40. Wisdom 1934, p. 37.
41. Dummett 1975, p. 97.
42. For a further discussion of this problem see chapter 2, section 1.
43. Note that this sentence form is restricted to descriptive, or indicative, utterances. See chapter 2, section 1.
44. Dummett 1975, p. 98.
45. It is worth pointing out once again that Grice is concerned with more than just linguistic meaning. See footnotes 23 and 26 of this chapter.
46. I do not mean to rule out theory building altogether for our concept of knowledge. However, before we attempt it, we need to explain what features of knowledge such a theory can illuminate. One might argue that knowledge too is "built up" and that theory building is applicable to this concept for this reason. However, if we distinguish the attitude of knowing from what is known, we can see that structure is present only in the latter.
47. McDowell 1980, p. 124.
48. In particular, McDowell has in mind some things written by Christopher Peacocke (1976) and P. F. Strawson (1970).
49. McDowell 1976, p. 44. On this change of tack compare Dummett. Talk of direct versus indirect approaches to the problem of meaning is mine, not McDowell's.
50. See in particular McDowell 1977 and 1980, sections 1–4.
51. McDowell 1980, p. 124.
52. McDowell 1980, p. 124.
53. I explain what I see to be involved in a reductive interpretation of the analysis of meaning in section 3 of this chapter and more extensively in chapter 3.
54. As I mentioned in chapter 1, section 1, the question of interpreting the analysis is intimately bound up with the issue of reconciling Grice's and more formal approaches to meaning. As the issues of both reconciliation and interpretation are raised by McDowell's remarks, my comments in the last two paragraphs may not be clear until the reader has read sections 3 and 4 of this chapter.
55. Evans and McDowell 1976, pp. xviii–xxiii. This is at least *one* interpretation of the point Evans and McDowell make in their introduction.
56. Evans and McDowell 1976, p. xix. See also Martin Davies 1981, chapter 1.
57. Schiffer 1982, p. 125.
58. For the distinction between primary and secondary intentions see chapter 2, section 2.
59. Strawson 1980, pp. 284–285. See chapter 2, section 1 below.
60. Armstrong 1971, pp. 433–434.
61. See Grandy and Warner 1986, pp. 9ff.
62. Evans and McDowell 1976, p. xxii.
63. Evans and McDowell 1976, p. xxii. This idea is further developed in McDowell 1980. Note that one can employ the metaphor of perception and at the same time give an account of underlying mechanisms. This, however, is not McDowell's way.
64. Bennett 1976, sections 50–53.
65. Bennett 1976, p. 160.
66. Bennett 1976, p. 172.

67. Bennett 1976, p. 172.
68. Bennett 1976, p. 172.
69. Bennett 1976, p. 171. Compare the original Gricean conditions, which I set out in chapter 2, sections 1 and 2.
70. Loar 1981, p. 251.
71. Strawson (1980) makes a similar observation in his reply to McDowell 1980.
72. Evans and McDowell have *two* preferences: one for the theory building approach to meaning and another for a non-Gricean account of communication.
73. In the light of this section, it is, strictly speaking, inaccurate of me to refer to Grice's work as a theory of meaning. Grice offers not a theory but an analysis of meaning.
74. Philosophical analysis as explication, employed to avoid difficulties, is also Quine's position. Quine, of course, would have no truck with analysis as conceptual unpacking. See Quine 1960, section 53, and also pp. 25ff herein.
75. Moore 1966a, p. 168. See also Moore 1966b and his "Reply to my Critics" in Schlipp 1952.
76. According to Susan Stebbing this terminology was first introduced by Wisdom. See Stebbing's essay entitled "Moore's Influence" in Schlipp 1952, esp. p. 528.
77. As opposed to "formal analysis," which is concerned with verbal expressions. See Moore's reply to his critics in Schlipp 1952.
78. Hence, Moore claims that philosophers may attempt to analyse, for example, the concept of causation (as Hume did, according to Moore) but not the concept of being a brother. See Moore 1966b.
79. Moore 1966b. In his reply to his critics (Schlipp 1952) Moore put the point in this way: not only must the expression used for the analysandum be different from that used for the analysans; expressions used in the analysans must explicitly mention concepts *not* explicitly mentioned by the expressions used in the analysandum.
80. In light of this aim we can see why we think there should be an *upper* limit on the amount of complexity allowed in the analysans as well: after a certain point complexity only obscures understanding.
81. There are two details apt to cause confusion if left unaddressed. The first is this. One might think that in an analysis the concepts mentioned on either side of the analytic biconditional should be from what may be called different categories. Thus, in the case of Grice's analysis we find semantic concepts mentioned in the analysandum and psychological concepts mentioned in the analysans. This is not necessary. It is not unusual to find analyses in which concepts in the analysandum are of the same category as concepts in the analysans. Consider, for example, Richard Grandy's attempt to analyse belief in terms of desire (1973). It may be that talk of levels encourages the view that analysis must cross categories. If so, this is a good reason to stick with my preferred talk of symmetry versus asymmetry. The second detail I should mention is this: It is sometimes suggested that reductive analyses mention on their right-hand side only concepts that are less obscure or less troublesome than concepts in the analysandum. I don't believe that this is a necessary condition of a reductive analysis. On this point see note 116 of this chapter.
82. See my discussion of McDowell's position in section 2 of this chapter.
83. Again see my discussion of McDowell's position in section 2 of this chapter.
84. See this chapter, section 1, where I suggest that Grice's concern is not so much with the issue of content as with the question of how utterances have their content. Understood in this way, we can see Grice's analysis as an analysis of

what it is for utterances to have their content. We can then think of the two interpretations of this analysis as follows: A reductive analysis is an analysis of the relation of having content: the way utterances have their content is definable in terms of the way propositional attitudes have their content. A reciprocal analysis is an analysis of the relation between the relation utterances have to their content and the relation psychological states have to their content.

85. Schiffer 1972, pp. 14–15.

86. To be exact, the problem arises if beliefs turn out to be attitudes toward sentences with public-language meaning. For more on this, see section 5 of this chapter.

87. Reciprocal analyses are not open to the charge of circularity; or, one might say, circularity in a reciprocal analysis is never vicious. Of course, even reciprocal analyses must beware of traveling in circles that are *too* small.

88. Schiffer 1982, p. 120.

89. Strawson writes, "For the classical method of analysis is that in terms of which, in our tradition, we most naturally think" (1970, footnote 1). And more recently Diane Ackerman writes, "Analyses are what many philosophers traditionally have tried to produce. . . . The process of trying to establish biconditionals of this sort of analysis is one fundamental philosophical process" (1986, p. 312).

90. So, for example, Quine writes: "This construction [Norbert Wiener's definition of an ordered pair] is paradigmatic of what we are most typically up to when in a philosophical spirit we offer an 'analysis' or 'explication' of some hitherto inadequately formulated idea or expression. We do not claim synonymy. We do not claim to make clear or explicit what the users of the unclear expression had unconsciously in mind all along. We do not expose hidden meanings as the words 'analysis' and 'explication' would suggest; we supply lacks. We fix on the particular functions of the unclear expression that make it worth troubling about, and then devise a substitute, clear and couched in terms to our liking, that fills these functions" (1960, section 53).

91. On this debate see Quine 1953; Grice and Strawson 1956; and Grice 1986, pp. 54–55.

92. Loar 1981, section 2.5 and p. 252.

93. For a discussion of this wider perspective on Grice's original work see section 5 of this chapter.

94. David Lewis, for example, claims that his theory of mind-body identity is the result of an investigation into the meanings of mental terms. He writes, "Physiology and the meaning of words leave us no choice but to make the psychophysical identification" (1972, p. 207).

95. Wiggins 1971a. A related idea of allocating different accounts of meaning to different "levels of meaning" is found in Harman 1968.

96. Wiggins 1971a, p. 20.

97. In 1971a, Wiggins does not discuss Grice's work on meaning (although he does mention Grice's work on implicature). When Wiggins makes this suggestion concerning semantics and pragmatics, he is considering the work of Austin and the later Wittgenstein as examples of use theorists of meaning. For a discussion of how Grice's work fits in with the work of these use theorists see section 1 of this chapter.

98. See McDowell 1977, and esp. 1976. See also my discussion of McDowell in section 2 of this chapter.

99. See, for example, Loar 1976.

100. This solution to (1) is mentioned by Davidson (1984f). It also seems to be accepted by Loar, see 1976, section 1.

101. See McDowell, esp. 1977.
102. Lewis 1983c, p. 173.
103. At least this appears to be so in Loar 1976. In section 3 of that paper Loar writes: "Notions like 'language' and 'means' should always be thought of as intrinsically relativized to a population of language users. The real semantical notions are not '*L* is a language', or '*S* means *M* in *L*', but '*L* is the language of population *P*' and '*S* means *M* in the language of *P*'. Clearly, *those* notions cannot be reduced formalistically to logical and syntactical notions. Facts about *use* of language in a population have to be introduced—and so psychological notions are needed in the analysis of semantical concepts" (1976, p. 150).
104. Loar 1976, p. 151.
105. I extract this fear from passages like the following: "There is a tradition in the philosophy of language which would locate all facts about the communicative intentions and beliefs of language users, and regularities concerning them, in *pragmatics* and not in *semantics*. Since the semantics of a language includes facts about the meanings or senses of its terms and sentences . . . , it would follow that these semantical notions are not to be construed as being about the communicative intentions and beliefs of language users. So, the nature of the semantics-pragmatics distinction is no mere terminological matter, but involves the question of the fundamental nature of semantic concepts" (1976, p. 149).
106. By Peacocke (1976) and Davies (1981), for example.
107. Loar 1976, p. 149. See section 1 of this chapter.
108. So Loar writes, "The concept of truth for beliefs would then serve as the foundational concept of truth, with the concepts of truth for sentences, statements and utterances derivative from it" (1981, p. 153). For a statement of the *range* of the Gricean account see section 5 of this chapter.
109. Loar 1981, p. 241.
110. See section 2 of this chapter.
111. This is true of the Gricean whether or not he adopts a reductive interpretation of the biconditional.
112. In a more recent paper, though, Grice professes a "strong opposition" to "a multitude of demons . . . bearing names like . . . Naturalism . . . , Reductionism, Physicalism, Materialism . . . and Functionalism" (1986, p. 67).
113. In particular, Stephen Schiffer and Brian Loar.
114. Schiffer 1982, pp. 127–128.
115. Schiffer 1982, p. 120. In this paper Schiffer argues as follows: There is no functional theory that defines both belief and meaning. Because of this and because Schiffer wants a functional theory of mind, he concludes that we must reduce the semantic to the psychological. In this way Schiffer supports his claim that the only viable reduction of the semantic to the physical is via a reduction of the semantic to the psychological.
116. Some philosophers have suggested that a reductive analysis of meaning in terms of the speaker's beliefs and intentions illuminates the more obscure concept in terms of the less obscure. But what I say in the text suggests that there need not be an assumption that one of the pair of concepts involved in an analysis is less obscure than the other. Even if the concepts are *equally* obscure, we will make progress if we show that the one obscure concept is nothing but a special case of another, equally obscure concept. Two problems will then have been reduced to one. If one were to press the claim and say that psychological concepts are less obscure than semantic ones, I can only think that this might seem so *if* by "less obscure" one meant something like "more tractable from the point of view of a

physical theory." Certainly philosophers like Schiffer and Loar have thought that the psychological is more tractable than the semantic from the point of view of physical theory, as I have explained in this section.

117. Loar 1981, p. 33.

118. Field 1978, for example.

119. Schiffer's term for a program that builds reductionist intent into Grice's original proposals for meaning. See Schiffer 1982, p. 7.

120. For Schiffer's proposal see his 1981a paper; for Loar's see 1981, p. 2. Very roughly, Schiffer takes beliefs to be relations to sentences in the language of thought, while Loar takes beliefs to be relations to sentences in the ascriber's language, non-semantically interpreted.

121. Loar 1981, chapter 9, esp. sections 9.2 and 9.4.

122. Loar 1981. In chapter 2, section 5 Loar proposes this dilemma in application to propositional attitudes. In chapter 10, section 3 he extends it to cover Grice's work on meaning.

123. Loar 1981, p. 43.

124. Loar 1981, p. 43.

125. Loar 1981, p. 41. Loar is here expressing a fairly common attitude towards anti-reductionist positions.

Chapter 2

1. See chapter 1, section 2.

2. For example, there is the problem of the psychological reality of the complex intentions mentioned on the right-hand side of the biconditional (see chapter 1, section 2). As this chapter will explain, we also need to address the questions of whether the conditions mentioned on the right-hand side of the biconditional are necessary or sufficient for speaker's meaning.

3. I shall draw mainly on the work of Grice and Schiffer.

4. Anyone well acquainted with the analysis will want to omit this chapter and turn to chapter 3, where I begin my discussion of the reductive interpretation of the Gricean analysis of meaning.

5. See chapter 1, section 2.

6. Stampe 1974, p. 283.

7. Stampe 1974, p. 283.

8. Grice 1957, p. 39.

9. In a more recent paper Grice proposes that we see nonnatural uses of "means" as a "descendent from"—in the sense of "derivative from and analogous to"—natural uses. Grice finds this preferable to adopting the view that the word "means" is ambiguous here. See Grice 1982, p. 232.

10. See chapter 1, section 1.

11. Of course an arm waving, for example, may technically be broken down into individual motions of the upper arm, forearm, hand, and fingers, but these elements in no way contribute to the meaning of the "utterance" as a whole. The case differs in this way from that of sentences of a language. The relevant structure of sentences is *semantic*.

12. Of course, meaning may be a property of an utterance on an occasion *in* a language as well. For a discussion of these issues see Grice 1969, section 1.

13. Grice 1957, p. 46.

14. It is intended, of course, that the analysis ultimately cover linguistic meaning (see chapter 1, section 1).

15. Grice 1957. By speaking, in the analysans, of the audience's "response," Grice allows that the response will vary with the force with which the speaker makes his utterance. In this chapter, I will mainly discuss the analysis only as it applies to descriptive or informative utterances. For a discussion of how to extend the account, see Schiffer 1972, chapter 4.

16. The examples in this and the following sections are taken largely unchanged from the literature so that the reader may more easily see how my discussion relates to the literature.

17. Several philosophers have questioned whether what follows is a genuine counterexample. See, for example, Schiffer 1972, pp. 56–57 and the more recent Recanati 1986, section 8. See also my discussion of this question in section 3 of this chapter, especially footnotes 53 and 54.

18. Note that formulation (3) introduces another important condition into the analysis: that the audience's recognition of the speaker's intention should function as A's *reason* for response r, rather than merely as a cause of r. See Grice 1957, pp. 46–47 and also Schiffer 1972, pp. 10–11 and 52–53.

19. Grice 1957, p. 44.

20. Grice 1957, pp. 44–45.

21. Compare chapter 1, section 2.

22. Of course, the presence of the intention to communicate cannot *guarantee* that there will be communicative uptake. I should also note that one may agree that the presence of appropriate intentions is what distinguishes nonnatural meaning from natural meaning without thereby accepting Grice's analysis of nonnatural meaning. For an account that opposes Grice's, see McDowell (1980). For a discussion of just how far McDowell may plausibly distance himself from an analysis like Grice's, see Strawson 1980.

23. The example is taken from Grice 1969. Note that the utterance in this example has imperative force. Schiffer offers another example, which has an utterance in the indicative. See Schiffer 1972, chapter 1, section 3.

24. This is taken from Schiffer 1972, pp. 13–14. Also see Grice 1969.

25. This common understanding is the basis of the speaker's expectations about his audience. See chapter 1, section 2.

26. Schiffer 1972, pp. 18–19. Like the counterexample involving torture by thumbscrews, this counterexample is also one in which the intended response is that the audience do such and such, rather than believe that such and such is the case. Another example can be found in Grice 1969.

27. See Schiffer's "Tipperary" example (1972, p. 22).

28. Grice 1969.

29. See also Schiffer's discussion of this suggestion (1972, pp. 23–26).

30. Grice 1969, section 3.

31. Grice 1982, pp. 238ff.

32. Grandy and Warner give another example from sailing: There is an optimal setting for sails that maximizes forward thrust but is difficult (if not impossible) to achieve when sailing due to wind shifts and changes in direction caused by the waves. See 1986, p. 5.

33. Schiffer 1972, p. 26.

34. See Schiffer 1972, p. 36.

35. Schiffer 1972, p. 39.

36. Schiffer 1972, p. 39.

37. Schiffer 1972, p. 39.

38. Charles Taylor (1980) suggests, in a very interesting review of Bennett's *Linguistic*

Behaviour, that the mutual knowledge condition in the analysis marks a significant difference between human and animal communication. By adding such a condition, we are acknowledging that human communication involves a quality that Taylor calls "entre nous," a quality not present in animal communication. Taylor concludes that there is a radical discontinuity between natural meaning (which animals achieve) and nonnatural meaning (which only humans can attain).

39. Loar 1981, p. 250.
40. Grice himself does not use this idea to defend the condition of mutual knowledge.
41. Harman 1974b. Harman does not put the point in terms of deceit.
42. Harman 1974b, p. 227.
43. Harman notes that Grice employs self-referential intentions in his 1957 work but drops this formulation by the time he came to write his 1969 paper.
44. Although Harman points up a gap in the analysis, he does not offer a counterexample to test his intuitions. Without such a counterexample it is hard to decide whether the absence of such further recognition is required for communication.
45. See Blackburn 1984, chapter 4.
46. Blackburn gives the following example to illustrate the unproblematic nature of self-referential intentions: "Imagine a certain kind of love affair. I want you to know *everything* about me. And everything includes, especially, the fact that I have this want. If you didn't know that about me, you might suspect me of concealment, and I wouldn't want that. There is no paradox here, and no regress either" 1984, p. 117. Note that Blackburn uses "intends" and "wants" as "stylistic variants."
47. In a footnote Sperber and Wilson argue that grasping a self-reflexive intention involves grasping a potentially infinitely long formula and as such is implausible. See 1986, pp. 256–257, footnote 20. See also Recanati 1986 for an interesting discussion of self-reflexive intentions in connection with the Sperber and Wilson footnote.
48. Recanati also chooses this option. See his discussion of what he calls "default reflexivity" in 1986, sec. 13, pp. 233–234. Default reflexivity is a descendent of Grice's original suggestion and is designed by Recanati to avoid the problems that Schiffer envisages for Grice's proposal. See Schiffer 1972, p. 26.
49. Schiffer 1972, chapter 3, section 5. Schiffer there gives two arguments to back up this alleged equivalence. In chapter 4 Schiffer proceeds to defend his position against what he calls the "Austin-Wittgenstein legacy." That legacy has it that utterances do *not* divide up so neatly into two mutually exclusive subclasses: statements and commands.
50. That is, I will follow the same policy I followed in section 2 of this chapter. Harman suggests a way of making the imperative out to be a special case of the indicative (1974b, p. 228). Notice that for the moment I have gone back to the analysis as it stands in formulation (8) rather than formulation (9).
51. Grice 1969, section 4.
52. Notice that (c″) is a formulation first adopted by Grice in his 1968 paper. It is also the formulation that Strawson uses in presenting Grice's position in his inaugural lecture (1970) and that led to McDowell's criticisms of Strawson's and Grice's position in his 1980 paper.
53. This problem also infects counterexamples (3), (4), and (5) above. In none of these cases do we want to say that S intends A's response to be brought about by means of A's recognition of S's intention to produce that response. See Schiffer 1972, pp. 43ff. Notice that there is no implausibility here if one thinks only of cases of *telling* (which appears to have been what Grice was thinking of, see Grice 1957 and the

discussion of formulation (2) above). Schiffer's point is that not all cases of meaning are instances of telling. Schiffer sums this up well in his 1982 paper, where he writes: "The completed definition would impose a requirement on the way in which S must intend his utterance of x to activate in A the belief that p. Grice's original account required that this be achieved by way of A's recognition of S's intention to produce in A the belief that p, but that condition is better suited to an account of *telling*. My preference is to have the definition require merely that, for some relation R' . . . , S intends his utterance to activate A's believing that p through A's belief that $xR'p''$ (p. 4).

54. Condition (*a*) should be read as follows: that there be some p such that S's utterance of x causes in A the activated belief that p for which he intends A to have the *truth-supporting reasons* that p. This replaces condition (*b*) of the analysis as it stands in formulation (8). That old condition is what lead to the implausibilities under discussion in this section. The new condition, (*a*), is essential to rule out various counterexamples (see footnote 18 and Schiffer 1972, pp. 55–56). Condition (*b*) ensures that A has reasons for his belief that p and that those reasons are truth supporting (rather than moral or prudential reasons for believing that p). Finally, note that the analysis as it stands in formulation (13) *allows* that in presenting Salome with the head of Saint John the Baptist on a charger, Herod meant that Saint John was dead. (See the discussion of this example following formulation (2).) As I noted in my earlier discussion of this case, some have not taken this to be a genuine counterexample and Schiffer is among them. If one wants to exclude this as a case of meaning, a small addition to the analysis will secure this. Simply add "the relation between S's utterance x and the belief that p that A is intended to recognize must not be such that S's utterance x will provide A with evidence that p without the mediation of S's intention in uttering x to produce in A the belief that p."

55. For a discussion of how each case is derived see Schiffer 1972, chapter 3, section 3.

56. Schiffer 1972, pp. 72–73.

57. Harman 1974b, pp. 128–129.

58. These counterexamples are taken from Grice 1969; Schiffer 1972, pp. 42–48 and 73–80; Ziff 1967; and Yu 1979.

59. Taking this line with counterexamples (*c*) through (*e*) leaves Schiffer free to say that in cases (*i*) and (*j*) the teacher and the purist did not mean something by their utterance or typed sentence.

60. Bennett 1976, p. 23.

61. Bennett 1985, pp. 620–621. Notice that Bennett uses '*x*' to stand for the speaker and '*S*' to stand for the sentence uttered.

62. See Grice 1982, pp. 238–239.

63. Grice 1957, p. 46. In this section I shall continue my policy of discussing only the indicative.

64. Grice 1968, p. 60. Notice that this account of timeless meaning builds on Grice's preferred analysis of speaker meaning, formulation (7).

65. Grice 1968, p. 61.

66. This is Grice's own example.

67. Grice 1968, p. 62.

68. Grice 1968, p. 62.

69. Schiffer 1972, p. 119. Notice that Schiffer builds on his preferred analysis, formulation (8), which contains the notion of mutual knowledge.

70. Schiffer 1972, p. 128.

71. The expression "M-intending" is used to abbreviate the analysans of the analysis of speaker meaning.
72. Schiffer 1972, p. 130.
73. Schiffer 1972, p. 136.
74. Lewis 1969.
75. Hume 1888, book 3, chapter 2, section 2.
76. This is from Schiffer's account of Lewis, Schiffer 1972, p. 150.
77. Schiffer 1972, pp. 151–152.
78. Schiffer 1972, p. 154.
79. Schiffer 1972, p. 156.
80. Searle 1971b, p. 46.
81. Grice 1968, p. 54.
82. Grice 1968, p. 63.
83. Grice 1968, pp. 63–64.
84. Grice 1968, p. 69.
85. Lewis 1969, chapter 5, section 1 and Lewis 1983c. What I am saying here is purely general. I am thus ignoring aspects of language such as indexicality, ambiguity, and mood.
86. Lewis 1969, chapter 5, section 2 and Lewis 1983a.
87. Lewis does not aim to relate grammars to speakers. For him it is sufficient that the language that speakers use is determined by a grammar.
88. Loar suggests that we say that a group's use of $\mathcal{L}$ is grounded in Γ just in case Γ enters into the psychological explanation of the linguistic competence of members of the group (1981, section 10.4).
89. Loar 1972, p. 5.

Chapter 3

1. For a discussion of the reconciliation see chapter 1, section 4.
2. For Grice's view see chapter 1, section 5.
3. See Schiffer 1981a and 1982.
4. Loar 1981.
5. This suggestion was put to me by R. Warner in correspondence.
6. And I doubt that it is. See chapter 1, footnote 116.
7. Holdcroft 1983, p. 148.
8. Evans and McDowell 1976, pp. xv–xvi.
9. Compare A. J. Ayer's formulation of phenomenalism: "The statement that this match-box exists must . . . be equivalent to some set of statements about sense-data. And to say, as the phenomenalists do, that physical objects are logical constructions out of sense-data is merely another way of expressing this. It does not mean that physical objects are literally composed of sense-data, or that physical objects are fictions and only sense-data real. It means simply that statements about physical objects are somehow reducible to statements about sense-data, or, as it is sometimes put, that to say anything about a physical object is to say something, though not necessarily the same thing, about sense-data" (1957, pp. 132–133).
10. Carnap has written that the confidence that it is in principle possible to reduce all concepts to the immediately given gives content to the idea of a "basic concept." He writes, "We are here concerned, in the main, with questions of epistemology, that is with the questions of the reduction of cognitions one to another" (1967, p. xvi).

11. Davidson 1984c, p. 127.
12. Davidson 1984d, p. 144.
13. Davidson 1984c, p. 127.
14. Although I reconstruct what follows from things Davidson has written, he nowhere defends his doubt in such detail.
15. For nonepistemological versions of this proposal see Schiffer 1972, p. 15 and Strawson 1970, p. 7. I discuss Schiffer's and Strawson's proposals in chapter 4, section 5.
16. Davidson 1984d, p. 144.
17. Davidson 1980c, p. 257.
18. Davidson adds to the assumption of holism the assumption of charity: we must maximize the number of *true* sentences we attribute to our subject. The second assumption is far from incontrovertible. See, for example, McGinn 1977b.
19. Dummett 1975, p. 127.
20. Dummett 1975, p. 138.
21. Consider what Davidson says: "This is only the beginning of the complications, however, for most emotional states, wants, perceivings, and so on, have causal connections with further psychological states and events, or at least require that these other states exist. And so, in saying an agent performed a single intentional action, we attribute a very complex system of states and events to him" (1980c, p. 255).
22. The process has been likened to solving a simultaneous equation. See, for example, Evans and McDowell 1976, xviii.
23. Bennett (1985) has recently made a suggestion along these lines.
24. Davidson himself has suggested that the radical interpreter begin his task by identifying those sentences the alien holds true (see Davidson 1984c and 1984d). Because we cannot firmly identify propositional attitudes without making some assumptions about the alien's language, at the outset the interpreter will be in a position to do little more than form *hypotheses* about what the alien holds true. This position conflicts with nothing else Davidson wants to hold and indeed strengthens his overall picture of radical interpretation.
25. Platts 1979, p. 92. Platts distinguishes these claims from a further thesis: an utterance is a piece of linguistic behavior only if it is intentional. Platts accepts this thesis and wants to distinguish it from claims (1) and (2), which he thinks are misguided.
26. Platts 1979, p. 92.
27. Peacocke 1976, p. 167.
28. Peacocke 1981, p. 45.
29. Neither Schiffer nor Loar adopts this way of dealing with the problem.
30. It is ironic that these two tasks should come apart for a Gricean, since Griceans heavily emphasize the role of speakers in meaning. See chapter 1, section 1.
31. Platts 1979, pp. 91–92.
32. See chapter 1, section 2.
33. Biro 1979, p. 248.
34. Davidson 1984d, pp. 143–144.
35. For this reason I did not say that the Gricean could accept Davidson's doubt, even though I repeatedly said that the reductive Gricean can accept a surface epistemological asymmetry between the semantic and the psychological. The Gricean can, of course, accept observations about both holism of interpretation and holism of the mental; what he cannot accept is the deep conceptual explanation of those facts I have introduced in this section.

36. Biro does not distinguish analysis from theory building. So while discussing his views I shall elide the distinction.

37. Biro 1979, p. 249. For a brief outline of Dummett's approach to meaning see chapter 1, section 2. This slogan of Dummett's (suitably adapted) *may* partially inform Platts's way of dealing with Grice's analysis.

38. Field 1978, p. 9.

39. An early statement of what I have in mind here can be found in Nagel 1965: "Physicalism will of course not require that these intensional predicates be identical simply with states of a person's body, narrowly conceived. An obvious case is that of knowledge, which implies not only the truth of what is known but also a special relation between this and the knower. Intentions, thoughts, and desires may also imply a context, a relation with things outside the person. The thesis that all states of a person are states of his body therefore requires a liberal conception of what constitutes a state—one which will admit relational attributes" (p. 111).

40. I assume here that we can in principle establish such correlations—a reasonable assumption in light of what motivates contemporary reductive philosophers of mind.

41. This position is sometimes called token physicalism to distinguish it from the type physicalism mentioned earlier.

42. Nagel argues like this in several places. See especially 1979a.

43. Nagel concentrates mainly on experiential states, but in one place he writes, "Not only raw feels but also intentional mental states—however objective their content—must be capable of manifesting themselves in subjective form to be in the mind at all" (1986, pp. 15–16).

44. Nagel 1979b, pp. 181–182.

45. Fodor 1981, p. 102.

46. Realism, of course, is not the prerogative of antireductionism.

47. Nagel 1979a, p. 166. Nagel points out that this way of stating the point has the character of a misleading analogy about it. The expression "what it is like" should not be understood to mean what (in our experience) it resembles; rather, it should be understood as "how it is for the subject himself" (p. 170, footnote 6). Note also that the expression "what it is like" appears originally in Sprigge 1971, and the expression "what it is like to be a bat" appears originally in Farrell 1950.

48. I should stress two points in connection with what Nagel is saying. First of all, Nagel is not concerned with the problem of other minds. In one place he writes: "I am not adverting here to the alleged privacy of experience to its possessor. The point of view in question is not one accessible only to a single individual. Rather it is a *type*" (1979a, p. 171). Secondly, Nagel stresses the *conceptual* nature of his claim. He writes: "My point, however, is not that we cannot *know* what it is like to be a bat. I am not raising an epistemological problem. My point is rather that even to form a *conception* of what it is like to be a bat (and *a fortiori* to know what it is like to be a bat) one must take up the bat's point of view" (1979a, p. 172, footnote 8).

49. This difficulty is one for psychophysical reduction, not reductions in general. For lightning or water the reductionist move in the direction of greater objectivity is unproblematic. Nagel writes: "It is possible to follow this path because although the concepts and ideas we use in thinking about the external world are initially applied from a point of view that involves our perceptual apparatus, they are used by us to refer to things beyond themselves—toward which we have the phenomenal point of view. Therefore we can abandon it in favour of another, and still be thinking about the same things" (1979a, p. 174).

50. Davidson's is only one of many arguments in the literature against a reduction of propositional attitudes. I choose to present this one here because of the affinities I see between it and Nagel's argument against the reduction of sensation. Davidson presents his argument most clearly in 1980a. Other statements of it can be found in Davidson 1980b and 1980c. For a more formal rendition of Davidson's argument see Hellman and Thompson 1975. For some other arguments to the same conclusion see McGinn 1978 and 1980.

51. See section 2 of this chapter.

52. Davidson 1980a, p. 217.

53. Davidson 1984e, p. 168.

54. Cf. Quine 1953: "As Pierre Duhem urged, it is the system as a whole that is keyed to experience" (p. 118).

55. Davidson 1980a, pp. 222–223.

56. See Davidson 1980a, p. 222 and 1980c, p. 257.

57. I say that knowledge of the physical leaves us "relatively ignorant" of propositional attitudes, since *token* physicalism (which Davidson espouses), allows that knowledge of the physical does give us knowledge of the physical *basis* of these propositional attitudes.

58. This is, nota bene, a supplementation of Davidson's view and should not be confused with it.

59. Quine 1960, p. 219. Davidson gestures toward a connection with Quine when explaining his notion of samesaying. See Davidson 1984e, p. 166.

60. Nagel 1979a, p. 179.

61. See especially Davidson 1984e. I assess this argument in section 3.

62. Note, however, the less pessimistic side of Nagel's views.

63. Once we accept that the semantical and the psychological are so interrelated, the principle of rationality (said by Davidson to be constitutive of the psychological) also becomes a principle which can be seen to guide the ascription of meaning to an individual. What another means and what he believes must be understood against a background of rationality. Rationality, then, can be taken to bind the psychological to the semantical and to pull both away from the physical.

64. I am restricting the discussion here to the case of *radical* interpretation. Of course, everything available to the radical interpreter is available to the interpreter in the home case as well.

65. Loar 1981, p. 140.

66. Loar 1981, p. 140.

67. Loar 1981, p. 141.

68. See Loar 1981, p. 141.

69. Loar claims that this "new level" will be revealed by a "theoretical psychology-cum-neurophysiology" and will detail a fine-grained functional organization (1981, p. 140).

70. Loar's reductionism is functionalist: psychological facts are functional facts. But for Loar functional facts are realized by physical facts, and functional roles must be specified in physical vocabulary. For this reason I will continue to speak of Loar's position as a kind of reductive physicalism. For a discussion of functionalism see chapter 4, section 4.

71. In other words, the Cartesian is a substance dualist. A substance, for Descartes, is the idea of a thing that needs only the concurrence of God to exist. See, for example, Descartes 1646, p. 52.

72. I discuss this Cartesian position in greater detail in chapter 4, section 1.

73. This Cartesian metaphysic is generally associated with the *psychological*. It is inter-

esting to ask what, on this picture, the view of semantics is meant to be. Are we to think that there is a separate semantical realm, on a par with the psychological? Or is the semantical to be reduced to the psychological, thereby achieving ontological economy?

74. I say "godlike" rather than "God" to avoid any implication of omniscience, etc. I mean simply to refer to some individual whose perceptual powers are suited to the immaterial substance in question.

75. I shall use the idea of godlike individuals to capture more than theoretical accessibility to this immaterial mental realm. I appeal to such individuals simply to capture in a vivid way the idea of a deep epistemological claim.

76. Nagel often remarks that his argument applies to the Cartesian position (though Davidson does not). See, for example, Nagel's discussion of "annexation" in 1979c, p. 211.

77. These two positions do not exhaust the moves the Gricean can make, though, as I shall soon argue, these positions are examples of the only *kind* of move the Gricean can make. This will become clearer in chapter 4.

78. Loar 1981, p. 203.

79. Loar 1981, p. 203.

80. Loar 1981, p. 2.

81. Some antireductionists are not at all uncomfortable with this conclusion. My point is simply that denying a Gricean reduction is consistent with accepting thought in the absence of language.

82. Properly understood, this claim is true. To see how it can be true despite certain claims by Griceans such as Schiffer and Loar, see the next section.

83. We have here instances of two elementary logical fallacies: denying the antecedent and affirming the consequent.

84. Field 1978, p. 52. Field is relying here on distinctions discussed in chapter 1, section 4.

85. Field 1978, p. 53.

86. Schiffer 1982, p. 154. "Meaning$_o$," is Schiffer's shorthand for public-, or outer-, language meaning; "meaning$_i$" is Schiffer's shorthand for inner-language meaning.

87. Loar 1981, p. 213.

88. Armstrong 1973, p. 35.

89. There is another difference in the formulation of this point by Schiffer on the one hand and Loar and Armstrong on the other. In their exchange Field and Schiffer do not distinguish between simple and complex beliefs. One may interpret Schiffer as saying that the Gricean can allow that the meaning of a sentence is dependent upon its outer, or public, meaning even for the *simplest* sentences. Loar and Armstrong think only complex or abstract beliefs may have such a dependence on public language. Schiffer may go along with Loar and Armstrong. But whether he does or doesn't, he will encounter implausibilities. If he sticks to his point in its most general formulation, he must deny thoughts to human infants and nonhuman animals. If, however, Schiffer follows Loar and Armstrong, he must implausibly deny the holism discussed in section 2 of this chapter, and he needs to reply to Field's objection of circularity applied to these simple thoughts.

90. See Davidson 1984e. I discuss Davidson's argument in the last section of this chapter.

91. Schiffer may or may not want to argue this way. See footnote 89 of this chapter. In the next section I consider one argument to the contrary, Davidson's, and I reject it.

92. Quine 1960, p. 213. Although I present this as Quine's comment on this semantic analysis of propositional attitudes, it is not at all clear that Quine took himself to be proposing an *analysis*. (The comment occurs in a discussion of a certain logical form for propositional-attitude sentences.) Whatever Quine's purposes, however, many other philosophers have adopted this as an *analysis* of propositional attitudes.
93. See especially Davidson 1984e and 1982.
94. Davidson 1984e, p. 157.
95. Davidson 1982, p. 326.
96. Davidson 1984e, p. 170.
97. Davidson 1984e, p. 170.
98. Norman Malcolm 1972–1973, for example, argues that the languageless can "think without having thoughts."
99. Davidson 1982, p. 326.
100. Davidson 1982, p. 326.
101. Davidson introduces the notion of surprise to characterize what he takes to be an essentially correct observation by Donald Weiss in his paper "Professor Malcolm on Animal Intelligence" (1975). In his paper Weiss describes some nonlinguistic behavior that, Weiss believes, should make us attribute not just thought but awareness of thought to this languageless creature. (Note that Weiss is responding to Malcolm. See footnote 98.) Oddly enough, Davidson describes the very case that leads him to introduce the notion of surprise as a case of being startled. I say this because Davidson holds that surprise is only exhibited by believers and to be a believer one must have a language. Remember that by hypothesis *Weiss's* creature has no language.
102. Bennett 1976, p. 52.
103. About educability Bennett writes, "If for a while *a* registers *P* whenever it registers that its environment is of kind *K*, and then later it does not register *P* in those circumstances because it has learned better, then *a* manifests *educability*" (1976, p. 84). Bennett goes on to explain and develop this notion of "learned better." He also suggests that we may want to add a condition of inquisitiveness to our account of belief (p. 86).
104. See Davidson 1982, p. 326.
105. Davidson 1982, p. 326.
106. In one place Davidson makes the following admission: "To complete the argument . . . I need to show that the *only* way one could come to have the subjective-objective contrast is through having the concept of inter-subjective truth. I confess I do not know how to show this" (1982, p. 327). Davidson concedes less in an earlier paper. There he writes, "This contrast [between true belief and false belief] can emerge only in the context of interpretation, which alone forces us to the idea of an objective, public truth" (1984e, reprinted from 1975).
107. Davidson 1982, p. 319.
108. My interest in Davidson's argument is mainly to show that one can reject a Gricean reduction without *having* to accept that languageless creatures can have no thought.

Chapter 4

1. This is an objection that I once heard Schiffer make in the course of a discussion on this topic in Oxford in 1978.
2. I use the phrase "the objective conception of mind" to mean the conception of

mind as an objective phenomenon. Note that my use of this phrase is not the same as Nagel's in his more recent work. See Nagel 1986.

3. See Taylor 1975.

4. See Nagel 1986, p. 14.

5. See my discussion of Nagel in section 5 of chapter 3.

6. Principle 60.

7. Commenting on the Cartesian model of mind, Gilbert Ryle writes: "Only the wearer knows where the shoe pinches. From this it is argued, plausibly but fallaciously, that there does indeed exist the hallowed antithesis between things and events which anyone may witness and the things and events which only their possessor may witness. Planets, microbes, nerves, and eardrums are publicly observable things in the outside world; sensations, feelings, and images are privately observable constituents of our several mental worlds" Ryle 1949, pp. 195–196.

8. Once we see that this is the picture, we can see why the idea of infallibility is inappropriate to this Cartesian conception of mind. Why shouldn't my perception of this immaterial realm be mistaken?

9. Characteristically, this perspective was of less concern to Descartes.

10. This possibility is not foreign to Descartes' own way of thinking of the mind, as is perhaps shown in a passage from a letter he wrote to More: "Though I regard it as established that we can't prove that there is any thought in animals, I do not think it is thereby proved that there is not, *once the human mind does not reach into their hearts*" (Kenny 1970, p. 244; my emphasis).

11. The reader should keep in mind the way I have appealed to such individuals when discussing the Cartesian metaphysic. See chapter 3, section 6, especially footnote 75.

12. By "directly presented" I mean presented without the intermediary of behavior.

13. This problem, *inter alia*, led Berkeley to reject the notion of *material* substance: "For, though we give the materialists their external bodies, they by their own confession are never nearer knowing *how* our ideas are produced; since they own themselves unable to comprehend in what manner body can act upon spirit, or how it is possible it should imprint any idea in the mind" (1710, pp. 73–74). For a good summary of further problems with Cartesian dualism see McGinn 1982, chapter 2, esp. pp. 23–25.

14. This receives a very important qualification in section 3 of this chapter.

15. At one point Loar asks the following very interesting question: If linguistic behavior is inessential in our theory of the propositional attitudes, why does it have an essential role to play in the ordinary attribution of those attitudes? His reply is that linguistic behavior alone has a structure relevantly isomorphic to the physico-functional structure of those attitudes (1981, pp. 140–141). It is interesting that Loar doesn't even consider the *subject's* perspective as essential, even to ordinary attributions of these attitudes.

16. Loar 1981, pp. 127–128. Do not be misled by Loar's reference to the "full picture of attitudes." The full picture for Loar is not a picture of what they are in themselves, but is a picture of what they are in combination with how we ordinarily understand them. The picture of what they are in themselves is, according to Loar, given by a functionalist theory of mind. For a discussion of his theory see section 3 below.

17. Loar 1981, p. 128.

18. Loar 1981, p. 128.

19. Loar 1981, p. 128.

20. In this section my central concern is with propositional attitudes, since only these are relevant to the Gricean enterprise.

21. Compare this with something always admitted by Griceans: the real question that must be decided when considering the reductive interpretation of the Gricean analysis is what account we are to give to the propositional attitudes.

22. Here I shall begin to fulfill the promise made in chapter 1, section 1, to explain how the Gricean account of meaning fits in with ideational theories of meaning.

23. See chapter 1, section 1.

24. At least one Gricean seems to be aware of his position. In *The Language of Thought* Fodor writes: "The present Gricean approach to communication is, however, mentalistic in a stronger sense as well. For it is asserted not only that non-behavioural processes mediate the communication relation between the speaker and his hearer, but also that communication actually consists in establishing a certain kind of correspondence between the mental states. It therefore seems to me to be comforting that this is what everybody has always thought communication consists in. We have communicated when you have told me what you have in mind and I have understood what you have told me" (1976, pp. 108–109). For an explanation of how this squares with the observation that the most prominent reductive Griceans are functionalists, see section 3 of this chapter. The reductive Gricean may want to hold the following: the semantic is reducible to the psychological, but the latter must be explicated by reference to its manifestation in behaviour. I explain why I do not think this is a coherent combination in section 5 of this chapter.

25. This and the following quotations are taken from Berkeley's introduction to *A Treatise Concerning the Principles of Human Knowledge*, sections 10ff (1710).

26. Dummett 1978a, p. 5.

27. Frege 1892, p. 59.

28. Frege 1892, p. 59. In his review of Husserl, Frege writes: "No one has another's mental image, but only his own; and nobody even knows how far his image (say) of red agrees with somebody else's. . . . It is quite otherwise for thought; one and the same thought can be grasped by many men" (1891), p. 79.

29. Frege 1967, p. 29.

30. I take this way of formulating the distinction between Frege and Wittgenstein from Dummett 1973, pp. 638–639.

31. The argument is in Dummett 1978a. See also Wittgenstein 1958, section 32.

32. This style of argument against what I am calling ideational theories of meaning is explicitly considered by J. A. Fodor (1976). Fodor aims to sidestep the learning issue by appeal to innateness. On the issue of understanding, his position is less clear.

33. Dummett 1978a, p. 7.

34. As Dummett himself seems to. See Dummett's William James Lectures, Lecture 8, pp. 48–49.

35. It may appear that this account is circular, but as it stands, so is Dummett's original account. This sort of circularity is only a problem, however, if one has reductionist ambitions.

36. The fact that the languageless can have thoughts that can be accounted for without reference to linguistic behavior would seem to be evidence that ontological asymmetry entails conceptual asymmetry (see chapter 3, section 9). It would also seem to leave room for a reduction of the semantic to the psychological *without* an objective view of mind. I explain why I think that neither of these conclusions can be drawn from what I say in section 5 of this chapter.

37. Dummett 1978a, p. 7.
38. Many Griceans and others have tried to address these problems in the last few years.
39. Functionalism is formulated in different ways by different functionalists. This intentionally vague characterization is taken from Block 1980b, p. 268).
40. For a statement of this central-state-materialist view of mind see, for example, Smart 1969 and Place 1969.
41. See chapter 3, section 5.
42. This allows the functionalist to be a Cartesian dualist. If immaterial stuff exists, it can realize a mental system just in case it is organized in the right way.
43. Note that variable realization is insisted upon by both functionalist and token physicalist. In other words, variable realization can be accommodated by reductionists and nonreductionists alike. For a discussion of variable realization without reduction see McGinn 1978 and 1977a.
44. Block 1980a, p. 177.
45. Lewis 1972, 1983a, and 1983d. Lewis's work takes as its point of departure the work of Frank Ramsey (1929). What follows is only a rough sketch of the Ramsey-Lewis proposal.
46. Lewis 1972, p. 212.
47. Block 1980b, p. 295. By "physicalism" Block means physicalism of the central-state-materialist variety.
48. It is only required that this financial system meet certain formal structural requirements and that there be some mapping from the personal psychological structure onto this economic one.
49. Block 1980b, p. 294.
50. Armstrong 1968, p. 84. Armstrong formulates his version of functionalism this way: "The concept of a mental state is primarily the concept of a state of the person apt for bringing about a certain sort of behavior" (1968, p. 82).
51. Loar 1981, p. 128.
52. Along with the idea that what the other observes is mere physical behavior, we should drop as well all talk of direct versus indirect access, to which the Cartesian conception of mind gives rise.
53. Sufficient similarity is a deliberately vague notion designed to stretch from those who have experiences and points of view of the same type as those of some given subject to those able to understand that the subject has experience but cannot appreciate the character and quality of that experience.
54. Or if they are committed not to a straightforwardly objective conception, then they are committed to one that is improperly subjective. For a discussion of this improperly subjective conception of mind see section 5 of this chapter.
55. An important difference between an objective and a subjective view of mind is this: according to the former, the mind may be thought of as something that is simply there and, hence, may be appreciated impersonally. According to the latter, the mind must be thought of as there for someone. This feature is as well captured by my objector's position as by my position, but one difference is that whereas my objector takes the mind as essentially there simply for the subject himself, I believe that we must understand mind as essentially there both for the subject proper and for other subjects. On my view, the mind is accessible through both introspection and behavior. This may be misleading. One way of thinking of a subjective conception of mind is by thinking of mind as a "proper sensible," that is, as there only for the subject. Seeing this as the essence of a correct view of mind, we may feel that we lose this essence if we allow that mind may be there

both for the subject and for other subjects. Allowing, as my position does, that the mind is accessible to more than one subject may make the mind appear more like a common sensible. This may explain both why my objector insists on leaving the third-person perspective out of his essential characterization of mind as a subjective phenomenon and why there is such a tendency to objectify the mind. Thus, my objector may insist that his position is the only one that really avoids an objective conception of mind. But it is a mistake to think that because there are two essential perspectives on the mind, the mind has thereby been assimilated to the status of a common sensible. It is not that mind is accessible through introspection or by the observation of behavior, but that it is there only for a subject, either through introspection or by the observation of behavior. Once we understand this, we are free to make essential reference to the third-person perspective and to maintain a properly subjective conception of mind.

56. In section 2 I allowed that the languageless may have thoughts which are manifest in their nonlinguistic behavior.

57. The position I am considering here is clearly different from the one I considered at the end of section 4. There the objector claimed to hold a subjective conception of the psychological but left behavior out of the picture. The objection I am now considering *does* make essential reference to behavior in its account of mind, and this is behavior *proper*. This objection disagrees with my position in that it makes no essential reference to *linguistic* behavior. The Gricean position I am considering in this section may be found in Bennett 1976. Bennett writes, "My programme [is to found] a theory of language on an account of meaning-intention-belief which does not itself presuppose that the subjects have language" (p. 96). He also writes, "Statements about minds are based upon facts about behaviour, and I shall never introduce any mentalistic concept without first displaying its behavioural credentials" (p. 3).

58. As I explained in chapter 3, not all reductive Griceans will or need to take this line. See section 9, esp. footnote 89.

59. This is explicitly stated by Schiffer (1972, p. 15), Strawson (1970, p. 7), and Bennett (1976, p. 271).

60. Schiffer considers such an objection from Searle (1970, p. 15). This is of course a criticism of the Gricean analysis only under its reductive interpretation.

61. Strawson 1970, p. 7.

62. Strawson 1970, p. 7 and Schiffer 1972, pp. 15–16.

63. This is Schiffer's version of the story. Schiffer 1972, pp. 15–16.

64. Compare the way political theorists sometimes appeal to the state of nature. Hobbes wrote of people coming together in the state of nature to form a social contract that enables men of a basically brutish nature to live together in peace. The appeal to such a contract was to justify certain practices current in his day and to clarify the individual's allegiance to them. Nozick (1974, chapter 1) also appeals to a state of nature when attempting to establish the rights of the individual and the limits of the state. Nozick explicitly states that his appeal to a state of nature is part of an attempt to give a *reductive* account of the existing political state. Nozick defends his strategy and explains that one way of pursuing a reduction is to start with the nonpolitical and to show how the political may be thought to grow out of it: "The more fundamental our starting point (the more it picks out basic, important, and inescapable features of the human situation) and the less close it seems to its result (the less state-like or political it looks) the better" (p. 7). Just as a Gricean reduction has its critics, so has this Hobbesian strategy. I believe Rousseau first argued that Hobbes's strategy may be circular: those appetites and

passions that the reductionist makes reference to are only available to those already living in society.

65. For an alternative account of communication, and a different story about the way language descended from these pre-conventional acts, see McDowell 1980.

66. Much work has been done to this end by Jonathan Bennett (1976). Yet Bennett seems to be confused about the status of his defence of the Gricean program. In particular, I have in mind section 79, where he confronts what I call the Davidsonian doubt. Bennett writes:

> Davidson has claimed that "making detailed sense of a person's beliefs and intentions cannot be independent of making sense of his utterances." I have tried to refute that; one wonders why Davidson is so sure of its truth that he is willing to assert it without argument. (He has much to say about the attempt to distill out separate belief and meaning components from the total import of a linguistic utterance; but that is a world away from the attempt to attribute beliefs where there is no language. General slogans such as "belief and meaning are interlocked" tend to blur that vital distinction.) Perhaps the word "detailed" is carrying a lot of weight. On the same page Davidson speaks of verifying without appeal to language "the existence of detailed, general, and abstract non-linguistic beliefs and intentions," and cites examples of "trying to learn without asking him whether someone believes there is a largest prime number." Is it assumed that the concept of language can be based on pre-linguistic concepts of belief and intention only if one could pre-linguistically attribute every belief which is expressed in language? I hope not . . . , but then what is the point of the example? (p. 271)

I argued in chapter 3 that the point of Davidson's example is twofold: first, it is an indication of a surface epistemological symmetry between the semantic and the psychological, and second, it is an indication of a deeper epistemological symmetry. Bennett seems unconcerned with the first point and clearly thinks that arguing that there are *some* thoughts that the languageless can possess is a way of denying the second. Of Bennett's discussion I would say this. First, even if Bennett is right about the attribution of thoughts to the languageless, this does nothing to affect Davidson's claim that there is a surface epistemological symmetry between the semantic and the psychological. And second, as I hope to show in this section, even *if* it is correct to attribute some thoughts to the languageless, this does not necessarily count against the antireductionist thesis.

67. If there are such semantically untainted propositional attitudes, then the Gricean analysis tells us how we can arrange these psychological pieces to yield something semantic. That the end result does not *appear* innocent is a mark of a good analysis.

68. I discussed one such argument, Davidson's, in the last section of chapter 3.

69. What I say here should be read against the background of chapter 3, sections 8 and 9.

70. Here I take up the challenge with which I ended chapter 3.

71. I don't know of any philosopher who actually holds such a position, but it is one that comes to mind when one considers what a Cartesian might say about the semantic.

72. Consider the following comment by Armstrong: "It seems perfectly possible that neurophysiological evidence should bear on the question whether a deaf-mute did or did not have beliefs or thoughts which he was unable to express. The identification of the nature of these beliefs from mere neurophysiological evidence is, no doubt, a piece of scientific fiction in the present state of neurophysiology. But it does show the logical possibility of an independent check upon claims like that of Ballard" (1973, p. 35).

References

Ackerman, D. F. 1986. "Essential Properties and Philosophical Analysis." In *Midwest Studies in Philosophy*, vol. II, edited by P. French, T. Uehling, and H. Wettstein. University of Minnesota Press.

Alston, W. P. 1964. *The Philosophy of Language*. Prentice-Hall.

Armstrong, D. M. 1968. *A Materialist Theory of Mind*. Routledge and Kegan Paul.

Armstrong, D. M. 1971. "Meaning and Communication." *Philosophical Review*.

Armstrong, D. M. 1973. *Belief, Truth, and Knowledge*. Cambridge University Press.

Ayer, A. J., ed. 1956. *The Revolution in Philosophy*. Macmillan and Co.

Ayer, A. J. 1957. "Phenomenalism." In *Philosophical Essays*, edited by A. J. Ayer. Macmillan: St. Martin's Press.

Bennett, J. 1973. "The Meaning-Nominalist Strategy." *Foundations of Philosophy*, vol. 10.

Bennett, J. 1976. *Linguistic Behaviour*. Cambridge University Press.

Bennett, J. 1985. Review of *Inquiries into Truth and Interpretation* by D. Davidson. *Mind*, October.

Berkeley, G. 1710. *A Treatise concerning the Principles of Human Knowledge*. In *Philosophical Works*. Dent, Everyman's Library, 1975.

Biro, J. 1979. "Intentionalism and the Theory of Meaning." *Monist*, spring.

Blackburn, S. 1984. *Spreading the Word*. Oxford University Press.

Block, N. 1980. *Readings in Philosophy of Psychology*. Harvard University Press.

Block, N. 1980a. "What is Functionism?" In Block 1980.

Block, N. 1980b. "Troubles with Functionalism." In Block 1980.

Carnap, R. 1967. *The Logical Structure of the World*. Translated by R. A. George. Routledge and Kegan Paul.

Caton, C. A. 1971. "Overview." In Jakobovits and Steinberg 1971.

Davidson, D. 1980. *Essays on Actions and Events*. Oxford University Press.

Davidson, D. 1980a. "Mental Events." In Davidson 1980.

Davidson, D. 1980b. "Psychology as Philosophy." In Davidson 1980.

Davidson, D. 1980c. "The Material Mind." In Davidson 1980.

Davidson, D. 1982. "Rational Animals." *Dialectica*, vol. 36, no. 4.

Davidson, D. 1984. *Inquiries into Truth and Interpretation*. Oxford University Press.

Davidson, D. 1984a. "Theories of Meaning and Learnable Languages." In Davidson 1984.

Davidson, D. 1984b. "Truth and Meaning." In Davidson 1984.

Davidson, D. 1984c. "Radical Interpretation." In Davidson 1984.

Davidson, D. 1984d. "Belief and the Basis of Meaning." In Davidson 1984.

Davidson, D. 1984e. "Thought and Talk." In Davidson 1984.

Davidson, D. 1984f. "Reply to Foster." In Davidson 1984.

Davidson, D. 1984g. "On the Very Idea of a Conceptual Scheme." In Davidson 1984.

Davidson, D. 1984h. "Communication and Convention." In Davidson 1984.

Davidson, D. 1984i. "Reality without Reference." In Davidson 1984.

Davidson, D. 1984j. "On Saying That." In Davidson 1984.

Davies, M. K. 1981. *Meaning, Quantification, and Necessity: Themes in Philosophical Logic.* Routledge and Kegan Paul.

Descartes, R. 1646. *Principles of Philosophy.* In *The Philosophical Works of Descartes,* vol. 1, edited by Haldane and Ross. Cambridge University Press, 1970.

Dummett, M. A. E. 1973. *Frege: Philosophy of Language.* Duckworth.

Dummett, M. A. E. 1975. "What is a Theory of Meaning?" In Guttenplan 1975.

Dummett, M. A. E. 1976. "What is a Theory of Meaning? (II)." In Evans and McDowell 1976.

Dummett, M. A. E. 1978a. "What Do I Know When I Know a Language?" Lecture held at the centenary celebrations of the Stockholm University.

Dummett, M. A. E. 1978b. *Truth and Other Enigmas.* Duckworth.

Evans, G., and J. McDowell. eds. 1976. *Truth and Meaning: Essays in Semantics.* Oxford: Clarendon Press.

Farrell, B. 1950. "Experience." *Mind.*

Field, H. 1978. "Mental Representations." *Erkenntnis,* vol. 13.

Fodor, J. 1976. *The Language of Thought.* Harvester Press.

Fodor, J. 1981. "Three Cheers for Propositional Attitudes." In *Mental Representations: Philosophical Essays on the Foundations of Cognitive Science.* Harvester Press.

Foster, J. A. 1976. "Meaning and Truth Theory." In Evans and McDowell 1976.

Frege, G. 1891. "Illustrative Extracts from Frege's Review of Husserl's *Philosophie der Arithmetik.*" In *Translations from the Philosophical Writings,* translated by P. Geach and M. Black. Basil Blackwell, 1952.

Frege, G. 1892. "On Sense and Reference." In *Translations from the Philosophical Writings,* translated by P. Geach and M. Black. Basil Blackwell, 1952.

Frege, G. 1967. "The Thought: A Logical Inquiry." In Strawson 1967.

Grandy, R. 1973. "Reference, Meaning, and Belief." *Journal of Philosophy,* vol. 70, no. 14.

Grandy, R., and R. Warner. 1986. *Philosophical Grounds of Rationality: Intentions, Categories, Ends.* Oxford University Press.

Grice, H. P. 1957. "Meaning." In Strawson 1967.

Grice, H. P. 1968. "Utterer's Meaning, Sentence-Meaning, and Word Meaning." In Searle 1971.

Grice, H. P. 1969. "Utterer's Meaning and Intentions." *Philosophical Review,* vol. 78.

Grice, H. P. 1982. "Meaning Revisited." In Smith 1982.

Grice, H. P. 1986. "Reply to Richards." In Grandy and Warner 1986.

Grice, H. P., and P. F. Strawson. 1956. "In Defense of a Dogma." *Philosophical Review,* vol. 56.

Guttenplan, S., ed. 1975. *Mind and Language.* Oxford University Press.

Hacker, P. 1972. "Frege and the Private Language Argument." *Idealistic Studies,* vol. 2.

Harman, G. 1968. "Three Levels of Meaning," *Journal of Philosophy,* vol. 65, no. 19.

Harman, G., ed. 1974a. *On Noam Chomsky: Critical Essays.* Doubleday Anchor.

Harman, G. 1974b. Review of *Meaning* by S. Schiffer. *Journal of Philosophy,* vol. 70, no. 7.

Hellman, P., and F. W. Thompson. 1975. "Physicalism: Ontology, Determinism, and Reduction." *Journal of Philosophy,* vol. 72, no. 17.

Holdcroft, D. 1983. "Meaning and the Background of Belief." In *On Believing: Epistemological and Semiotic Approaches,* edited by H. Parret. Walter de Gruyter.

Hume, D. 1888. *Treatise of Human Nature.* Edited by L. A. Selby-Bigge. Oxford University Press, 1960.

Jacobovits, L. A., and D. D. Steinberg, eds. 1971. *Semantics: An Interdisciplinary Reader in Philosophy, Linguistics, and Psychology*. Cambridge University Press.

Kemmerling, A. 1986. "Utterer's Meaning Revisited." In Grandy and Warner 1986.

Kenny, A., trans. and ed. 1970. *Descartes: Philosophical Letters*. Oxford: Clarendon Press.

Lewis D. K. 1969. *Convention: A Philosophical Study*. Harvard University Press.

Lewis, D. K. 1972. "Psychophysical and Theoretical Identifications." In Block 1980.

Lewis, D. K. 1983. *Philosophical Papers*, vol. 1. Oxford University Press.

Lewis, D. K. 1983a. "How to Define Theoretical Identifications." In Lewis 1983.

Lewis, D. K. 1983b. "Mad Pain and Martian Pain." In Lewis 1983.

Lewis, D. K. 1983c. "Languages and Language." In Lewis 1983.

Lewis, D. K. 1983d. "An Argument for the Identity Theory." In Lewis 1983.

Loar, B. 1972. "Sentence Meaning." B. Phil. thesis, Oxford University.

Loar, B. 1976. "Two Theories of Meaning." In Evans and McDowell 1976.

Loar, B. 1981. *Mind and Meaning*. Cambridge University Press.

Locke, J. 1690. *An Essay concerning Human Understanding*. Edited by A. D. Woozley. Fontana Library, 1964.

McDowell, J. 1976. "Truth Conditions, Bivalence, and Verification." In Evans and McDowell 1976.

McDowell, J. 1977. "On the Sense and Reference of a Proper Name." *Mind*, vol. 86.

McDowell, J. 1980. "Meaning, Communication, and Knowledge." In van Straaten 1980.

McGinn, C. 1977a. "Anomalous Monism and Kripke's Cartesian Intuitions." *Analysis*, vol. 37, no. 2.

McGinn, C. 1977b. "Charity, Interpretation, and Belief." *Journal of Philosophy*, vol. 74, no. 9.

McGinn, C. 1978. "Mental States, Natural Kinds, and Psychophysical Laws." *Proceedings of the Aristotelian Society*, suppl. vol. 52.

McGinn, C. 1980. "Philosophical Materialism." *Synthese*, vol. 44.

McGinn, C. 1982. *The Character of Mind*. Oxford University Press.

Malcolm, N. 1972/73. "Thoughtless Brutes." *Proceedings and Addresses of the American Philosophical Association*, vol. 46.

Moore, G. E. 1952. "Reply to my Critics." In Schlipp 1952.

Moore, G. E. 1966. *Lectures on Philosophy*. Edited by C. Lewy, George Allen and Unwin.

Moore, G. E. 1966a. "The Justification of Analysis." In Moore 1966.

Moore, G. E. 1966b. "What is Analysis?" In Moore 1966.

Morris, C. 1938. *Foundations of the Theory of Signs*. Chicago University Press.

Morris, C. 1946. *Signs, Language, and Behavior*. Prentice-Hall.

Nagel, T. 1965. "Physicalism." In O'Connor 1969.

Nagel, T. 1979. *Mortal Questions*. Cambridge University Press.

Nagel, T. 1979a. "What is it like to be a Bat?" In Nagel 1979.

Nagel, T. 1979b. "Panpsychism." In Nagel 1979.

Nagel, T. 1979c. "Subjective and Objective." In Nagel 1979.

Nagel, T. 1986. *The View from Nowhere*. Oxford University Press.

Nozick, R. 1974. *Anarchy, State, and Utopia*. Oxford University Press.

O'Connor, J., ed. 1969. *Modern Materialism: Readings on Mind-Body Identity*. Harcourt, Brace, and World.

Odgen, C. K., and I. A. Richards. 1923. *The Meaning of Meaning*. Routledge and Kegan Paul.

Peacocke, C. 1976. "Truth Definitions and Actual Languages." In Evans and McDowell 1976.

Peacocke, C. 1979. *Holistic Explanation: Action, Space, Interpretation*. Oxford: Clarendon Press.

Peacocke, C. 1981. "The Theory of Meaning in Analytic Philosophy." In *Contemporary Analytic Philosophy*, edited by G. Flistad. Martinus Nijhoff.

Place, U. T. 1969. "Is Consciousness a Brain Process?" In O'Connor 1969.

Platts, M. 1979. *Ways of Meaning: An Introduction to a Philosophy of Language*. Routedge and Kegan Paul.

Quine, W. V. O. 1953. *From a Logical Point of View*. Harper and Row.

Quine, W. V. O. 1953a. "Two Dogmas of Empiricism." In Quine 1953.

Quine, W. V. O. 1960. *Word and Object*. MIT Press.

Quine, W. V. O. 1977. Review of *Truth and Meaning*, edited by G. Evans and J. McDowell. *Journal of Philosophy*, vol. 74, no. 4.

Ramsey, F. 1929. "Theories." In *Foundations*, edited by D. Mellor. Routledge and Kegan Paul.

Recanati, F. 1986. "On Defining Communicative Intentions." *Mind and Language*, vol. 1, no. 3.

Ryle, G. 1949. *The Concept of Mind*. Penguin Books.

Schiffer, S. 1972. *Meaning*. Oxford: Clarendon Press.

Schiffer, S. 1981a. "Truth and the Theory of Content." In *Meaning and Understanding*, edited by Parret and Bouveresse: Walter de Gruyter.

Schiffer, S. 1981b. "Indexicals and the Theory of Reference." *Synthese*, vol. 49.

Schiffer, S. 1982. "Intention-Based Semantics." *Notre Dame Journal of Formal Logic*, vol. 43.

Schiffer, S. 1987. *Remnants of Meaning*. MIT Press.

Schlipp, P. A., ed. 1952. *The Philosophy of G. E. Moore*. Tudor Publishing Co.

Searle, J. 1970. *Speech Acts: An Essay in the Philosophy of Language*. Cambridge University Press.

Searle, J., ed. 1971. *The Philosophy of Language*. Oxford University Press.

Searle, J. 1971a. Introduction to Searle 1971.

Searle, J. 1971b. "What is a Speech Act?" In Searle 1971.

Smart, J. J. C. 1969. "Sensations and Brain Processes." In O'Connor 1969.

Smith, N. 1982. *Mutual Knowledge*. Academic Press.

Sperber, D., and D. Wilson. 1986. *Relevance: Communication and Cognition*. Basil Blackwell.

Sprigge, T. 1971. "Final Causes." *Proceedings of the Aristotelian Society*, suppl. vol. 45.

Stampe, D. 1974. "Towards a Grammar of Meaning." In Harman 1974a.

Stebbing, S. 1952. "Moore's Influence." In Schlipp 1952.

Stevenson, C. L. 1944. *Ethics and Language*. Yale University Press.

Strawson, P. F. 1956. "Construction and Analysis." In Ayer 1956.

Strawson, P. F. 1964. "Intention and Convention in Speech Acts." In Searle 1971.

Strawson, P. F. ed. 1967. *Philosophical Logic*. Oxford University Press.

Strawson, P. F. 1970. *Meaning and Truth*. Oxford: Clarendon Press.

Strawson, P. F. 1980. "Reply to McDowell." In van Straaten 1980.

Tarski, A. 1944. "The Semantic Conception of Truth." *Philosophy and Phenomenological Research*, vol. 4.

Tarski, A. 1956. "The Concept of Truth in Formalized Languages." In *Logic, Semantics, and Metamathematics*. Oxford: Clarendon Press.

Taylor, C. 1975. *Hegel*. Cambridge University Press.

Taylor, C. 1980. Review of *Linguistic Behavior*, by J. Bennett. *Dialogue*, vol. 19.

Van Straaten, Z., ed. 1980. *Philosophical Subjects: Essays Presented to P. F. Strawson*. Oxford: Clarendon Press.

Wallace, J. 1977. "Only in the Context of a Sentence Do Words Have Any Meaning." In *Midwest Studies in the Philosophy of Language*, vol. 2, edited by P. A. French, T. E. Uehlig, and H. K. Wettstein. University of Minnesota Press.

Watson, J. B. 1919. *Psychology from the Standpoint of a Behaviorist*. Lippincott.

Wiess, D. 1975. "Professor Malcolm on Animal Intelligence." *Philosophical Review*, vol. 84.

Wiggins, D. 1971a. "On Sentence-Sense, Word-Sense, and Difference of Word-Sense." In Jacobovits and Steinberg 1971.

Wiggins, D. 1971b. "Reply to Alston." In Jacobovits and Steinberg 1971.

Williams, B. 1978. *Descartes: The Project of Pure Enquiry*. Pelican Books.

Wilson, N. L. 1970. "Grice on Meaning: The Ultimate Counter-example." *Nous*, vol. 4.

Wisdom, J. 1934. *Problems of Mind and Matter*. Cambridge University Press.

Wittgenstein, L. 1958. *Philosophical Investigations*. Basil Blackwell.

Yu, P. 1979. "On the Gricean Program about Meaning." *Linguistics and Philosophy*, vol. 3, no. 2.

Ziff, P. 1967. "On H. P. Grice's Account of Meaning." *Analysis*, vol. 28.

Index